Praise for
THE UNDERTO

"A riveting, vividly detailed collage of political and moral derangement in America, one that horrifyingly corresponds to liberals' worst fears."
—Joseph O'Neill, *New York Times Book Review*, Editors' Choice

"One of my favorite nonfiction writers anywhere, just an incredible writer, and an incredible reporter. [*The Undertow*] is I think, among his best work ever."
—Chris Hayes, *All In with Chris Hayes*

"[Jeff Sharlet's] stories are as necessary as they are harrowing. The writing is explicit and expansive, almost cinematic, like looking at a battlefield from above. Altogether, it's a rare achievement, a cultural-political book that is literary. . . . [*The Undertow*] has a narrative arc that captures the fever pitch of the past decade."
—Ann Neumann, *Guardian* (UK)

"I deeply appreciate Sharlet's mythic-religious approach, and how it enables him to capture what other journalists miss. Data can only tell half the story, and usually the half that's less interesting. Add to that the book's welcome ambition, both as journalism and literature. This is no mere compilation of bullet points. This is journalism-as-art, attempting to capture the mood of the nation at this fraught moment, so that others in the future may know how it felt to live through the present. Hopefully there will still be readers then."
—Adam Fleming Petty, *Washington Post*

"Much has been written about the figure of Trump: his biography, his appeal, his hold on the Republican Party. Some too have written about [Donald] Trump's antecedents in the broader conservative movement. But Sharlet offers something new. . . . As Sharlet chases [Ashli] Babbitt's ghost across a fractious landscape, he documents a new kind of civil war. States do not face one another on the battlefield; there is no rebel government. Instead, the battlefield is everywhere, and combatants have, in a sense, already seceded from the United States. That the secession occurred in their minds makes it no less real. They are armed, and they are backed, too, by power and money. They have successfully enthralled a major political party, and their allies are capturing courts and state legislatures. The other side is still catching up to the danger it's in." —Sarah Jones, *New York* magazine

"Jeff Sharlet's startling, Didion-esque *The Undertow: Scenes from a Slow Civil War*, with its CinemaScope landscapes and slightest of hopes, visits the dirt lanes and country rallies where Christian nationalism threatens." —Christopher Borrelli, *Chicago Tribune*

"Incomparable. . . . The weekend Donald Trump wrongly claimed he'd be 'arrested' within a few days, as his incitements to supporters to get violent kept coming, I found myself thinking about the best and most disturbing nonfiction book I'd recently read: Jeff Sharlet's *The Undertow: Scenes From a Slow Civil War*. It's both perfect and impossible to describe. . . . This amazing book makes all of it into tragic sense."
—Joan Walsh, *Nation*

"[*The Undertow*] is a foreboding drive through the backroads of the country's rising militancy. From campy Trump rallies and a memorial service for the January 6 insurrectionist Ashli Babbitt to a televangelist's church in Miami and a self-declared prophet in Omaha, Sharlet takes a hard, unwavering look at the nation's guns-and-Bibles underbelly." —James Sullivan, *Boston Globe*

"Jeff Sharlet is one of our essential guides through the Age of Trump, that fascist nightmare and what he describes . . . as the 'Trumpocene.'"
—Chauncey DeVega, *Salon*

"[*The Undertow*] induced a physiological response similar to the one I experienced while reading Joan Didion's *Slouching Towards Bethlehem*. Both books are mood-altering, mind-altering odysseys. . . . Sharlet is a kind of anthropologist of the Trumpocene, and the richness of his dispatches derives from his ability to inhabit a broad range of sensibilities and psychologies." —Elizabeth D. Samet, *American Scholar*

"A literary anthropologist looking at society and its ills, pondering what it means and how we got here. It's that curiosity and energy that comes across in his writing, both smart and easy to read while also packed with context and information." —Kevin Koczwara, *Esquire*

"[Sharlet] may be unusually hopeful for an author invoking civil war in his subtitle, but [he] is not deluded. . . . [A] dark travelogue of a nation of 'simmering violence' in which QAnon-influenced rabbit-holers stalk perceived enemies, often without making headlines. . . . He wants readers to feel empathy for . . . those he met along the way. Some of them might be 'worst of the worst,' but ultimately we need to understand the right and its vulnerabilities." —Stuart Miller, *Los Angeles Times*

"More than any book about Trump or Trumpism, *The Undertow* takes us on an extraordinary journey inside the fascist imagination, from the grifters and con artists who profit from commodifying far-right propaganda and memes, to the seemingly ordinary people who have embraced it as an expression of what it means to truly be American." —Sarah Posner, *In These Times*

"Of all the recent books I've read about the threats to democracy in America . . . none have hit me at quite the level of Jeff Sharlet's new book, *The Undertow*. More than all the academics citing surveys seeking to explain 'the authoritarian personality' or pundits sketching the contours of hyper-polarization, Sharlet manages to convey something more visceral while also intuiting where current developments on the populist right are heading." —Micah L. Sifry, *Connector*

"*The Undertow* suggests that two things separate the current [rightwing] movement from past iterations: guns and proximity to power. . . . *The Undertow* is an ear to the ground, recording the seemingly disconnected notes of what for many armed Americans is a coordinated symphony of revolution." —Randy R. Potts, *Commonweal*

"A fine and troubling book. . . . The witness, [Sharlet], does not argue with his interlocutors. The witness mainly shows: here is the shape of desire—guns, power, war, a strongman. . . . Here may also be the shape of heartbreak." —JoAnn Wypijewski, *New Left Review*

"A distinctive, brilliant, and poetic study of Amerikaner fascism. . . . *The Undertow* is part travelogue, part prose poetry, part first person journalistic inquiry, part participant observation, part personal memoir, part history, and part horror story. . . . This is an at once beautiful and terrifying book." —Paul Street, *Counterpunch*

"Harrowing, heartbreaking, scary, but also bleakly funny in a theater-of-the-absurd way, *The Undertow* is a *Wisconsin Death Trip* for the Trumpocene, a graveside elegy on the edge of the burn pit that used to be—if only aspirationally—a democracy." —Mark Dery, *4Columns*

"At once heartbreaking and quietly hopeful, *The Undertow* navigates the slow-motion collapse of America with compassionate reporting and acute, devastating prose. These dispatches immerse readers in the currents threatening to pull a nation apart, while skirting the nihilism that could drag us under." —Jessica Bruder, author of *Nomadland: Surviving America in the Twenty-First Century*

"In these reports from America's different corners there comes a feeling for why we're so broken and what it might take to heal. Brilliant, lucid, incisive, meticulously reported—Jeff Sharlet is at his best here even when we are not."
                                        —Alexander Chee, author of
                                        How to Write an Autobiographical Novel

"Jeff Sharlet's rich narrative prose unpacks a worldview in which US democracy is an existential threat. These essays are an essential read for all Americans."   —Jason Stanley, author of *How Fascism Works: The Politics of Us and Them*

"That America is deeply divided is undeniable. Yet underneath this polarization lies a rich tapestry of human experience, stories of individuals inspired by myths, driven by fears, and searching for meaning. At once unexpectedly sympathetic and profoundly disquieting, Jeff Sharlet's work shows how the task of binding our nation together is a daunting one, but the fate of American democracy depends on it."
                —Kristin Kobes Du Mez, author of *Jesus and John Wayne: How White Evangelicals Corrupted a Faith and Fractured a Nation*

"Brilliant, humane, and incisive, Jeff Sharlet illuminates the numerous fault lines of a fractured nation. His meticulous reporting connects the dots on a stark but hopeful journey."
                        —Wajahat Ali, author of *Go Back to Where You Came From: And Other Helpful Recommendations on How to Become American*

"A riveting, insightful reading of 'Real America'—the fearful, violent, and sometimes chaotic lives of people who are caught in a maelstrom of social, economic, and racial tensions. Weaving religion, hate, hope, and fear into stories that catch us unaware, Jeff Sharlet confronts us with the realities of the shifting American psyche—a must-read in order to understand the conflicting voices and tensions in America today."

—Anthea Butler, author of *White Evangelical Racism:*
The Politics of Morality in America

"Sharlet's books require the kind of reportage that feels both immersive and terrifying—his work takes him deep into uncomfortable territory, holding a mirror up to the world we think we live in to reveal another place altogether. That's what *The Undertow* promises: a deep dive into the religious dimensions—and fanaticism—of American politics. From a conference for incels to the celebrated martyrdom of a Capitol rioter, Sharlet's new book will be a must read for everyone looking to understand how the country got to where we are."

—Emily Firetog, *Literary Hub,*
"*Lit Hub*'s Most Anticipated Books of 2023"

"Poetic descriptions of America's landscape and history punctuate Sharlet's unsettling insights into the undercurrents of fear, isolation, and anger coursing through the country. It's a jaw-dropping portrait of a country on the edge."   —*Publishers Weekly*

"A frightening, wholly believable vision of an American cataclysm to come—possibly soon."   —*Kirkus Reviews*, starred review

"A grim but necessary examination of democracy's potential assassins, leavened by Sharlet's incredible storytelling and acute observations."   —*Booklist*

THE
UNDERTOW

THE
UNDERTOW

>‹

Scenes from a Slow Civil War

JEFF SHARLET

W. W. NORTON & COMPANY
Independent Publishers Since 1923

For information about permission to reproduce selections from this book, write to
Permissions, W. W. Norton & Company, Inc., 500 Fifth Avenue, New York, NY 10110

For information about special discounts for bulk purchases, please contact
W. W. Norton Special Sales at specialsales@wwnorton.com or 800-233-4830

Manufacturing by Lakeside Book Company
Book design by Chris Welch
Production manager: Lauren Abbate

Library of Congress Control Number: 2023948615

ISBN: 978-1-324-07451-9 pbk.

W. W. Norton & Company, Inc.
500 Fifth Avenue, New York, N.Y. 10110
www.wwnorton.com

W. W. Norton & Company Ltd.
15 Carlisle Street, London W1D 3BS

1 2 3 4 5 6 7 8 9 0

Contents

III. Goodnight, Irene: On Survival

Prelude:
Our Condition

Throat clearing such as this prelude usually accounts for a journey that ends with the book in your hands. But this book is written from the middle of something, a season of coming apart. A friend said that it feels sometimes now as if we are bobbing in the sea, surrounded by sharks, but I misheard. I thought he said "sharps." I pictured myself pulled by the undertow into deep water, jagged with needles and knives and razors and broken glass—like that of the window through which Ashli Babbitt, a subject of this book's title essay, attempted to climb when she invaded the Capitol on January 6, 2021. Babbitt, shot for her trouble, was a fool who pursued her own death. And yet, many of us might say the same of ourselves. The peril in which the country finds itself now is not natural; it is in the broadest sense of our own American making.

My friend offered another metaphor: "When you're in the trough, it's hard to see the crest of the next wave." He meant it is hard to see hope, but I could only think that what we see as we rise with the water is that the next wave will be bigger, and the one after that bigger still. And if we make it to shore? There's the smoke of wildfire, like that which filled so much of the Western sky as I drove across the country near this book's end; and the rain such as that which falls in the valley to which I came home, harder now than in recorded history, flooding land that hasn't been underwater for fifteen thousand years; and all the many smaller signs of the climate "crisis" that is increasingly simply our condition. I think, for instance, of the headline this morning in my local paper: a winter fair that the town next door has long celebrated on the ice of a pond will not take place this year, or next. The ice is no longer "viable." The experts—the U.S. Army Corps of Engineers maintains a laboratory for the study of cold here, and in years past they would bore through the pond's ice to show children the stages of freezing—say it will not be reliably "viable" again. No more winter fair, no more marching bands on the frozen pond.

Such a small loss! But a real one. This book of stories of difficult people doing terrible things is a register also of grief and its distortions, how loss sometimes curdles into fury and hate, or denial, or delusion. Especially delusion. The first time I found myself at gunpoint was twenty years ago, a sheriff who pulled a fake weapon without identifying it as such. I was as scared as you might expect—and scared, too, when, driving across the country near this book's end, I kept meeting men with guns who said they might "have no choice" but to draw them soon. Bluster, or anticipation? Fact or fiction? The pointlessness of such distinctions was the sheriff's point. He grinned when I jumped in fear: "See now," he said, "that just goes to show how things that aren't real can still hurt you." He meant, he said, that had I held a toy like that myself he would have shot me.

The sheriff's stunt was a performance, and so, too, are the subjects of the stories that follow. Power is always of its moment. But coursing through the undertow now are certain recurring lies, chief among them that of Whiteness, into which so much else is drawn: desires, jokes, games, money, schools, anger. My capitalization of "Whiteness" in this book is no undue honor. It's visibility. White people need to be *more* visible? Yes—to themselves, argues Princeton historian Nell Irvin Painter, author of *A History of White People*. "White Americans have had the choice of being something vague, something unraced and separate from race," she writes in *The Washington Post*. "A capitalized 'White' challenges that freedom, by unmasking 'Whiteness' as an American racial identity as historically important as 'Blackness.'"

Many of the stories that follow are about performances of Whiteness, the delusions with which it disguises and reveals itself. There is a difference, though, between delusion and imagination—that's the hope of this book. I've tried to pull a thread of imagination through these pages, to notice moments of generosity, small solidarities, genuine wit, actual funny, real sorrow and love. Although this book is "about" a period of dissolution the documentary filmmaker Jeffrey Ruoff has described as "the Trumpocene," it's anchored against the undertow of these times at its beginning and end by such stories—of real sorrow and love—from other days of struggle. They are portraits of singers, their best songs forgotten or worn smooth by time and seemingly safe. Such is the effect of the undertow, which too often pulls our voices beneath. The losses these chapters chart are just as real as those of the pages in between, and deeper. But so, too, is the care for one another to which the songs these singers sang once summoned us.

I've named the first and final sections of the book for two of those songs. Harry Belafonte's "Day-O," turned by the tide of American Whiteness into a charming novelty tune, which still carries within it for those who'll listen a kind of secret code, a current of resistance; and "Goodnight, Irene," sung now as a lullaby but once upon a time given voice as an elegy, a song of mourning, which, its first singers knew, is essential to survival. In between, a middle section: "Dream On," named for an Aerosmith song, "classic rock," a real banger. Trump put it in heavy rotation at his rallies, where the truest believers, the most far gone, would sometimes spin to it, arms akimbo, lost in fantasy.

We will need new songs if we are to make it through what is to come—what is already here. I am not the one to write them. My hope is less than that: only that this book may reveal fault lines within our fears, in which others will find the better words our children may one day sing.

I

Day-O
On Hope

✕

Voice and Hammer

Once, more than half a century ago, he was the handsomest man in the world. A radiant man. It was a matter of bearing, of voice and gesture and timing. He had that high, buttery baritone, nothing special really, except, he says, "I knew how to use it," and that smile, the genuine pleasure that seemed to roll off the so-called King of Calypso in soft little waves, and those eyes, bedroom but darker, almost cadaverous but alert, ready. The eyes revealed the simmer inside. "This hard core of hostility," a director once said, comparing him to Marlon Brando. That mesmerizing anger. "He's loaded with it."

And now? In a diner he asks a kid in a ballcap where he's going to college. The kid raises his brim and squints—*Who are you?* At a museum he tries to chat up a guard from Jamaica, where down by the docks he had learned to sing as a boy. The guard murmurs and smiles. *Old man*, the guard says with his eyes.

One day we're walking up Broadway in Manhattan with his wife, Pam. She admires a Porsche, antique and teal. "What year do you think it is?" she asks. Sixty years old but nearly a quarter century his junior, Pam is his youthful bride. He walks over to the car's owner: a rumpled White man, wearing khaki shorts and a mint-green Izod, plugging coins into a meter.

The old man takes out his money roll. It's fat and bound by a gold clasp. "How much?" he rasps. His voice sounds familiar but scraped, like rocks beneath sand.

The Porsche's owner looks at this stranger, his skin the color of dark honey, with a half-smile of alarm. "Uh . . ."

The old man grins, a shining, slightly crooked expression. It's like a light turning on; you can almost hear the White man think, *Wait—you're still alive?*

"How. Much."

The White man twitches. "One hundred thousand dollars?" he says, just in case Harry Belafonte—it's Harry Belafonte!—isn't joking. Harry Belafonte pats the White man's shoulder and moves on, keeping time with his carved wooden cane. "I'm going to tell my wife you tried to buy my car!" the man chirps after him.

One day Belafonte tells me, "I'm taking you to a movie." There's a documentary about his life called *Sing Your Song*, an elegant testimony that doesn't quite bridge the peculiar gap between Belafonte's past, when he was labeled "subversive" and spied on by the FBI, and his present: a golden oldie who used to sing folk songs with a Jamaican accent, a "national treasure." "Our heritage." How did that happen? To him? To us? What have we forgotten?

"I've seen *Sing Your Song*," I tell him.

"That's not the movie," he says. He won't tell me its name. He and Pam and I pile into a cab and shoot downtown to a theater. Invitation-only: the families of the movie's stars, there for a special screening of a documentary, *Zero Percent*, about a prison college program called Hudson Link at Sing Sing. The program's director, Sean Pica, is waiting. "Mr. B!" Pica says, bouncing on his toes. Pica is a graduate himself. He earned his high school, college, and master's degrees inside. "I grew up in the town of Sing Sing," he likes to say. That's where he learned about Harry Belafonte. "I'll tell you about Mr. B," he says. At Sing Sing, five times a day, every man's in his cell for a head count. One man missing, the whole prison shuts down. Belafonte's there one afternoon to meet about thirty incarcerated students. Almost four p.m. Head count approaching. "Gotta wrap up," the deputy of security tells Belafonte. "Gotta get these men back to their cells."

Belafonte waits a beat. Stares. Smiles. Mesmerizing. "We'll take another fifteen minutes."

"But—" goes the deputy.

"We will take another fifteen minutes."

He's Harry Belafonte.

That's how it happens: four p.m., no count—not at Belafonte's table, not anywhere in the prison. Pica couldn't remember anything like it. "I *love* Mr. B," he says. "He's the guy who stopped the clock."

›‹

Don't get stuck on the bananas. You know the bananas. *Day-o! Day-o-o-o. Come Mr. Tally Man, tally me banana.* "Day-O," or, "The Banana Boat Song," was the hit that made *Calypso*, Belafonte's third album, the first LP in history to sell a million copies. 1956, the same year a White boy from Mississippi released a record called *Elvis Presley*. Belafonte outsold the so-called King. This fact is important to him. Even now, eighty-four years old, his left eye wandering, his right hand curled around the head of his walking stick ("a phallic symbol," he observes), his still-great frame folded into the front row of another darkened screening room, just us and Pam this time.

Belafonte was first. First Black man to win a Tony; one of the first to star in an all-Black Hollywood hit (*Carmen Jones*, 1954); first to star in a noir (*Odds Against Tomorrow*, 1959, which he also produced); first to turn down starring roles (*To Sir, with Love*; *Lilies of the Field*; *Porgy and Bess*; *Shaft*) because, he said, he'd play no part that put a Black man on his knees or made of him a cartoon. We're here in this screening room to watch a forgotten hour of television for which he won the first Emmy awarded to a Black man for production, for being in charge. He produced it, scripted it, cast it, and starred in it. In 1959 it was certainly the most radical hour of network television ever broadcast. It may still be. It is the best hour of television I've ever seen. When I found it in a film archive, I thought it would be more of what I believed I already knew about the man. The albums I'd bought were labeled "easy listening," or "folk," from the days when folk meant harmonizing trios in matching sweaters. Then I watched. My eyes went wide. I think I gasped. I was wearing the archive's cheap headphones, sitting at a monitor in a dark room. Other researchers hunched over screens, all our faces flickering blue. I laughed. I slapped the desk. My eyes watered. Goddamn. I felt like I was watching a different past, one in which the revolution *had* been televised. *Goddamn.* As if that was what TV was for. A signal.

December 10, 1959, 8:30 p.m., live. Kids across America are groaning because the night's entertainment, *Zane Grey Theatre*, White men with six-guns, has been displaced by, of all things, Revlon. Makeup. Miss Barbara Britton, the sponsor's blond hostess in ball gown and pearls and white gloves up to her elbows amidst crystal cases of Christmas possibilities, introducing "the exciting Mr. Belafonte," the dreamiest and safest Negro in America, sweet as Nat King Cole and so much prettier.

At least, part of that was true. "From the top of his head right down that white shirt, he's the most beautiful man I ever set eyes on," said Diahann Carroll, who costarred in *Carmen Jones*. His beauty was a kindness. It was golden, encompassing. Where Elvis stood center stage and pushed, Belafonte, a bigger man—six-two, 185 pounds—curled his shoulders around his Cadillac chest and seemed to a certain demographic to be promising the spotlight to Miss Barbara Britton, to Mrs. America, to the married White womanhood of the nation, if she could gather the courage to come up onstage and join him. An offer, not a proposition.

But that's not what made him a star. It was this: Elvis was going to seduce you. No, that's a euphemism. Elvis, legs jittering, wanted to fuck. Belafonte, fingers snapping, seemed like he'd be seduced by *you*, he'd really see you, and then you'd make love.

It pisses him off, even now. "People saying it in line," he rasps, sweetening his voice to mimic the White women who presumed he could be theirs for the taking: "'I'll tell my husband, *I'll leave* you *in a minute*, he'"—Belafonte—"'*can put his shoes under my bed anytime*.' Never stopping to debate whether I would like to do that." He was a sex symbol, he got that. But what kind? A man or a "boy"? Lover or servant?

Miss Barbara Britton fades to black and *Tonight with Belafonte* begins: a harsh charcoal drawing of a man so twisted, so fixed in nothing but pain that he's barely recognizable. Belafonte. *Ca-chink*. A beat. *Ca-chink*. A beat. Not a drum but a tool, like metal striking stone. *Ca-chink*. *Ca-chink*. Eleven times the hammer falls, and then the light comes up, a spot on Belafonte. "Voice and hammer, that's it," the old man murmurs now, watching himself then. Behind him, seven bare-armed Black men, biceps like cannonballs, shoulders heaving, let their hammers fall. Their chains hang from the darkness above—vertical, huge, heavy links, like anchors. Belafonte's center stage, his signature outfit—high, tight mohair pants, a sailor's double-loop belt buckle, a tailored shirt of Indian cotton open almost to his navel—made over into a prisoner's rags. His right hand is a claw and his left is a fist; his eyes are blackness and his legs are wide, his feet planted. He begins to sing. A hard dragging snarl. *I don't want no bald-headed woman, she too mean lord-lordy, she too mean . . .*

"Bald-headed woman," Belafonte snickers now, in the screening room, thinking of the products his sponsor wanted to peddle. "Revlon." He snorts.

It's a chain-gang song. Belafonte had found it ten years earlier, and he'd been holding it back for just this moment, waiting to sing it on the mountaintop of his stardom. He found it on a record nobody listened to back then, a chain gang recorded live. Found it in the Library of Congress, flat-broke Harry bumming his way down to Washington to sit in a room with big black headphones framing his unsmile, soaking up songs that made more sense to him than the pop on the radio. "Make me mean," he murmurs, echoing the line.

On the screen, there's a twitch in his narrow hips. His hands, rigid, frame his crotch. The thrust is no longer pretty, not Elvis or Belafonte, not any kind of singer.

"How simple," he murmurs now. "How very simple."

Belafonte bangs his stick on the screening room's carpeted floor, his grin as gorgeous as it was in 1959 but stripped by age of its smooth padding, the boyish cheeks, plain now as what it always was: fury.

I say, "You changed the lyric." On the original recording, "bald-headed woman" is "jet-black woman."

Belafonte looks at me like I'm a fool. "I changed lyrics on *everything*. Like that thing upstairs?" Earlier, we'd watched a happier Harry, singing a song called "Hold 'Em Joe" on Jackie Gleason's *Cavalcade of Stars*, Caribbean costume and the all-White June Taylor Dancers prancing as Belafonte leads a donkey onstage. It made me wince. A donkey. I wasn't reading the code. Early on Belafonte intuited that African American music, Caribbean music, is nearly always encrypted with meanings. "All our songs are filled with metaphor and filled with subtext, and we're always codifying," he says. "You know what 'Hold 'Em Joe' is?" He grips his stick. "It's a phallic song. 'My *donkey*'? Here I was, doing the song known by millions of people in the Caribbean as one thing, and I'm on the most popular show in America singing the same song. I made 'em think it was a song about a *donkey*." He laughs. Cackles. The donkey's a metaphor, but so is the phallus for which it stands. Metaphors all the way down, from donkey to defiance to the root, humanness. Not in the abstract, the ideological or the spiritual or the moral, but in the flesh: a body: a human being.

Belafonte nods toward the screen. "Let's play it."

The hanging chains tumble down and the first number ends with a close-up of Belafonte's boot on the iron heap. But the next song's a whisper, the guitar behind him just a little strum.

Sylvie . . .

Pause.

Sylvie . . .

I'm so hot and dry.

Sylvie . . .

Sylvie . . .

Can't you hear,

Can'tcha hear me cryin'?

" 'Sylvie,'" he says now. "When I heard this at the library, by Lead-belly, it was a children's song." Leadbelly was Huddy Ledbetter, the ex-con *LIFE* magazine once called "Bad N-----," the genius from whose twelve-string guitar not just Belafonte but Woody Guthrie, Pete Seeger, and dozens of others learned the truths of the old songs. Leadbelly really had worked on a chain gang, but what Belafonte took from him wasn't "authenticity." It was the simple idea that you could take any song and make it your own. His "Sylvie" doesn't sound like Leadbelly's; it's slower, sadder, sharper.

Sylvie say she love me
But I believe she lie
She hasn't been to see me
Since the last day in July.

"I made no connection with purism," he says. "I looked at the art of it and I said, '*Goddamn*. How long has this room been here? Why didn't I ever see this wing of the house of life?'"

For the rest of the show, Belafonte roams the house. Ballads and kids' songs and comedy songs and work songs, "Jump in the Line" and "Mo Yet" and "John Henry." Odetta's national debut singing a version of "Waterboy" that could drive nails into the cross. The camera cuts to her in a spotlight, and the visual alone makes your breath stop, because she doesn't look like anything you've seen on television. Because she's fat. Not fat like a gospel singer, that ready role for a big-voiced big woman on TV, but too fat, beautiful but probably not healthy, angry-eat-too-much-because-you-hurt fat, and she stands on the stage in that stark spotlight in a plain A-line frock, her shadow her only accompaniment, and she plays her guitar like it's the rock and she's the hammer.

"God," Belafonte says, watching it now. He remembers how he got this big, dark-skinned, angry woman on television. "Heavy voice, heavy color," he says. It was at a meeting with the account executive for Revlon, Madison Avenue. "I got some guests," Belafonte tells him. "And the first and most important guest is Odetta."

The ad man waits for more. Belafonte stares. Finally the ad man blinks. "Ah, what's an Odetta?" he says.

"Well, I don't know," Belafonte answers. "She looks a little bit like Paul Robeson."

That was a name you didn't even say out loud then, a star—*Showboat, Othello, The Emperor Jones*—gone radically Red. "The Russia-loving Negro baritone," one newspaper called him.

"Uh-huh," murmurs the ad man. He'd been thinking maybe a sultry soprano like Lena Horne. Light-skinned.

"And she sounds like him too," adds Belafonte, deadpan.

"Oh," says the ad man. He's responsible for the hour of primetime television Revlon has bought and turned over to Belafonte, who, by the way, will not be singing "The Banana Boat Song" and has also decided that he won't accept commercials.

"Oh my God," says the ad man.

Belafonte grins now and says what he thought then: "Swallow that shit, motherfucker."

And they did. Belafonte had negotiated one of the first pay-or-play contracts in the business. He'd get paid whether they used it or not. Revlon's money was already gone.

So Belafonte had an Odetta, and the first Black dancer with Balanchine's New York City Ballet, and two then-unknown bluesmen named Sonny Terry and Brownie McGhee, and a young director named Norman Jewison, whom Belafonte had plucked from a dead end after Jewison had been fired—by Revlon—just weeks before. Jewison, who'd go on to become a three-time Oscar nominee, thought he had nothing left to lose; he'd already lost. That was how Belafonte liked it. Bottomed-out and mad. He had a voice, a dancer, a camera, and his own almost supernatural control of the stage. What he needed, he concluded, was a church. A temple. Because he wanted Miss Barbara Britton to understand what this really was. Not a song and dance—not *just* a song and dance—but—"you see it?" he asks me, and through his eyes, then my own, I do: A judgment. He could have built a gallows, but no—he chose a church. He built a church, right onstage. High modernist, nothing but a line, an angular arch, his singers sitting in the pews, Belafonte one among them and now Odetta rises up like the tide, singing "The Walls of Jericho," gospel made over as fight song.

"Pause it for a minute," Belafonte says. He's not a believer, never was.

For him it's political. He can't forgive the church the slave catechism taught by traders of flesh: "Your redemption lies in heaven at the right hand of God," he recites, his voice filled with contempt. "Never rise up against your oppressor. Don't rebel." But that was just the surface. Beneath it, or maybe within it, were other meanings. "Bible readings, telling stories, passing information. You planned all the escapes in church. You sang your songs in code. Slave codes." Then as now, he says. Every spiritual he sang on TV or in a concert hall was a message about this world, not the next. "All these songs were about the coming of justice, the coming of a greater social truth." He considers, smiles, the edge that doesn't so much cut through his earnestness as mark its boundaries. "I'm sorry I'm not singing Bob Dylan's 'Blowing in the Wind,' or whatever, all the protest songs out there. I'm singing this. And if your humanity is touched by this, then I got you where I want you."

This is where he wants you: the last number, he's standing on a pillar surrounded by his singers and dancers, looking down on them like a preacher. "I'magonnatellyouaboutthecomingofthejudgment!" And then he comes down into the crowd and gathers them up and wheels them around to a ramp rising from the stage—"There's a better day a-coming," he sings, the jazz inflection speaking the grief of the days behind—marching up the ramp, a blues stomp, the camera rising and dipping, almost all one shot, Belafonte first leading the crowd then overwhelmed by it, a mass of men and women of all races growing to fill the screen, singing the old gospel like it's the new power, here and now, this world and not the next.

Did you see that fork of lightning?
Fare ye well, fare ye well!
Can you hear that rumbling thunder?
Fare ye well, fare ye well!
Then you see them stars a-falling!
Then you see the world on fire!

Cut to the chandelier of the Revlon room, White couples in tuxedos and gowns, the evening's hostess in pearls. "Well!" says Miss Barbara Britton. "Have you ever heard anything like it before?"

›‹

In 1959, Belafonte was playing Vegas for $50,000 a week. Every night he looked out across a sea of White faces. Most Black people couldn't have afforded the show even if Vegas hadn't been segregated. But TV? Black folks had TVs. One night on television reached more Black people than a year of Sundays at the Apollo, Harlem's legendary theater. TV, Belafonte thought, would be his hammer. He'd use the idiot box to break chains. Revlon ordered another five specials.

But after just one more show, Charlie Revson, scion of Revlon, had a problem. "The White guys down in the South don't want it," he said. "They'll black out the station." It was the dancers, the backup singers. Some Black, some White. Choose, said Revson; no mixing. He figured Belafonte would probably prefer the color, but Revlon wanted to respect his freedom. You're the artist, Mr. Belafonte. So choose: Black or White.

On the street and up in his apartment, in a taxi and in a diner booth, here in this screening room, Belafonte will tell me this story over and over. Not because he's forgotten but because it's one of the moments to which, in age, he chooses to return. "I said, 'See you around, and goodbye forever.'" He smiles, shark-toothed generosity. "See you around." The words with which he set himself free.

"Instead of being a grateful nigger, walking in and saying, 'How wonderful you gave me this,' I'm sitting there saying, 'No. See you around.'"

He still got paid. Pay-or-play: A check from Revlon for $800,000 showed up at his office that afternoon, the price of keeping America's biggest Black star off TV.

"Fear and consequences," says Belafonte. He pushes himself up and eases out of the screening room like he's carrying the cane just for fashion, one hand brushing the wall along the archive's dark hallway.

><

Harold George Bellanfanti Jr. was born in New York on March 1, 1927. His father was the son of a Black Jamaican mother and a White Dutch Jew, and his mother, Millie, was the daughter of a Black Jamaican father and a White mother. They were both undocumented immigrants. They kept no family pictures; Millie feared they might serve as evidence. Of what? Hard to say. Proof of their island past? Every so often she changed their family name. A letter here, a letter there, enough to disappear among the files, rounding down the syllables until they became the Belafontes.

His father, Harry Sr., cooked on the banana boats that sailed between New York and the Caribbean. Millie worked as a maid and sometimes a dressmaker. She was stern and Jamaican-proud, raised on a Black island with a history of revolt. Harry would stand beside her among hundreds of other Black women dressed in their Sunday best every day, beneath the stone arches up past Ninety-Seventh Street, where the train tracks come up from underground. White women would inspect Black women, pick the day's help. Sometimes a White woman would let him follow his mother into the backseat of a giant automobile. One Saturday evening in a kitchen on Central Park West one of those White women slapped Millie. He remembers the sound, the crack of a hand against his mother's face. His aunt, working that night, too, had to wrap her arms around Millie to keep her from going for a knife.

Sundays after Mass, Millie would take him to the Apollo to hear Count Basie or Billie Holiday or Ella Fitzgerald. On the street he'd see Duke Ellington, Langston Hughes. But his heroes were gangsters. White ones, because that's who filled the screen: James Cagney, Edward G. Robinson. And there was his uncle Lenny, a numbers boss he once watched knock out a beat cop for mouthing off. Harry liked that. Millie worried. Seven years old and her boy already knew how to swagger, how to curse and fight dirty. Ran from a White boy just once, to keep his shirt clean for the school play, and even then, he went back. "To stomp the guy." There was a gang called the Scorpions, another called the Spiders. "We fought with bottles, garbage cans, rocks, hands, and feet." Millie read the odds. She put him on a banana boat, sent him to his grandmother. White-skinned and blue-eyed, his grandmother lived in a house on stilts in the country, surrounded by plantains and mangos and yams. "I was a great night gazer," he'd recall. "I used to climb up in a mango tree and lie back and eat mangoes and look through the leaves at the sky."

He rode the banana boats back and forth between Harlem and Jamaica for two years. Jamaica saved him. "Black people saw people from Jamaica as the Jews of the Black world," he says. They were educated; they pushed. "You look at us, Malcolm X and his island roots, Sidney Poitier and his island roots. Look at Stokely Carmichael, 'Black Power' coming from his Trinidadian mouth." On the docks, from banana loaders and fishmongers, he learned to sing mento, the Jamaican music out of which reggae grew, and a more accurate name than calypso for the source of the music he later sang. In the streets, in Harlem, he learned to gamble. For a while he tried to pass. Sometimes he watched his mother cry. He fought, he drifted; sometimes he sang. He dropped out of school. When he was seventeen, he went to a movie called *Sahara*. War movie, Bogart, but more important a Black actor named Rex Ingram, who plays a Sudanese soldier fighting with the Allies, a Black man who tackles and suffocates a Nazi, a White man, pale as the moon, on that big silver screen. *Yes!* thought Belafonte. That was what he wanted.

He joined the Navy, 1944, and was sent to a camp called Robert Smalls, after an enslaved man forced to work on a Confederate ship in the Civil War until he commandeered it and sailed it to freedom. Eighty years later, Camp Robert Smalls was still segregated. Many of the Black seamen were older, some had been to college. They schooled Belafonte, fed him pamphlets. One man passed on a copy of W.E.B. Du Bois's just-published *Dusk of Dawn: An Essay Toward an Autobiography of a Race Concept*. Du Bois was even better than Rex Ingram. Belafonte wanted more. He swung on an officer, a White man, and went to the brig. He found other books, more Du Bois. When he returned to Harlem, he kept reading. He worked as a janitor. That's what he'd be, he thought. A janitor who read, a man with a broom wise to the world.

One day a woman who lived in his building gave him a pair of theatre tickets. He couldn't afford a date, so he went alone. The company was called the ANT, the American Negro Theatre. He'd never heard of it. He'd never heard of any theatre. And this theatre was in a library, the Schomburg—a whole library dedicated to Black people. The play was called *Home Is the Hunter*, a story of Black veterans returning to Harlem. He knew them. He was one of them. He could play these parts. An actor, he thought—maybe *that* was what he could be. He used GI Bill money to enroll in the New School's Dramatic Workshop. His classmates were Tony Curtis, Walter Matthau, and a young Marlon Brando. Sidney Poitier, another young West Indian actor he'd met at the ANT, was his best friend. "This bright, tough cookie who knows where jugular veins are located," Poitier—who in 1964 became the first Black man to win an Oscar for best actor—would later write of Belafonte at twenty-one.

"Sidney radiated a truly saintly calm and dignity," Belafonte would respond. "Not me."

Belafonte's hero, Paul Robeson, showed up at one of his first plays. He began singing as an actor, performing in agitprop theatre on behalf of the 1948 leftist presidential candidacy of Henry Wallace, alongside Seeger and Guthrie. He made his professional debut in 1949 at a mobbed-up jazz club where he'd become a regular, a musical obsessive who'd bring scripts with him to study in the dim, smoky light while jazz greats jammed into the morning. The musicians took pity and, over his protest, got him a gig singing during an intermission. It was just a money thing; they knew he really wanted to be an actor. And maybe they knew he had that all wrong. He needed a band. Al Haig, a pianist who played for Lester Young, Dizzy Gillespie, and Miles Davis, volunteered to back him. When Belafonte took the stage one Tuesday night in a secondhand blue suit he'd bought for the occasion, introduced as "a new discovery, Harry Bella Buddha!" his throat dry and his hands sweating and his mind reeling not with doubt but certainty—*I don't belong here*—Charlie Parker's bass player, Tommy Potter, slipped onstage. Then came Max Roach on drums. And finally Charlie Parker himself picked up his saxophone. Bella Buddha was a nobody, and he had the best band in jazz. He sang "Blue Moon," he sang "Stardust."

Belafonte knew what he brought to the combo: a warm but untrained voice, limited range, and a preternatural sense of timing. Not musical timing; the beat and pause of a showman. The musicians heard it in that first song. "Somebody once said to me, 'Do you consider yourself an actor or a singer?'" he says now. "And I said, 'By all measure I consider myself an actor. And I will tell you something else, my claim to arrogance. I think I'm the best actor in the world.' 'Well, that is arrogant. How do you draw that conclusion?' 'I've convinced you I'm a singer.'"

The papers started calling him the "Cinderella Gentleman." He bought new clothes, he crooned, he cut records. Brando envied him. Henry Fonda followed him from gig to gig. Maybe, Belafonte thought, this was what he had been looking for.

He married a woman he'd met in the Navy, Marguerite, and they had the first of two girls, and he made enough money to live in growing style. But it felt wrong. After shows he'd go backstage, look in the mirror. He wore a tuxedo. He sang to order. He had a pretty face—interchangeable with a dozen others. What he sang wasn't jazz. It wasn't anything. "Pop ditties," he thought, and the thought wasn't kind. "Junk," he thought. In 1950, he took a booking at a club in Miami called the Five O'Clock, his first trip below the Mason-Dixon line. "Land of the Jews," his manager reassured him. "The segregated South," Belafonte responded. The club gave him a handful of passes, the paperwork necessary for a Black man to move about town after curfew, and a special dispensation to perform for White people at a club that'd only let him in the back door. Not just any White people, either. White women, lonely women who wanted him as a Black fantasy at a remove. "As long as I was onstage, crooning love songs, I had a certain power over them," he'd write in his memoir, *My Song*. "But when the lights came up, I was just another colored man hotfooting it back to Colored Town—or else." He made up his mind that night. He was done. The club offered him a raise, but he walked. He had no idea how he'd make a living, couldn't foresee *Calypso* or all the awards, the stages he'd make his own that no African American had stepped on before without a broom. None of that seemed possible for a Black man. Crooning was his main and seemingly only chance. It was that or poverty. He said no just the same.

He plowed his savings into a hamburger joint in the West Village called the Sage. He and his partners bought wholesale from the grocery store and fed hard-luck cases for free. As a business, the Sage was a disaster. But as a scene? Tony Scott, a clarinetist who'd played with Billie Holiday, was a regular. A cantor taught Belafonte folk songs from Israel. The Village Vanguard, where Leadbelly was playing the music Belafonte wanted to sing—"raw, gritty, American songs"—was just down the street. Sometimes, those songs were right in the Sage. "We'd just stop everything and sing right there," Belafonte says. It was the beginning of his second act.

When Belafonte played Carnegie Hall in 1959, he opened with one of those raw American songs: "Darlin' Cora," about a boss who called him "boy." His friend Pete Seeger, along with the Weavers, had opened with a version of the song at Carnegie three years before, but they'd played it loud and fast. Seeger, a Harvard boy, had been blacklisted, disappeared from the top of the charts, and he sang the song like an assertion: *I am*. Belafonte's anger was more deeply aged. He let the song simmer, backed by a trotting guitar.

> *I ain't a man to be played with,*
> *I ain't nobody's toy.*
> *Been working for my pay a long, long time . . .*

He leans on the word and the guitar lopes into a gallop:

> *Well I whupped a man, Darlin' Cora*
> *And he fell down where he stood*
> *Don't know if that was wrong, Darlin' Cora*

He stretches her name out, singing over the dead man's body:

> *But Lord, it sure felt good!*

›‹

He always made it feel good. Strip a half century of camp off *Calypso* and it's one of the most lilting grooves recorded. It's the music of Pax Americana: island holidays for the middle class, nightclubs for workingmen and -women. The most successful Black musician in history had made the nation hear him on his own terms, had made them love him for singing his own song. Forget the "Day-o" in your mind. Shuffle the songs, start with the "hoooo-*uh*" of "Dolly Dawn" or the high, falling cascade of "I Do Adore Her" or the perfect rhythm of "Man Smart (Woman Smarter)." *Then* go back to "Day-o" and listen to the pleasure and the edge, the code within the act.

"What I did," Belafonte says, "what made conscious political sense, was to say, 'Let me have you love me because I will show you my deeper humanity.'" He beats out the "Banana Boat" rhythm on his desk. "If you like this song so much that I can engage you into singing it, delighting in it, I've sold you a people, a region, a culture. If you look more deeply into that region, that culture, those people, you'll see a lot of things that have to do with oppression, with slavery. The song is a *work* song. It's a protest song." Calypso is Trinidadian music, derived from West African kaiso by slaves who used it to mock their masters. Belafonte tilts his head back, eyes half-closed, and opens his palms, becoming a Kingston dockworker. "'I want to get home. I want to drink a rum. I want to get out from *under*.'"

We've been talking in Belafonte's living room for an hour when his wife, Pam, reminds him he has a phone interview about his new memoir with *Essence*, a fashion-and-lifestyle magazine for African American women. Belafonte puts the reporter on speaker and nods at me to listen. The interview doesn't start well.

"Did you learn anything about yourself through the writing process?"

"Yep." Silence.

But after a while he starts riffing on perfunctory questions, veering from entertainment to art to politics. The reporter interrupts him; he continues; she interrupts again. Three times he tries. *Essence* wins.

"Before I let you go, this is a magazine for Black women. Could you talk a little bit about what you love about Black women?"

Long pause. Belafonte's first wife was Black. His second, the woman with whom he spent most of his life, was a White dancer named Julie Robinson. When Belafonte married her in 1957—around the same time he was starring opposite Joan Fontaine in *Island in the Sun*, the first Hollywood movie to feature a romance, a kiss, between a Black man and a White woman—the outcry was so great he wrote a cover story for *Ebony* magazine called "Why I Married Julie." White critics said it was an integration scheme, only the word many of them preferred was *miscegenation*, what the Klan considered racial abomination, the only result of which could be "mud people." And not just the Klan; Robert F. Kennedy deemed Belafonte's interracial marriage, opposed by 96 percent of Whites—as if his love life was subject to public survey—to be "a sign of instability," proof that he was a "questionable character." Black critics, meanwhile, accused him of betraying the race, and specifically Black women. It was a big enough issue that *Ebony* ran an article with the opinions of Thurgood Marshall, A. Philip Randolph, Mahalia Jackson, Louis Armstrong, Duke Ellington, and Roy Wilkins, head of the NAACP, among others. "We didn't marry to prove a social point," wrote Belafonte. "We did it for love."

More than half a century later, he's being asked the same question. "Now," he says, "you ask me what do I admire most about Black women. What I most admire in *a* woman who faces oppression is her willingness to be smart and cunning in overthrowing that oppression. Other than that, Black women don't hold very much more than all women. Because—"

"I do thank you so much for your time with this," the reporter interrupts. "Is there *anything* else you wanted to say?"

"*Yes*. We have a culture where to tell the truth is not an easy thing to do. Every day we wake up we do our minstrel act. And our minstrel act means we put on the mask. We put on our burnt cork. And we grin like we know we have to grin to get through the day even though there's a rage inside of us."

It sounds like the reporter is trying to break in. Like she wants to get away from this crazy old man. Like she can't hear the confession. Because Belafonte, what he's trying to tell her is he corked up too. The donkey's a metaphor, sure, metaphors all the way down, but up top, on the surface, it's still a donkey on a stage: an act. "Everybody does it," he tells the reporter. "It's the American theme."

He pauses, and the reporter seizes her chance: "Have a terrific rest of the day!"

><

Belafonte was twenty-nine when he met Martin Luther King Jr. in the basement of Abyssinian Baptist in Harlem. King was twenty-seven. "He was shorter and stockier than I expected," Belafonte writes in *My Song*. But then, he hadn't expected much. "You don't know me," King had said when he'd called and asked for the meeting. Belafonte thought he did: just another hustler working his Bible routine. "One of the first things that I said to Martin was, 'I gotta tell you right now, I understand your mission, I hear what you're saying, but I gotta tell you, I'm not the church.'" There's a picture of the meeting in Belafonte's apartment. Just two men in a bare basement that doubled as a Sunday school, complete with a blackboard. A singer and a preacher; New York and Georgia; the Old Left and a new vision of freedom with a little wooden table between them and a couple of folding chairs. Belafonte's in a dark suit, hands folded, listening. King's leaning just a little bit forward, trying to rope a star. "I need your help," he's saying. "I have no idea where this movement is going.

I'm called upon to do things I cannot do, and yet I cannot dismiss the calling."

They spoke for three hours that day, the beginning of a relationship that would become one of the deepest in each man's life. "There was an almost invisible electricity," was how Sidney Poitier described the bond. "Almost mystical." Belafonte was converted—not to the gospel, about which he'd argue with King to the end, but to the cause as King understood it. "I wasn't nonviolent by nature," Belafonte writes, but the more time he spent with King the more he believed nonviolence wasn't just a strategy. It was a way of life. It was something he could do with his anger.

As for what he could do with his money, one of the fattest bank accounts in pop culture: bankroll a revolution. He tapped every celebrity he knew for a donation, but none matched the flow of funds from his hands into every corner of the movement. He became one of its biggest donors, "took only what he needed for his family and turned the rest of the money over to King," writes historian Steven J. Ross. He underwrote the Freedom Riders and paid bail money whenever needed and provided much of the backing for the Student Nonviolent Coordinating Committee, the younger, more radical alternative to King's Southern Christian Leadership Council. He kept the lights on at the movement's meetings all over the country, and he was King's liaison to the Kennedys; Bobby and Jack relished Harry's style. He paid King's bills and hired a secretary and a driver for King's wife, Coretta, left home alone with their four children. And when King was in New York, he stayed in Belafonte's twenty-one-room apartment, a hideout from even King's closest allies.

"Nobody knew it was there," Belafonte says. "Nobody knew his number. Nobody knew anything. He had his own key, he had his own bathroom, he had his own entrance." King would slip in late, and Julie Belafonte would bring out the Harveys Bristol Cream they kept for him. King always marked the bottle with a line. It was a joke, or maybe it was a border between the world outside and his secret retreat at Harry's.

Some nights they'd talk tactics and strategy, some nights it was the go-slow Kennedys and Bull Connor, the White supremacist police boss of Birmingham, Alabama. Sometimes they'd just crack each other up. *Who am I?* one man might say, miming a pompous strut. *Oh, man, that's gotta be Abernathy,* and they'd both double over in giggles. Across the hall from that photograph of King and Belafonte meeting for the first time, there's another picture of the two of them at Harry's, the rarest of images of King: busting a gut with laughter, eyes squeezed shut, not the noble Christ figure we're used to now but a fat, jolly Buddha.

Some nights King wrote. He'd scratch out something on a yellow legal pad, put on his MLK suit and leave for a fundraiser, return to the apartment, sip some sherry, become Martin again, write a few more words, crumple the page and toss it. "Before it hit the floor, my hand was there like Willie Mays," says Belafonte. "'Don't throw that out! Hold on, man! That's your *writing*.'" He'd smooth the wrinkled pages and store them away, the sacred texts of a man he insists even now must not be deified. King, to Belafonte, was a comrade.

There were death threats and bomb scares and arson attempts. When you marched in front, next to King, you had to be ready to die. Belafonte's closest call came in 1964. He'd tapped the stars—Frank Sinatra, Henry Fonda, Marlon Brando, Joan Baez—and his own funds to raise money for the Mississippi Freedom Summer's voter-registration drive. Then three activists disappeared. On August 4, the FBI found the bodies. James Chaney, a twenty-one-year-old Black man from Mississippi, and two White men from New York, twenty-year-old Andrew Goodman and twenty-four-year-old Michael Schwerner. They'd been shot; Goodman had been buried alive; Chaney was castrated. That night one of the leaders of the voter drive called Belafonte. Change of plans. Originally, volunteers were to work two-week shifts. Now they were going to stay—every one of them. They needed more money.

"How much?" Belafonte asked.

"At least fifty thousand dollars," the activist said—within three days. There was no way a Black man in New York could wire $50,000 to a civil rights activist in Mississippi. It'd be like sending a death warrant. Somebody would have to hand deliver. Cash. Belafonte called Poitier: "They might think twice about killing *two* big niggers," Belafonte told him. When they landed in Jackson, a handful of activists hurried them into a Cessna that took them to a dirt runway in Greenwood. As soon as they stepped off the plane, the pilot wheeled around and took off. Belafonte remembers a single lightbulb dangling over a gate to the dirt road beyond; Poitier believes there may have been two. "Blacker than a hundred midnights," Belafonte thought, a line he remembered from a poem by James Weldon. When they got into the car—its finish sanded down to dull its shine— a pair of headlights across the field popped on, then another, and another, more.

"Federal agents," Belafonte told Poitier.

"Agents my ass," said their driver. "That's the Klan." The driver, a man named Willie Blue, made straight for the lights. At the last second, he veered off. "Faster, man!" shouted Belafonte. Uh-uh, said Willie Blue. Deputy would pull them over and they'd wind up just like the three boys the feds pulled out of the river. The three boys who, they'd later learn, had been chased just like this, by a lynch mob led by local lawmen. The car jolted. A truck had rammed them. It jolted again; the car shuddered, the night dark and wet and hot pouring in through the windows, Belafonte and Poitier twisting round toward the glaring lights as if their star power could stop them. It's okay, said Willie Blue. As long as they could stay in front, the men in the truck couldn't draw a bead.

Close to town, a convoy of activists came out to meet them. Hundreds of activists, White and Black, were waiting in a dance hall. The applause, remembers Belafonte, was like nothing he'd ever known. He let the crowd fall quiet. Just Mississippi night. Then he sang.

Day-o! Day-o-o-o!

He changed the words.

Freedom, freedom, freedom come an' it won't be long.

When the song was over, Belafonte held up a black doctor's bag and dumped $70,000 in small bills on a table.

><

The loveliest image of Belafonte I've seen is in a CBS News broadcast of the 1965 march from Selma, Alabama, to Montgomery, the original capital of the old Confederacy. The third march. The first, March 7, 1965, "Bloody Sunday," ended in a cloud of tear gas and a blur of blood on a bridge across the Alabama River. Maybe you've seen the picture: a woman beaten nearly to death, unconscious, in the arms of a man who looks like he's singing a song, or weeping, or both. The second ended with the crushed skull of a White minister from Boston. The third set out 8,000 strong on March 21 and came around a corner of six-lane Dexter Avenue in Montgomery four days later with 25,000 souls. That was the day King gave the speech now known as "How Long, Not Long"—

I come to say to you this afternoon, however difficult the moment, however frustrating the hour, it will not be long.

But before the speeches, songs. Belafonte at a podium on a flat-bed truck parked crosswise in front of the capitol, towering and broad in a dark zip-neck sweater, his arm around a blacklisted folk singer named Leon Bibb, who's waving a little American flag with a sly smile, and Mary Travers of Peter, Paul and Mary, who's twitching her perfect platinum bangs, wearing a tight white sleeveless shirt and tighter black-and-white check pants, swinging her hips in front of a seated MLK, who's trying to peer around her. If you grew up on "Puff the Magic Dragon," you probably don't know how absurdly sexy Mary once was. They all were, all three of them on that flatbed truck, desire and redemption and, in the middle, Mr. B, so beautiful he could be the solution to an equation. Solve for x, if x equals physical perfection. Behind them, hunkered in the capitol, the tragic little troll-man of segregation, Gov. George Wallace. Wallace didn't come out for Belafonte's show. Said he did not care about the 25,000 on his doorstep or the television cameras all over the world. That didn't matter to Harry, Leon, and Mary. They'd already won, and they'd sing their song wherever and whenever they wanted. And they did, and they sang it terribly—maybe the worst rendition of "Michael, Row Your Boat Ashore" you've ever heard, their voices ragged and breaking into laughter and bumping into one another, Joan Baez off on the side soaring way too high above them. That didn't matter, either, they were so tired and so glad, Leon, Harry, and dazzling Mary.

How long? Not long.

I ask Belafonte about that moment one day at a diner near his apartment. We've been talking about the decades since those years with King, since the April 9, 1968, march in Memphis Belafonte led in King's place, holding the hands of King's fatherless children, after the bullet of April 4.

In Belafonte's speech that day, recorded by network news, you can hear him fighting to hold on to the vision. "In the hope," he says, "that the White world, in its bestiality and its decay, in its inability to understand the meaning of the Black movement, in its inability to understand the compassion that Black people are bringing to them, that the White man will be able to come to his senses. Because we find it increasingly hard to deal with his intellect, to deal with him in the sociological sense, but perhaps, after this, we might be able to appeal to his soul. Because that's all that's left."

And then he walked away.

"Did you ever struggle with it?" I ask. Nonviolence, I mean.

"What do you mean, 'did I ever'? That's all I struggle with, as a matter of fact." He keeps all of King's speeches on his computer. "I get in a real tough moment, I go into my computer, sometimes I don't even know which one it is. I just need to hear his voice. It's not self-asphyxiation. I'm not praising a deity. I'm living with a man that I remember." He turns his head, smiles, then frowns. "Now that you've elected not to be around here." He's addressing Martin. "Which was a very selfish thing to do."

There's doubt in Belafonte's voice. A note of confusion. How long? Not long. But it's been more than four decades now, and the movement he helped make he believes has been stolen, turned into an uplifting story, a Hollywood fable with a happy ending that isn't yet real.

In early 1968, NBC asked Belafonte to take over *The Tonight Show* for a week. He agreed, as long as he had the freedom to choose his guests. Odetta, Aretha, Lena, RFK. Of course King. "We came out. I said, 'Martin, I was waiting for the tic.'" A tic King developed on the eve of the Birmingham campaign. Belafonte twitches in imitation. "What happened to it?"

"Well," says Martin, "it's gone."

"When did it leave?"

"When I made my peace with death."

Belafonte slumps in the booth. "I don't know if I've made my peace," he says. Sometimes he feels the loss of King as if it's fresh. Not like you might have felt it if you were alive then, or, if you weren't, like when you were a child in school and you first learned of the story

and followed its terrible arc from Selma to Montgomery to Birmingham and finally to that balcony in Memphis. Not like that but like
one of those frozen moments in history, a gunshot cracking through
your imagination. As if imagination existed not for the sake of wonder but as a kind of clay with which to take impressions of the incre-
ments by which the world is always, slowly, drawing a razor across its
own neck. It's not the grief that's fresh for Belafonte, it's the gap: the
awful absence of the *other* imagination, the what-might-have-been-
but-is-not. What is left, in the place of that other imagination, is this
still-beautiful, still-raging old man sitting across from you in a diner
on the Upper West Side, turning his ravaged but still-seductive voice
away from you to address the absence: "Now that you've elected to be
gone." Speaking to King as if he were here, sharing a lunch of clam
chowder and raspberry soda. Here and not here.

><

Belafonte wants to tell me—or maybe Martin—about a movie he
never made, probably never could have made.

Amos 'n' Andy. Not like *Bamboozled*, Spike Lee's postmodern riff on
blackface, but *Amos 'n' Andy* as a history of minstrelsy going back to
the beginning. It was the director Robert Altman's idea. A movie of
a minstrel show. White men in blackface who mimicked every brilliant song, every joke, every true story ever told by a Black soul: stole
it all and played it again, as both tragedy and farce, tragedy because
it was farce.

"It's about the mask," Belafonte says, speaking in the present tense
like he's talking strategy and tactics, sipping Harveys Bristol Cream.
"It's about how much time people spend being false, how often we
façade our behavior. Nobody's better at that than the minstrels. And
in them I see all of us. Everybody's in the minstrel show. Behind the
mask, you can say and do anything. The Greeks did it. Shakespeare

used it when he wrote the jester. Those he could not give the speech to, he created the jester to say it. All of America's problems are rooted in the fact that we're all jesters. Not one of us truth-tellers. So how do you get to the truth? Well, how do Amos 'n' Andy do it? What's behind the mask?"

This: In the mimicry and the falsehood, you can still find the roots of the song. "The art for me is how do you bend it your way?"

Maybe it couldn't be done. He told Altman, "You're going to get us both fucking killed. Black people gonna be completely outraged. Don't go to Black people with blackface. And White people know it's politically incorrect. There's no audience."

Altman said, "Except everybody."

Belafonte's quiet. Then: "But Altman left me here all alone." Altman died in 2006. Belafonte shakes his head, talking to no one now. "Everybody's in the minstrel show. Everybody's a minstrel act."

He dismisses most of his records; he never managed to capture what mattered about his shows, the way he had of shaking people, "all this rage coming out in this song that compelled them to find out what was this anger about and then to understand that it was the voice of a human being telling a story of the moment"—that never quite made it to vinyl. He's ambivalent about the movies. *Carmen Jones*, a breakthrough for Black actors? "Huge disappointment." Even the movement. "We created slogans, we created songs, we created *metaphor*," he'd lamented when we'd first met. "We created all sorts of things. And now you come back years later, and the language is still out there, but now they've *coopted* it."

Who's they? You. Me. Even Belafonte. We're all a part of the act. We dissolve the past into the inevitability of the present, as if this world of ours had to be. As if there were no others, slipping away from us, even now.

"The question you asked," I say, "was how do you be a truth-teller?"

Belafonte deadpans: "Find out what the reward is for truth-telling." He means, Martin found out. You get killed.

I say, "Maybe you get to stand on a stage in Montgomery at the end of a long march and sing a couple of songs."

"That's the best stage there is. Because in all these things there was death right afterward. Very successful march, boom, Medgar Evers murdered. March on Washington, then four little girls." The Sixteenth Street Baptist Church bombing in Birmingham. "Every time," he says.

After that day in Montgomery, Klansmen murdered a mother of five who was driving marchers back to Selma. "After every great victory, a great murder."

Then it clicks. The code. The murder is the blackface. It's the cork. It's the minstrel show, the act replayed, second time perverse.

"They're gonna let you know you didn't win," Belafonte says. That's why he's been so angry, so long. It's what keeps him alive. "Where your anger comes from," he says, "is less important than what you do with it."

What do you do with it? What he's always done. You take it from the top. You sing your song again, until they hear it like it's the first time. You make it your own, and then you give it away.

2

On the Side of Possibility

I have on my desk before me a spine-cracked paperback copy of a collection of stories called *The Pagan Rabbi*, by Cynthia Ozick, first published in 1971. This edition seems to have shared close quarters at some point with a broken pen; the edges of its pages are gilded with blue ink. The cover depicts the title story's eponymous subject, a black-hat rabbi with a purple shirt and a rose clutched in his hand, his head in profile beneath the tree that has become his lover. That's what the story is about: a rabbi who falls in love with a tree. On the back of the book there's a red discount sticker, "$1.00." And next to it, beneath a picture of Ozick, another sticker: "OWS." I have another copy of this book, but I picked this one up for that sticker. OWS. Written across the edges of the pages is the legend "OWS Library."

OWS, in the autumn of 2011, stood for Occupy Wall Street. How to account for this odd movement that for a brief moment—before it was crushed, its debris hosed off the street—seemed even to the cynical like it might herald a shift? Occupy was dedicated to "soft regime change," explained one of its founders. When pressed for the meaning of such a phrase, he offered instead a poem in the form of a picture, an image devised by a sleek, satirical magazine called *Adbusters*, for the movement they hoped to dream into being: a ballerina balanced in attitude croisée derrière between the shoulder blades of *Charging Bull*, the iconic idol of Wall Street snorting in bronze, with a crowd of riot police in gas masks staggering in smoke behind her. "Dear Americans," *Adbusters* tweeted, "this July 4th, dream of insurrection against corporate rule." *Insurrection*, a word that did not then bristle with threat. Indifferent to dates, this uprising began instead on September 17, in a block-long granite plaza tucked between anonymous skyscrapers a few blocks away from Ground Zero, which had once been the site of the Twin Towers before 9/11 erased them. That morning of 9/17, 2011, this plaza filled with some 2,000 protesters; that night, 200 stayed, some number of whom would remain, reinforced by growing numbers, until the night of November 15, when hundreds of New York City police officers, a helicopter thumping overhead, forced the reporters out and then in the dark erased it all, trampled the tents and people within them, smashed the kitchen and kicked over the drums and broke the books' spines.

But before that! In the fall of 2011, occupations sprouted in parks and public squares everywhere. One of the premises of the movement was the idea that we are still strangers to democracy, that maybe we have not yet lost for good what we have not yet achieved. The occupations proceeded from the conviction that we live in a kind of political vacuum, not unlike the paradoxical "privately owned public space" in which it began in Lower Manhattan, a gray zone between a corporation and the government that provides it with police power. Occupations were literally about re-filling a hollowed-out public sphere with an actual public of breathing bodies. In Atlanta, Woodruff

Park was renamed Troy Davis, for a Black death-row convict widely believed innocent but executed nonetheless on September 21, four days into the occupation; in Oakland there was Oscar Grant Plaza, named for a young Black man killed by police in 2009. There were at least 1,000 occupations, a gritty spiral jetty of anarchist punks and construction workers, cooks and nannies and librarians—lots of librarians—and Teamsters and priests and immigrants, "legal" and otherwise. Some occupations drew tens of thousands, most a few hundred, some no more than one earnest soul on the side of the road with a sign that said WE ARE THE 99%.

What did they want? They made no demands. They drove the press and even the politicians who might have been allies—"it expresses the frustrations the American people," said President Obama—mad by refusing the very idea of demands. They met nightly in "general assemblies" to which you elected yourself simply by being there. They made decisions by consensus. They wanted a better world; they thought they might start building it in a gray park in lower Manhattan, close to Wall Street, which they never did in fact occupy.

The "OWS Library" was one of the movement's most remarkable creations. It began as a row of boxes containing donated books, mostly well-used paperbacks like my *Pagan Rabbi*, and it became a row of tables alongside the northeast corner of the park, a collection of several thousand—cataloguing was as never-ending as the stream of donations—maintained by a group of volunteer librarians, one of whom slept on an air mattress beside the reference desk. He wasn't there as a guard: At this library, books were free for the taking. Howard Zinn's *A People's History of the United States* got taken almost as fast as it could be shelved. My *Pagan Rabbi*, I'm guessing, had been lingering for a while, tucked between a romance novel and a mass-market paperback of *A Canticle for Leibowitz*, a 1960 sci-fi classic about a monastic order dedicated to the preservation of books in a postapocalyptic age. *Canticle* is about scarcity. This library wasn't.

"Books are no longer like commodities here," another librarian once told me at two a.m., standing near his sleeping colleague. "We've had to give them away." One word for that is *surplus*, but a better word—the biblical word, the rabbinical word—is *abundance*.

Abundance not just in fact but as something that is felt is what most of the media seemed not to notice about the Occupy movement. That's reasonable, given that the movement was born in opposition to the "1 percent," whose minimum annual household income averaged then more than $1.5 million, an impressive sum that is nonetheless too small to convey the proportion of the nation's wealth—nearly half—in their control. But the old frame of the haves versus the have-nots does not convey the joyousness of the experience of Liberty Park. I'm not sure when I first felt that joy, but I know when I named it for what it was: one night lying on a sleeping pad beneath a thin blanket, hemmed in by my just-met friend Austin, a teacher of autistic children who left the park for work every day at 7:30 a.m., and his girlfriend and her girlfriend, reading my newly acquired copy of *The Pagan Rabbi* by the yellow sodium light of the city's permanent illumination. Purists call that light pollution, but filtering through the feathery leaves of Liberty Park's honey locust trees, it was lovely. More than lovely; bathed in its amber glow I felt like one of five hundred little Christs, if by "Christ" you'll allow me to refer not to divinity itself but to one of its more wholly human representations, Andres Serrano's 1987 photograph *Piss Christ*. Appreciating what happened in Liberty Park requires a mental shift akin to the one necessary to see *Piss Christ*—an image of a plastic crucifix submerged in the artist's own golden urine—as not blasphemous but a strange breed of beautiful. I don't mean ideologically beautiful, some baroque idea one admires for the complexity of its inversions. I mean gorgeous. Breathtaking, breath-giving, at the same time.

The title story of *The Pagan Rabbi* begins with two men, friends from rabbinical school. The narrator, no genius, becomes instead of a rabbi a furrier. The pagan rabbi, meanwhile, Isaac Kornfeld, "a man of piety and brains," hangs himself from a tree in a public park with his own prayer shawl. Instead of writing a suicide note, he composes a theological treatise in the form of a love letter. Isaac had, it turns out, fallen for the tree, and this being Cynthia Ozick, the love was consummated.

The *why* of Isaac's love is, of course, weird, or wonderful, or both, depending on your feelings about transcendentalism and tree hugging. But the story is more about the narrator's attempt to comprehend his nature-loving friend's dying declaration that "there is nothing that is Dead. There is no non-life." And when the narrator grasps the rabbi's feeling—glimpses it, really, for it's impossible to hold—it returns him to childhood. Not wonder, but its opposite:

> It was the crisis of insight one experiences when one has just read out, for the first time, that conglomeration of figurines which makes a word. In that moment I penetrated beyond Isaac's alphabet into his language. I saw that he was on the side of possibility: he was both sane and inspired. His intention was not to accumulate mystery but to dispel it.

Such were the intentions of the Occupy movement. It should come as no surprise that those intentions did not transmit well through CNN or the column inches of the *New York Times*—that, working off these sources, a skeptical student at the college where I teach said to me, "I can *feel* the excitement, but I don't know if I can articulate why." She liked an Internet video that compiled footage of beautiful women at Liberty Park. "It looked more like celebrating than protesting," she observed. But most of what she'd seen on TV was police beating people, or people screaming because they'd been beaten by police. She suspected there was more to it. "I don't think I've experienced democracy in a physical way," she said. It sounded intriguing: *physical democracy*.

Her inability to reckon with what was happening in Liberty Park and, to greater and lesser degrees, across the country, was not the result of a media conspiracy, as many protesters charged. It was not a problem of TV talking heads executing orders from on high to make the dissidents look like fools. In fact, the protesters *were* fools—but in the holy tradition, the one that speaks not truth to power but imagination to things as they are. The American press, with its geography of public and private spheres, its love of contests, was built for a different reality. Pragmatically so; it's the reality in which we find ourselves constricted.

Movements are born from the problems of everyday lives, but they're not limited by them. "We're not in ordinary time," a writer visiting Occupy Nashville told me. "This is movement time."

She wasn't speaking in slogans. What she meant was a sort of slow motion, sped up, outside of the flow of minutes and days, the temporal experience suggested by the Christian theological term *kairos*, ritual time, a moment that is unique and suffused with moments past. Holidays are a kind of kairos. Each is its own, but for celebrants it is also all the iterations past that they can remember, and all the holidays of the future, anticipated, imagined.

So the Occupy movement was a holiday. There is nothing frivolous about that. Holidays are not escapes; at their best, they deepen our experience of things. Consider the rituals of this one: The marches, yes—many saw those on TV, and many have themselves marched for one thing or another. Then there was the police violence, for the White middle-class majority a more exotic experience. Pepper spray blinds, but it has a way of clarifying the issues. But that, too, is still ordinary stuff. The media knew how to report that. You have to push further.

To the OWS Library, for instance—the ritual of simply taking a book, with no money or identification changing hands. The ritual is something like this: "Here. I have a story. You can have it too." So you sit on the stone steps into the park and read for a while. Ozick describes the shiksa bride in "The Pagan Rabbi," and the way she "danced without her shoe, and the black river of her hair followed her." And Ozick records this exchange between the narrator and his bride:

> "After today she'll have to hide it all," I explained.
>
> Jane asked why.
>
> "So as not to be a temptation to men," I told her. . . .
>
> "It's a very anthropological experience," Jane said.
>
> "A wedding is a wedding," I answered her, "among us even more so."

>‹

Present tense, now, because the apocalypse—not just an end, but an "unveiling," per its original meaning, and thus a beginning—is always now. Dusk falls, cars honk, the jackhammer the city has set to racketing across the street competes with the thumping aural blur of the drums down at the southwest edge of the park. *Bongos* is too fun a word for that ceaseless noise. There's a celebrity of some sort beneath the three giant red girders bound together into a public sculpture on the southeast corner called *Joie de Vivre*. Is it Susan Sarandon? "I just watched *Rocky Horror* last night," says a policeman, delighted. A line begins to wind around the kitchen at the heart of the park—2,000 served daily—and the halal carts and smoothie carts and veggie carts rev up for evening supper, and the smells of falafel and grilling meat settle in with the Hasidim who, as evening comes, seem to flock to the park, their politics moot (a wink is all one will give me by way of explanation), some of them singing in Yiddish and Hebrew, some of them circling the perimeter along with a certain kind of well-weathered middle-aged man, scoping but not leering, contemplating, doubting, wondering. "I don't know what these kids are doing," says an old guy named Walt. "But I want to—I don't know what these kids are doing." He keeps shuffling around.

"Mic check!" somebody yells. "Mic check!" come a dozen replies. "Mic check!" goes the single call again. "MIC CHECK!" a hundred voices holler.

This is the "human microphone," an adaptation of the old church style of call-and-response for the NYPD's rule against amplification, taken up after the police flattened a speaker holding a megaphone. One person speaks, the crowd repeats, everybody hears the crowd and their own voices. Born of everyday hassle, it has become one of the movement's most absurd and ingenious maneuvers, its inherent humor and brevity undercutting the wordy earnestness that usually makes political meetings unbearable.

"My concern," says a speaker.

"MY CONCERN," booms the crowd.

"Is deeper—"

"IS DEEPER—"

"—than sleeping bags!"

"THAN SLEEPING BAGS!"

The politics of the human microphone are implicit: We will have to collaborate for any of us to be heard. And its effectiveness is stunning. As the evening's general assembly, the daily ritual of deliberative democracy, begins, you find yourself repeating things you don't agree with. And you watch the inevitable cranks and complainers who are forced to repeat the crowd's pleas even when the crowd is pleading for them to let the meeting proceed. You become intimately aware of language, the first means by which we share imaginations.

The meeting moves faster than most town-council meetings. A half hour is spent on, say, a proposal to spend part of the general fund on more sleeping bags, or bins to aid in cleanup efforts, or whether to allow a visiting movie star to jump the "stack"—the speaking line. The answers come relatively fast: yes, maybe (more debate is required), no. Each answer brings applause, some whoops, a shout: "Consensus!"

Maybe you didn't believe in consensus, but now here it is, before your eyes, on the tip of your tongue. It feels good. Not like a task; like a creation. Every decision in the general assembly is a story, every member of the general assembly its author.

Of course, that's not really true—there are always dissidents, angry ones, grumblers, people with "better ideas." And what kind of story is it, anyway, that can't travel? Can this kind of decision-making go beyond a crowd of a few hundred? How far? A few thousand? A million?

Tomorrow they'll try again. For now, there is cake: kitchen volunteers stepping over bodies, moving through the dissipating crowd with great platters of it, fluffy and frosted.

At ten p.m., the quiet hour agreed upon with the local community board, noise ebbs, stretches out like a thin tide moving off to sea, and people begin repairing to their sleeping bags. After a beer with a few 99 percenters at a fireman's bar around the corner, I stop by the comfort station for some bedding and lie down beneath the honey locust trees with *The Pagan Rabbi*. The night, cooler but softer than the day, is the ritual at the marrow of the movement. Like the human mic, it's an adaptation. The police said no tents. So we all sleep together, so deep in the funk of several weeks' camping that the smell becomes normal, so close to strangers that the strange becomes comfortable, so tired beneath the trees, the lovely honey locusts a-shimmer in the yellow sodium, that our books fall upon our noses sometime in the early morning.

What time it was, I couldn't tell you.

II

Dream On
On Vanity

X

3

Heavy with Gold

The First Campaign

"It's coming," said Kim, her face flushing beneath her flowing white hair. The long rectangle of the open hangar doors seemed to thrum, space waiting to be filled. And then, slowly, unstoppably, the plane nosed into view—a giant *T*, a giant *R*, a *U* and an *M* and a *P*, the plane swelling from its tip to its girth to its wings, filling completely the field of our vision: "Trump Force One."

We had been waiting five hours by then, standing crushed together on the concrete floor of a hangar at a regional airport in Youngstown, Ohio, cycling through Candidate Trump's rally playlist, swaying together to Elton John's "Tiny Dancer," hopping to Billy Joel's "Uptown Girl." We hadn't really known what to do with the aria, Pavarotti's "Nessun dorma," but we sensed that it was grand— "This is special!" said a woman behind me. Such was the mood, the deep pleasure of waiting derived not just from the speech to come but from a building sensation of togetherness, rolling vibrations of solidarity and giddiness and anticipation.

"First protester," Kim's husband declared, soon after we were packed in next to one another close to the podium. "I've got dibs."

Kim wore a pink top and a heart-shaped sapphire ring; the rest of her jewelry was turquoise and swirling green malachite. For a beat she gave her husband a look, the serious kind—then it cracked, and she beamed with the sweet comic timing of a couple long in love. "Oh, Gene!" she said.

Gene looked down on his lady with a sly smile. "I'm gonna beat the shit out of him," Gene promised, "and get on CNN."

Not likely; CNN had been confined like the rest of the press to a cage far behind us, a prop for the passion play to come. That didn't matter. The joy of punching, real or imagined, is the ideal of action, an inner feeling made incarnate. "He stands up there and says what we all think," Gene said. "We all want to punch somebody in the face, and he says it for us." We envisioned it: knuckle, soft cheek. "You know you do," Gene said.

Kim nodded and said, "I do," like a vow. She patted my arm. It felt maternal. "We all do," she said. Then she tugged my sleeve, pulling me toward her. There was something, she told me, she'd been wanting to say for a while. About Hillary. "Don't you think," she whispered in my ear, "she looks like she's been rode hard and put up wet?"

So the conversation circled for hours, like the Rolling Stones songs on heavy rotation, "political" to the same extent that "Sympathy for the Devil" is a pop song. Sex and violence and the comic grotesque; that was the surface. Beneath it a longing more profound. When a preacher nobody knew took the podium and started crying, "He's worthy! He's worthy!" the crowd knew he meant God and Trump and them all at the same time, and when the preacher shouted, "Praise Him!" they did. And when he finished his sermon—sharp with crime and heroin and missing children, prophecy and Trump and the father-nation—and said, "His name is Jesus and he approves this message," they laughed, delighted by the preacher's joke because it was just for them. The Stones resumed, midsong, "Let's Spend the Night Together," but nobody minded the contradiction, sex and the sacred, because it wasn't a contradiction, it was the completion of the sentence they'd all been thinking but hadn't known how to say out loud: "greatness," by which they meant the end of shame.

Then, at last, it came: Trump's 727, heavy with gold. A group of women who had been sucking lollipops for the duration, to keep their mouths wet—security did not permit water—screamed: "Oh my God! Oh my God!" Gene said, "That's it, all right." The heavy guy next to me said: "That is a *big* plane. I gotta admit, that is one big plane."

It was. Liberals giggle over the innuendos of Trump but the believers are more sophisticated, they embrace not just the manufactured hope of a political rally but also the lust, the envy, the anger of our bluntest selves, transformed by a mighty plane and the man inside— "He owns that," moaned a girl behind me—into something greater.

The Trump stairs rolled slowly toward the plane. A servant bolted them on. And then we stared, our eyes bound to the diagonal silver bar of the plane's door. We did not will it to turn. We waited, as if it were a minute hand on a clock suspended.

><

American politics tends to produce a limited emotional range, mostly positive, peppered with indignation. But Trump scrawled across the spectrum: not just anger but rage; love and, yes, hate; fear, a political commonplace, and also vengeance. It didn't feel political. Politicians have long borrowed from religion the passion and the righteousness, but no other major modern figure had channeled the tension that makes Scripture endure, the desire, the wanting that gives rise to the closest analogue to Trumpism: the prosperity gospel, the American religion of winning.

Trump was impious, but he didn't reject faith. Instead, he returned it to the roots of Christian business conservatism, which is where he had been all along: Norman Vincent Peale's 1952 bestseller, *The Power of Positive Thinking*. Since Trump announced his candidacy, he had been talking about Peale, "my minister for years" (Peale died in 1993), but long before that—before he began declaring on the campaign trail that "nothing beats the Bible, not even *The Art of the Deal*"—the book that beat them all for Trump was Peale's. In Iowa, Trump held up the Bible his mother gave him, but it was *Positive Thinking* that Trump inherited from his developer father, Fred. In the books he claimed to have written, Trump invoked a personal trinity: his father, Fred, "a rock," who taught him "toughness"; his mentor, Roy Cohn, the Red Scare mafia lawyer who taught him how to get away with anything "without admitting any guilt"; and his childhood pastor, Peale. As a child, Trump has said, he watched Billy Graham on television "for hours and hours," but what he took from it was merely method, the hard sell presenting as a soft one. It was from Peale that Trump learned "a very positive feeling about God," he "wrote" in his stream-of-consciousness campaign book, *Crippled America*, "that made me feel positive about myself." The point wasn't God; it was him, Donald J. Trump, alpha and omega. Peale, Trump boasted, "thought I was his greatest student of all time."

The irony of Trump's religion, mostly mocked as a campaign put-on, was that it was one of the few consistencies in his life. Of course, consistency doesn't equal depth, but then, to "God's Salesman," as Peale marketed himself, depth was a distraction. *Positive Thinking*—still in print and popular—"makes no pretense to literary excellence," Peale wrote, "nor does it seek to illustrate any unusual scholarship on my part." "Positive Thinking" isn't about serving God; it's about using God, through what Peale called "applied Christianity," to achieve "a perfected and amazing method of successful living." The method is like a closed loop, a winners' circle of the soul. "The man who assumes success tends already to have success," Peale wrote, a tautological spirituality as instantly recognizable in Trumpism as the drumbeat of his words: *success, perfect, amazing.* For Peale, and Trump, these were magic words, the very utterance of which gave them the singular truth Trump derived from *Positive Thinking:* self. "BELIEVE IN YOURSELF!" Peale began the book, and the rest was commentary, fables of status drawn from the lives of sports heroes and businessmen, "competent spiritual experts" whose authority was demonstrated not by quoting Scripture but through the visible evidence of their success.

Peale's "positivity" has diluted into the air of the American myth of the businessman-redeemer. It was what Trump transmitted; what his followers received, though, was shaped for believers and unbelievers alike by the prosperity gospel that surpassed Peale. Peale's message resonated in its time most with the affluent—those, like Trump himself, who saw themselves as winners. The prosperity gospel recasts the same promise to those, like Trump's followers, who feel lost.

On the surface, the prosperity gospel is a simple transaction. It begins with a kind of sales demonstration, a preacher who shows you his wealth as evidence of his anointing. He's blessed; and you can be too. All you have to do is invest. How? The usual way: You give him your money. Only, your money is just a metaphor for your faith, and the good news promised by the prosperity gospel is that faith will be repaid in kind. "Miracles" will release you from the bondage of debt or obliterate the tumor you didn't even know was forming within you. The Christian Right that has so long dominated the political theology of the United States emphasizes a heavenly reward for righteousness in faith and behavior; the prosperity gospel is about what Peale might call "amazing results" you can measure and count. The old political theology was about the salvation to come; the Trump religion was about deliverance, here and now.

The deal—belief in return for relief, belief as a form of relief—is as old as religion, too fundamental to human consciousness to dismiss simply as a con. Pray for rain, sacrifice to the gods, keep kosher—you needn't believe to recognize the power of trading devotion for the hope of well-being. What the prosperity gospel did was regulate the exchange, something like the medieval selling of papal indulgences. Kenneth Hagin, one of its modern founders, called it "the law of faith," as real as the laws of physics. This wasn't the Protestant work ethic. It wasn't about "works" at all. Rather, it proposed supernatural intervention as a force you could direct through faith, as revealed through tithing and by putting the wealth that resulted on display. For the prosperity pioneer Oral Roberts, that included one of the largest bronze sculptures in the world, the sixty-foot-tall praying hands at the entrance to the university that bears his name. For the perfectly named Creflo Dollar, one of the following generation's most popular prosperity preachers, it was the $65 million Gulfstream G650, for which his ministry asked its followers to make donations and "love offerings."

Roberts was White; Dollar is Black. What the prosperity gospel offered as a model for the followers of Trump was what they imagined was a means for transcending race: colorblindness. Pastor Mark Burns, a Black prosperity-gospel minister from South Carolina, explained it this way in his opening prayer for Trump in Indiana: "It's horrible, horrible, how they're trying their best to make sure you and I focus on race and our color, and not the only true color that matters!" There is no "Black person," he continues, no "White person," no yellow, no red; "there is only green people!" He froze his face in a giant grin. "Green is money!"

Trump's religion was that of Norman Vincent Peale, but the religion of Trump was even bigger, a more amazing prosperity gospel, secularized. All that was ugly within it, the violence and the hate, was part of an expression of the sense of lack that Trumpism fed and to which it responded. It was, in its deepest sense, about desire. About wanting. Wanting things, yes, wanting the "green," wanting jobs; and also wanting to feel safe (from threats real and imagined, the actual decay of the welfare state and "Black crime"), wanting to feel brave (that is, like a man, as seen in the movies, or like a woman, in love with such a man), wanting to feel like a winner. Wanting to feel like Trump. Trump knew his followers wanted what he had, and that what Trump had, that for which the plane and the gold and all the "green," too, were merely symbols, was the freedom from want, economic and racial. Trump did not want, Trump was. "Is Trump strong?" Trump asked rhetorically. Those constrained by ordinary manners heard in the question evidence of insecurity. His admirers heard rejoicing. Trump's strength *was* his strength. Why not take pleasure in power? It feels good to be strong. It was, for the believers, those whom Trump called, "my people," a blessing.

><

After the rally I drove to the only bar still serving food and found myself sitting across from three people talking about Trump. Mike was a union electrician, Shawn a dispatcher, and Jackie a nurse. They were all White. "Definitely a racist," Shawn said of Trump. That did not appeal to him, he insisted. So who was he voting for? "Definitely Trump." Mike was a probably, Jackie wouldn't say, but she recoiled when Shawn teased her about Hillary Clinton. She seemed to be sliding toward Trump. Only the bartender was holding firm for the Democratic Party. He couldn't believe his friends were crossing over. "Trump's not just a racist, he's a fucking psychotic racist!"

"So are half the people who walk into this fucking bar!" Shawn shouted back.

"But they're not running for president," said the bartender.

"OK," said Shawn. "What about Michelle Obama? She's a racist."

"What?" said the bartender. "One, no she's not, and I don't know what you're talking about. Two, it doesn't fucking matter, because Michelle Obama isn't running for president."

"Well," said Shawn, grinning as he wound up what he considered a zinger, "she sucks the president's cock, don't she?" It was the essence of Trump's rhetorical style: vulgarity masquerading as candor. That the accusation made no sense only made it, in Trumpian terms, more "perfect," since, lacking any appeal to logic, it could not be rebutted.

The bartender did not try. He sighed and slapped another round of sickly sweet fireballs, shots of cinnamon whiskey, on the bar, glancing at a party including both Black and White people he hoped was out of earshot. He, like me, was White. We both rolled our eyes at Shawn's racism rather than confronting it, which is to say we cowered in what is sometimes called White privilege.

Shawn celebrated by moving, Trumplike, to the subject of his own genitalia. "Ten inches, baby!" he hollered. "Tell 'em!" he implored Jackie. Jackie wasn't talking.

Three Asians walked into the bar. Shawn suggested sending them a round of sake. Mike, whose adopted little sister was Korean American, said, "That's racist." Shawn agreed and repented. He said he did not *want* to be racist. It just came out of his mouth sometimes. It felt too easy. He said he did not want Trump to be racist, either, because when he was—"*when?*" muttered the bartender—it made it harder for Shawn to resist such thoughts, and they were not the thoughts he wanted. "I don't want fucking thoughts!" What he wanted, he said, was a better job, the kind of job Youngstown used to be known for.

That was what Mike wanted too. We drank another round of fireballs. Mike's "probably Trump" began inching toward certainty. He said it was about roads; Youngstown's were crumbling, and Trump was supposed to be a builder. He said it was about wages; union, yes, but still he struggled, and "free trade," which he believed Trump opposed, did not make it easier. It was about what you looked at every day when you woke up and walked out of your house and drove to work. Youngstown, he said, was a fucking shithole. "That's the way it is," he sighed.

Another round. "Ah, fuck it," Mike said. He suddenly roused himself, rising up from the bar. "I don't care if you're racist!" he shouted at a room by then nearly empty but for us. "If you'll just bring back one fucking steel mill!"

Shawn nodded, seriously, and raised his glass. Solidarity forever. Together they drank to the beautiful dream of the steel mills Trump had promised to revive. The steel mills they both knew, they allowed, were not really coming back. No politician could perform that resurrection, but at least Trump *said* he would. "Don't it feel good, at least, to believe?" asked Shawn.

›‹

"He takes what we all say on the back porch and puts it on the front page," a White woman named Kate Worthington told me at a Trump rally in Fountain Hills, Arizona, a wealthy White-flight refuge of gated communities forty minutes from Phoenix. She was a designer of women's bicycling fashions, dressed in a flowery skirt and a breezy white top as if for a Sunday brunch. We met when she inserted herself into my conversation with a White man named Nohl Rosen, who'd come to the rally strapped with a Glock on his thigh to fly the "thin blue line" flag of police solidarity. Worthington wanted her picture taken with him. Together they looked like the means and the end, the scowl and the smile of Trumpism. Rosen, speaking of the "lumps" Trump's people might give the disruptors, said, "There's nothing wrong with kicking a little ass!" Worthington beamed. She

liked the rough talk too. She called it the "human moment" of a
Trump rally, those little eruptions of feeling when Trump gave voice
to that which Worthington could never say: "I'd like to punch him
in the face," for instance, or, smacking his fist into his palm, "boom,
boom, boom."

The violence of Trump's rhetoric was not at odds with its secular
religiosity; it was what made his fantastical wealth imaginable, with
Trump as a medium between the emotions we all struggle to control and the power to act on them. The "human moment" was when
Trump, who was by his wealth freed from the concerns of ordinary
people, nonetheless felt what his followers felt, said what they wished
they could say. The mainstays of his rallies were parables, in which he
channeled such sentiments into full-fledged, multivoiced dramatic
scenes. Trump played every role. There were three scenes in rotation;
if Trump worked off a set list, they might be labeled "The Call," "The
Snake," and "The Bullet."

In "The Call," he played President Trump, bringing American
companies home through sheer force of will over the phone—or else.
This was his parable of strength. In "The Snake," he read the lyrics
of a 1963 song of that name by a Black civil rights activist, Oscar
Brown, made into a hit in 1968 by a Black soul singer named Al Wilson. Trump usually introduced it without attribution as a poem. It
was his parable of danger. "Think of it," he said sometimes, "when
we think of people coming into our country, who we don't know
who they are." He drew out that last word, a long, almost whimsi-
cal "aaarrr." Then, through four stanzas, he toggled between the
personae of a wounded snake and a "tender woman" who cradles it
to her bosom. Finally Trump-as-the-tender-woman cried, "'I saved
you . . . / And you've bit me even, why? / You know your bite is poison-
ous and now I'm going to die!' Trump-as-the-serpent hissed, "'Oh
shut up, silly woman!' said the reptile with a grin / 'You knew damn
well I was a snake before you took me in!'"

Camp came easily to Trump, and he had an unusual gift for making it earnest. Reagan had it, too, but as the better actor he more inhabited his role without visible contradiction. Reagan's favorite movie was *High Noon*, a story of an ordinary man who rises to greatness in response to circumstance. Trump's favorites include *Citizen Kane* and *The Godfather*, stories of titanic ego that the rest of us can marvel at but never truly grasp. Given our limits, we tend to endow those born to a scale beyond our imagination with elements of grandeur. Trump's genius had been to recognize that he could capitalize on both, the power and the comedy of the overblown ego. As with a tent revivalist, camp might have undermined Trump's gravitas, but it amplified his gravitational field. Gravitas is somber; somber is dull; and dull, to Trump, was impotent. Gravity is a force, and Trump made his own. The speaking style Trump's critics called crude—the smirk, smile, snarl, and shrug; the digressions; all that was "very, very, very big," "amazing" or "huge"—represented to his followers not vanity but the public intimacy of a man utterly himself. He did not try to claim, "I'm like you." His promise, his selling point, was that he was better than you. Not a servant; a leader. The one who acts. His mode was physical, shaped as much by gesture as by words: the chop, the finger pointing up or jabbing out, the turning away. When he delivered a phrase he knew the crowd loved—"Get 'em outta here!"—he swallowed their response with a Grinch-like grin. When the noise swelled—"So much love!" he'd croon—he spread his arms wide and turned the broad blue back of his $50,000 suit away, Trump acknowledging that Trump was the greatness they craved.

The darkest set piece in Trump's campaign lineup, a parable of strength and danger combined, was the monologue I call "The Bullet." You can see Trump perform it in the video of a rally he held in Dayton, Ohio, in March 2016, the day after protesters shut down his rally in Chicago. "Fuck Chicago!" yells a supporter.

Trump grins, pointing a finger at the man. He holds up a fist to show its size, a move played for laughs and power: He's telling us, as he did on the debate stage, about the size of his genitals. He gets away with it because he's joking. Except that he's not. "But just to finish on torture," he continues, although he hasn't yet begun. "I started by saying they're chopping off heads. Because you have to do a little bit of warm-up." So he talks some more about terrorists "chopping off heads," how hard it is to win when you have "rules." Then more about "chopping off heads," then the problem with laws, then more chopping, chopping, and finally the choppers sitting around at the end of a long day of chopping—let's say three heads—talking about us.

"Can you imagine what these people say about the United States? How weak we are?"

We're warmed up now.

"There's a story I tell," he says. "This is when we were strong." The crowd cheers. Many have heard it before. He asks if they want to hear it again. "Should I tell it?" He asks three times.

It begins with a horse, and on the horse there's a general. The year is 1919; the place is the Philippines; the general is John J. "Black Jack" Pershing. "A beautiful-looking guy," a beautiful white horse. Trump does not name the war (the rebellion of the indigenous Moros). It's not the point. "Tremendous terror problem," that's what you need to know, and that the terrorists are Muslims. The point is Pershing's solution:

They catch fifty terrorists.... Today we read 'em their rights, take care of 'em, ba ba [the audience boos], we feed them the best food, make sure they have television, we give 'em areas to pray, it's a wonderful thing. We're wonderful people. We're wonderful, wonderful, stupid, stupid people [laughter]. So General Pershing, tough, tough guy ... fifty terrorists ... what happens

is he lines 'em up to be shot. [A man shouts, "Yeah!"] Lines people up to be shot. . . . And as you know, swine, pig, all of that is
a big problem for them. Big problem. He took two pigs, they
chopped them open. [Trump chops his hand.] Took the bullets
that were going to go and shoot these men. [Holds up an imaginary bullet pinched between thumb and finger.] Took the bullets. The fifty bullets. Dropped them in the pigs, swished them
around [swishes] so there's blood all over those bullets. [Cheer-
ing.] Had his men, instructed his men [voice rising] to put the
bullets into the rifles [thumps lectern]. They put the bullets
into the rifles and they shot [he shouts the word; another man
shouts, "Yeah!"] forty-nine men.

He tells it again, puts the imaginary bullets into an imaginary
rifle and shoots his imagined forty-nine Muslims. "Boom."
He leans forward, squints, and runs his words together:
"a-pig-infested-bullet-in-each-one."
A woman shouts, "Yeah!"
Then, Trump says, they dumped the bodies into a mass grave—
he waves his hand across the podium, sweeping the corpses in—and
threw the gutted pigs on top of them. They took the final bullet—
he holds it up again—and they gave it to the last man. "And they
said, 'Here, take this bullet'"—he mimes handing it over—"'go back
to your people'"—he jabs a finger at the last man's "people," and yet
another man shouts, "Yeah!"—"'and explain what we just did!'"
Trump pauses. The crowd cheers. "This is history, folks." (It's
fiction, but to Trump that doesn't matter.) He's not going to say
whether it was "good" or "bad." We can choose to win, or we can
choose to lose. "We have to do," he says, "what we have to do." It's who
we are. Winners.

›‹

"Look, Dad," said a beefy boy, damp with sweat beneath his tousled chestnut curls, "snipers!" He pointed at two buildings bordering the park. Sure enough, there were men on the rooftops, surveying the thousands of Arizonans who had poured themselves into the vivid green bowl of Fountain Park in Fountain Hills. We were waiting for Trump. It was supposed to hit 91 degrees. There was a lemonade stand back by the metal detectors, but the crowd was too dense to move. There was nothing to do but sweat and stand. And listen. "Tiny Dancer." "Uptown Girl." Pavarotti.

The father shaded his eyes. So did I, and so did the tall man next to me, Marty, with whom I'd inched forward in the half-mile line for hours that morning. Marty worked in the desert that recommenced at the town line, and maybe it had dried him out, because he had just so many words. "Secret Service," he muttered.

I disagreed. "Look at the tan uniforms," I said. "I think those are Joe's men."

"Joe," in Fountain Hills, was Sheriff Joe Arpaio, nationally known for the boiling-hot tent-city jails he joked about as concentration camps, his theory of sexual humiliation as a form of rehabilitation and his "saturation patrols" in Latinx neighborhoods in search of "illegals," a practice that led to a 2013 federal court ruling against him for racial profiling and unlawful detention. Trump was particularly proud of his endorsement.

Marty considered. Yep. "Joe's."

"Awesome," the boy said. His dad smiled.

Rumor held that you could see Arpaio's house from where we stood. Rumor held that Arpaio had cleared bunks in his tent city for any protesters. Rumor held, one woman said, that Arpaio kept Fountain Hills "clean." What did this mean? "It's landlocked," Marty volunteered. In Arizona, that seemed as if it would be a given, but what he meant, he said, was that Fountain Hills—incorporated only in 1989—was surrounded by Indian reservations.

Only he didn't say *Indian*; he mouthed the word. That's how Marty and his lady, Carol, talked about people they didn't like: in whispers. "They don't like White people," Carol said. "They keep to themselves." She twirled a finger to indicate the ring of Indians out there beyond the town line. She had seen their reservations. "The Indians are"—she leaned in, dropping her voice even lower—"are filthy."

But Joe, she said, kept the town clean.

The rally was scheduled for eleven, but it wouldn't begin until after twelve, and most of us had been there since eight, seven a.m. We held our Trump signs over our heads to shield our reddening faces from the sun, we squinted at helicopters—local news? Sheriff Joe's?— and traded tales of Trump's Sikorskys, said to be lined with gold and creamy leather just like his plane. Like a beautiful living room. Trump's flying living room—imagine the splendor!—would thump- thump-thump above the protesters like in the movies, Bob Hope in Vietnam, it would swoop round the fountain on which we fixated, telling one another that Mr. Trump was paying for its nonstop gush- ing just to make the day special.

And then, close to two p.m., Trump at last took the stage. Trump never tried to dress like a common man, never the stiff new blue jeans or uncomfortable plaid of a politician playing "Heartland," but today he was tieless, his white shirt open beneath a navy blazer and a red Make America Great Again cap pulled down so low you couldn't see his eyes.

"Whoa! Whoa!" he shouted. "Man!" Behind him the mountains, before him a sea of red faces. The crowd unshaded their eyes. An elderly woman beside me with a pink-and-white Trump cap propped atop her floppy sun hat rose to her toes.

Trump began with a recitation not of winners but of losers. Most of all "the establishment." "They don't know how to win! They hav- en't won in a long time," he said, growling through a litany of defeats. Each one cranked the crowd higher. The excitement at the beginning of a Trump rally at first seemed negative, but it was a necessary prelude to Trumpian positivity, a method Trump could have borrowed directly from Norman Vincent Peale: "First," Peale wrote, "it is important to discover why you have these feelings of no power." Trump counted the reasons. "Bad things happening!" he shouted. "Crime all over the place!" Yes, exclaimed the crowd, because "crime all over the place" is the reason towns like Fountain Hills exist, a walled cluster of walled clusters in which people dream of the biggest wall of all.

"You had the killing of Kate, the killing of Jamiel," called Trump, chopping his hand down with the names. The crowd knew who they were. Kate Steinle, a pretty blonde, out for a walk on a San Francisco pier when an undocumented immigrant from Mexico shot her for no reason—a killer, the man in front of me shouted, who'd been "deported six times!" (Five, in fact, but to those who love the martyred dead such numbers mean no more than the fact that the immigrant, who admitted responsibility—a ricochet from an accidental shot—was fully acquitted.) And there's Jamiel Shaw, a Black high school football player shot and killed at seventeen by an undocumented immigrant who mistook him for a gang member, his father's support for Trump, now, proof to Trump's believers that the message wasn't about race, it was about "illegals," "animals," a different species altogether.

"So many killings!" Trump shouted, slicing his hand up and down. That morning it was Kate and Jamiel, later that afternoon, at another rally in Tucson, it would be "the veteran, a female," and the crowd there would know who he meant. Marilyn Pharis, age sixty-four, murdered with a hammer, "raped and sodomized and killed," Trump would say; and the crowd would cheer because only Trump spoke the martyrs' names, even when he couldn't remember them. *Thousands*," he would say and then, holding up a finger, his voice dropping into a deep and deliberate monotone: "It's gonna *end*."

There it was: the positivity, not a promise or a prediction. A fact.

"I guarantee you this," Trump told Fountain Hills. "Nobody, and I mean nobody, is gonna mess with us anymore." "USA!" the crowd chanted. "I love you too," Trump crooned. "I love you! I love you!" Trump! Trump! Winning, now. "NAFTA," he sneered. The crowd booed. "We will make great deals!" The crowd cheered. Trump deals: "You do 'em one at a time, folks," he said, mincing, holding his thumb and finger apart to show something small, deals he would crush as he was crushing his primary rivals. "One at a time," he said, putting one down and picking one up: Little Vietnam, Little Japan. "One at a time. And if they misbehave"—the crowd's cue to laugh—"if they don't treat us properly, we terminate. We put 'em in the shed. And then"—he shrugged—"maybe they come back."

Everything was winning from then on. He took out a folded-up copy of "The Snake"—it appeared to be handwritten—and drove past the question of temperament ("Act presidential! Act presidential!" he said, mimicking his wife, Melania, and his daughter Ivanka).

But then, instead of reading "The Snake," he opted to make "The Call." He put his fist to his ear like a phone. "Hello? This is the president," he said, like a boy making a prank call. He didn't even need to tell the crowd what he would say next. "It's so much fun for me!" he cried. "I love doing it! Please don't take that away!"

Take it away? They planned to give it to him: the power to Make. That. Call.

"So I call up," he continued. "I say, 'Listen, here's the story.'" He'd tell the executive on the other end—this time from Carrier, the air-conditioner company that had recently announced plans to lay off 1,400 people and build a factory in Mexico—that he had seen pictures of their new facility, he loved it, it was beautiful, but, again, "here's the story": Every A/C that comes across the border would be taxed 35 percent. "And I will get a call within twenty-four hours," Trump went on, exultant. "And he will say to me, the head of Carrier, he will say, 'Mr. President, we've decided to stay in the United States.'"

The crowd cheered as if it had already happened. Which, in a sense peculiar to the church of Trump—in which in the ecstasy of confidence itself was the ultimate win—it might as well have.

To the right of me, the crowd rippled: hands in the air, pushing a small circle of young Black men and a White boy with a DUMP TRUMP T-shirt, hands ripping it off him. I squeezed closer. One of the Black men hurtled sideways, falling into the man in front of me. Like dominoes we started to go down. The press of bodies kept me standing, but my arm swung behind me, and I hit an old woman. She smiled at me, neither hurt nor afraid.

When I looked again, the fight was gone. So, too, the disrupters, tugged away by security. We flowed into the empty space, that much closer to Trump, who rolled on, deep into a crescendo of victories. In every aspect of our lives, he said; so much, he said, at every level, all the time. The memory of the fight dissolved into his tide of good feeling, as if the dream of violence, Trump's and the crowd's, had simply been a prelude for the winning to come. It was filling them already, now that the losers were gone, vanished, as if loss itself, the very concept of grief, had been disappeared.

4

Ministry of Fun

The First Service

Usually the church comes first, then TV. For most of televangelism's history, that's how it's worked. But Vous Church was born on an Oxygen channel reality show featuring beaches, bikinis, and screaming fans, called *Rich in Faith*. Even then, the titular Rich, Pastor Rich Wilkerson Jr., was already almost famous, having at only thirty years old officiated the since-dissolved wedding of Kanye West and Kim Kardashian. This was long before Kanye became Ye, the antisemite, back when he was still beautiful, a star in whose light Rich basked. The happy couple wore Givenchy; Pastor Rich, impeccably stubbled, wore a vestment of white and gold. He had also "guested" on another Kardashian production, the E! network's *Kourtney and Khloé Take the Hamptons*, and attended to the soul, such as it may be, of Justin Bieber.

Vous may still be, in Pastor Rich's terms, a "baby church," but when I visited, Rich was already filling three services every Sunday. Each was staged to perfection, from the neo-emo praise band to the climactic baptisms in front of a DJ spinning in the courtyard. At the first service I attended, Rich was preaching about John the Baptist, whom he calls the "original Christian hipster." First, though, he wanted to talk about Leonardo DiCaprio, as seen in the 2013 film adaptation of *The Great Gatsby*, the movie poster of which Rich re-created, featuring Rich, as the "The Great Gospel." Rich loves talking about Leo, because he looks like Leo. Or rather, he insisted, Leo "looks like *me*." The *guests*—the term Rich prefers to *members*—always laugh, because at Vous it's not vanity if it's true.

Vous is short for Rendezvous, a weekly youth service Rich hosted for eight years at his father's megachurch before "planting," as he put it, his own "seed" in the form of Vous Church, an urban resettlement satellite of the suburban mothership. It met in a repurposed middle school, José de Diego, in Miami's Wynwood district, once a neighborhood of warehouses and factories bordered by the dilapidated housing of those who worked in them. Now the warehouses and former factories are art galleries and restaurants. The dilapidated housing is still dilapidated housing. Ninety-six percent of José de Diego students live beneath the poverty line. The church did not keep such statistics, but it seemed likely that at least that percentage of its "guests" are above it. Almost nobody from the neighborhood attended. "I was nervous," one White guest said of his first time. He'd heard stories of people being "killed for their sneakers" in this part of town. "But then you walk through those doors"—guarded by a cop in a cruiser when church is in session—"and it's like you're moving into a different world."

The aesthetic is "mini-mega," big-church spectacle at intimate scale, "intimacy" being a term of theological marketing for such ventures. It is achieved with the help of pulsing lights, a little fog, a lot of throb. There are no hymns. The "praise songs" are indistinguishable from secular Top 40, the music too denuded of signifiers to belong to an actual time and place. Certainly not the auditorium of this desperately poor middle school, which used to store textbooks on the stage—Vous cleared them out—and which used to have a mural-in-progress before Vous painted it over in black and gray. Then Vous installed a $100,000 sound system, to which it kept the key. On Sunday mornings, a crew arrives early. To erect velvet drapes and lay down oriental carpets, to erase the school and replace it with—it's hard to say what it is. When they close the drapes, when blue and purple light fills the room and ripples through the mist and thumping bass, you could be in any megachurch in the world.

This morning at Vous, Rich was wearing beige ankle-high suede boots, black skinny jeans, and an untucked soft-cotton blue tee beneath a short black jacket. A thin gold chain looped down over his pecs. No pulpit, no cross; just Rich working the stage. He hunched over like he was rapping, bobbing up and down, and then he straightened and spread his long arms, sampling the fundamentalist vernacular from which Vous was born. It was a tonal change—from "yo bro" curling out of a crooked grin to a glottal, shouted utterance of "God" comprising at least two syllables, maybe three: *"Gaw-w-d!"* Then he dialed it back around to the Rich who keeps it real on television.

"He"—Leo—"is the greatest actor of our generation, hands down!" *Mmm*, murmured the guests. A few years ago, Rich said, he had been in L.A., driving with a friend, when he saw Leo. "I said, 'Stop the car.'" His tone was OMG. "I said, 'PULL OVER!'" Rich followed Leo into a bar. Nobody was there but Leo and three of his friends. "So I walked in there and I got nervous, and I"—he mimed rubbernecking, his mouth and eyes wide—"I walked right past him."

He needed to prepare. "So I'm in the bathroom, trying to pump myself up. Preach to myself a little bit, you know? I look in the mir-ror: *Rich. You got this, bro. You got this. This is your moment. This is divine appointment.*"

He was half joking, but only half. Rich is the son of a preacher who is also the son of a preacher. Rich's father, Rich Wilkerson Sr., is the pastor of Trinity Church, one of the largest megachurches in subur-ban Miami. Rich worked there until he launched Vous—financed by his father. "When it comes to money," Rich Sr. tells the camera on *Rich in Faith,* his face as smooth as his son's, his hair as full of color, "he hasn't had to pay the bills." Rich Jr.'s spiritual authority is rooted not in his knowledge of suffering but in his removal from it; he is blessed and unabashed.

But once, at least, he was, if not lost, a little shy. Contemplating Leo, he stayed hidden for fifteen minutes. Then, "as soon as I walk out of the bathroom, I'm telling you, we have, like, a *moment.* Our eyes *connect.* Like, locked in. Like, *ME.* And Leo. Like, whoa! Honestly, I feel like the *Titanic,* the music starts." He sang like Céline Dion: "*Whereeeeeeever you arrrrre…*"

Back in the car, Rich's friend asked how it was. "*Life-changing.*" What had they talked about? "Nothing."

This was what Rich called "a collision with Christ." The guests laughed cautiously. Rich's voice became low and throaty. He whis-pered from his heart to bring the moral home: "Don't walk on by." He meant Christ. Leo isn't Christ, but the principle is the same: that of an encounter that leaves you transformed. The way you walk, the way you talk, the way you think. "You don't even look the same!" He imitated his guests' confusion: "'Like, what do you mean, I changed my look?' *Yeah.*" A beat. Get ready. The crooked grin: "You went from a *frown*—you turned it upside down!"

›‹

"Obedience," said Pastor Rich, gazing upon Biscayne Bay from his penthouse balcony, "is our job." And Pastor Rich obeys; he always has. He strayed once as a teen, resolving to kiss as many girls as he could at a party, but then he met his wife, DawnCheré—also a Pentecostal scion, the daughter of Louisiana football and Christian royalty—and together they saved themselves for marriage. DawnCheré admitted that for the first year of matrimony, their sex was a "2," but now, she said, it is a "10," which is God's reward for those who trust him. Rich trusts; it's easy. "I'm not," he mused, "the prodigal son."

He came of age televangelically on what he calls "world Christian television," TBN, the largest Christian television network. In high school there was some "cussing," some "sassing," but when he was seventeen, on tour in Australia with Rich Sr., God spoke to him. For most, this is a moment of intensity; Rich doesn't remember what God said. "It wasn't very emotional," he said. He cracked a glowing grin.

Rich's most precious inheritance, which he honors through regular workouts and excellent skin care—both featured on *Rich in Faith*—is his genes: broad shoulders and lithe frame, the slightly off-center curve of a widow's peak that amplifies the arch of his brow and the tilt of his smile. "My pastor," comments one of his 941,000 Instagram followers, with double heart-eyed smiley-face emojis. *Hot*, another expresses with twin fire emojis in response to one of the hundreds of selfies he posts as part of his ministry. Even critics acknowledge that he is an exceptionally good-looking man. For "causing women to lust," a follower posts an ironic trio of thumbs-down emojis below one of his bare-chested Instas: Pastor Rich on horseback, wearing a white cowboy hat and skinny jeans, ripped just-so across a taut upper thigh.

Superficial, yes, but by design. Every few years, the secular press produces an astonished report of a preacher who embraces pop culture. But so it has always been, each era of American Christendom giving rise to competitive strains of faith, one that curses the culture, one that coddles it. Sometimes the latter is liberal, but more often it reveals the shallowness of liberalism's aesthetic trappings, the ease with which secular music and fashion and art can be repurposed to serve a religion of control—over sex, over emotion. Such is the surge of hipster Christendom. We live in the age of its great multiplying, ministries with one-word names such as Status and Mosaic and Reality and Shine, or two words made into one, CityBeat, TheCause, and, most famously, Hillsong. Most leave untouched fundamentalism's core convictions—opposition to abortion and sex outside of marriage (which is between a man and a woman) and also to false gods (meaning all but their own). Instead, they rebrand the presentation. Rich is only the most mediagenic of what *Complex*, a pop-culture magazine for "sneakerheads" (Rich collects designer kicks) has described as a "new wave of stylish pastors," just as a young Billy Graham was before him and Billy Sunday before *him*, stripping away the Bible's subtler teachings to draw the masses. Rich Jr. is the latest avatar of a tradition common to Christianity and capitalism, the so-called new-and-improved. His new is burnished with vestiges of the artisanal; "vintage," Rich likes to say, meaning that which is artfully rendered to reference an idea of the old. It's like sampling from a song you've never actually heard.

Rich wasn't really a fan of Kanye West, the man whose brand made Rich nationally known, when they first met in 2013. "I mean, I liked 'Jesus Walks,'" Rich said. But Rich was a regular at LeBron James's Miami boutique, Unknwn, which was cofounded by entrepreneur Chris Julian, who attended Rich Sr.'s megachurch. Kanye shopped there too. One Sunday, Julian texted Rich Sr. a "heads-up" that he was bringing Kanye with him to Rich Sr.'s church that morning. Rich Sr. was suffering from back troubles, so Rich Jr. preached in his place. "There are no coincidences," he told me. God, he believes, puts people where they need to be.

For three Sundays, with Rich Jr. onstage, God put Kanye in the pews. They became "good friends," and then "really good friends." Explaining his decision to have an actor portray "White Jesus" during "Jesus Walks" on his *Yeezus* tour, Kanye told a radio station, "I had a friend of mine that's a pastor there as we started discussing how we wanted to deliver it. My girl even asked afterwards, 'Hmm, is that weird if Jesus comes onstage?'" Kanye said his pastor told him no. "People play Jesus. You know what's awesome about Christianity is we're allowed to portray God."

When Kanye chose Kim to be his bride in 2013, he asked Pastor Rich to officiate. Six months later, Rich, styled by Allison Depriestre of Paris, bound them in holy matrimony before two monolithic slabs of white roses and peonies estimated to have cost $136,000. The party began in Versailles and proceeded by private jet to Florence for the nuptials. Kim's gown, designed by her friend Riccardo Tisci, was said to have been given its own five-star hotel room and to be worth $500,000. Lana Del Rey sang at the rehearsal dinner, Andrea Bocelli at the ceremony. At Kanye's request, Rich spoke simply—"about Jesus," Rich told celebrity reporters, "which is who we serve." Then they ate cake. Vanilla and berry, ornamented with real gold, a confection seven feet tall. Cost estimates for the week ran from $5 million to $12 million, possibly more than $1 million for each of the seven years the union endured.

When Rich published a book in 2015, *Sandcastle Kings: Meeting Jesus in a Spiritually Bankrupt World*, Kanye designed the jacket, beach-sand beige with a giant gothic "SK." "The church, throughout history, has always called upon the world's greatest artists," Rich told Rapzilla.com, placing Kanye's two-letter graphic in the tradition of Michelangelo.

At Rich's penthouse—270-degree views of the water and the city, new condo high-rises under construction all around them—I asked Pastor Rich why so many stars—Kanye and the Kardashians, Bieber and Selena, athletes from the NFL and the NBA—clustered around his ministry. "They're my friends," he said. "I don't talk about my friends." No, but he instagrammed them. Did they sense that he is, in advertising parlance, "a creative"? No, he said, *art* is a word that intimidates him.

Maybe it's what there is not: much of anything. To the spiritual void that is celebrity gloss, Rich responds with a blankness of his own. To the turbulent theology that is Kanye's most vital music, Rich is merely a sample. He is, like the Apostle Paul, all things to all people—especially the beautiful ones. Descended from a Pentecostal tradition of "spiritual warfare," educated at a prep school founded by D. James Kennedy—one of the last century's Christian Right chieftains—Rich himself is post-culture war. He *could*, he allowed, talk the five points of Calvinism (memorizable as an acronym, TULIP, the first letter of which stands for "Total depravity," as in our natural condition). But he'd rather just "do life," awesomed by God. Of sin he said, "I think we think about it not as much as you might think we think about it." Of social justice, he said, "the moral conversation is one I don't get into." His church is diverse but he deflected my attempts to engage him on White evangelicalism's history of racism by dismissing it as "deep." Not cool. Then he just smiled; we were sitting on the balcony, it was dusk, gray-violet over the water. His teeth were radiant. "I think *fun* is a big word," he said.

It was time for a photo shoot. He fixed his hair and checked his shirt, not, he wanted me to know, because he is vain but because "fashion is the language of our culture." Fashion is evangelism. "We're on a mission, always," DawnCheré said. She spotted a lick of gelled hair breaking free and raised her hand, then pulled it back. "He never lets me touch his hair."

><

Every Saturday morning, Rich gathers his inner circle, the "Vous Crew," a few dozen beautiful people, mostly young professionals, at his penthouse to plan the coming week. It's part logistics meeting, part Bible study. But the Bible is hard, its stories old, so this week they were starting what would be an immersion into one of Rich's favorites, the bestselling *Seven Habits of Highly Successful People*. "I've read it, like, nineteen times," Rich told me. Sitting in front of a big flat-screen television that was silently showing images from the church—Rich, Vous, Rich, Vous—Rich, wearing a denim shirt by a designer called Fear of God over a white tee, began with Psalm 1. Since most of the Vous Crew had brought their copies of *Seven Habits* instead of the Bible, Rich recited the psalm from memory. He interrupted himself to make the key point: "I love this line," he said, shaking his head and grinning: "'Whatever he does'"—a righteous man, that is—"'prospers.' Prosperity *follows* him." What do you need to do to be righteous? "It's how I walk, how I sit, how I talk—these are, like, lifestyle things."

"So good, so good," murmured DawnChéré. We'd gathered in the open-plan penthouse—exposed pipe, brushed concrete—between her white baby grand in one corner and her wedding dress hanging as an ornament on the other side, near a white chair covered by a white fur throw and her minimalist desk, on which stood two white candles and a sculpture in white of the head of a gazelle. That morning, DawnChéré was wearing a tight white tee and strappy silver sandals with heels. She's very slender; you see it in her arms, crossed, her head held in her palm as she watches her man, murmuring approval. As a preacher's wife, she was part of his presentation. To Rich's performance of Christ-driven intensity, she brought gentle mockery and the gaze of a woman in love.

Rich believes that your lifestyle is the product of your habits.

Good habits equal a good lifestyle equals "righteousness," not so much a morality as a look. And if you are righteous—if you look good—prosperity follows. Where there is prosperity, there is "positivity," since what's not to be happy about if you are rich in fact as well as faith?

To be fair, Rich believes prosperity is relative. For him it's a penthouse, for another it might be simply—well, Rich doesn't really know. Knowing poor people is not his calling. Poverty, in his theology, is like a bad habit. The happiness that flows from wealth, meanwhile, is a just reward. Happy people are good people.

It is, he said, simply a matter of "taking control," of separating your "haves" from your "bes." For example, you may *have* a terrible boss at work. Such circumstances, Rich said, you should relegate to a circle of "no concern" to allow you to better focus on who you want to *be*. You could *be* more grateful to your boss for giving you a job. It's up to you. "Anytime you think the problem is out there," he said—he gestured at the window, and the city below, one of the poorest in the country—"that is the problem." The good news was that the solution is within you: lifestyle choices.

"So good," said Rich, pumping his fist.

"*So* good," agreed the disciples, tapping the lesson into their phones.

><

After the meeting, Pastor Rich's assistant, Chris Lopez, pulled up to Rich's building in Rich's Jeep. Chris had worked in real estate, and he'd developed a sideline selling and renting homes to Vous members who'd just moved downtown. "It's almost become a ministry itself," he said. He oversees dozens of Vous ministries and hundreds of volunteers, and sometimes he's Rich's driver.

On *Rich in Faith*, Rich drives an Audi Q7, but for his thirty-first birthday, DawnCheré commissioned Miami's Luxuria Bespoke Auto to revitalize and customize the Jeep Wrangler his parents gave him when he turned seventeen. Matte black, its windows tinted, its giant wheels kicked out from under the chassis. It looked like it had been built for a death squad.

That morning, Vous was having its monthly volunteer event, "I Love My City," at a men's homeless shelter, but the homeless men were nowhere to be seen. Where they were, Rich didn't know. Their absence was practical. Vous needed room for the volunteers who came from downtown condos or drove in from the suburbs. It was also spiritual. It felt more "authentic" to be in a shelter, said a Vous volunteer who'd moved to Miami a few weeks before, and at the same time—surrounded by affluent hipsters—"safe."

The day's "heart"—as in what Rich calls "a heart for the city"—would take three forms. One group was going to bring diapers and clothing to a women's shelter. The next was going to hold a pizza party, with karaoke, for a small number of homeless men. (With great fanfare, about a half dozen wary-looking men were ushered in, each seated at a table and surrounded by Vous volunteers eager to "relate.") The third group would conduct what they call the laundromat ministry. What this entailed wasn't clear. Chris, who had been designated my handler, did not want me to find out. He didn't explain why. So I decided I'd follow Rich and DawnCheré. But they had lunch plans, and I wasn't invited. And since the only homeless man I could get close to said he didn't know who these people were or why they wouldn't leave him alone, laundromat ministry it was. The group's leader, Tiago Magro, a tall, bearded artist wearing a black-and-white leopard-print tunic, gave me the address in Little Havana. Chris called when I was minutes away. "This was not the agreement," he said. Chris's idea of "the agreement" seemed to be that I was not to wander beyond Chris's supervision. "Do not enter the laundromat," he told me. Again: "*Do not enter the laundromat.*"

I entered the laundromat. A life-size painted statue of Saint Lazarus, depicted as a beggar leaning on a crutch, presided over the washing machines. The volunteers were spreading the gospel: with quarters. The laundromat ministry, it turned out, revolved around the assumption that people who use laundromats must be so poor that they would appreciate strangers offering them spare change, at which point the Vous volunteers could begin evangelizing. But everybody in the laundromat had their own quarters and they mostly spoke Spanish, which the Vous volunteers mostly did not. There were alarmed looks when the volunteers tried to grab the customers' clothes; they wanted to help fold.

Finally, they found two takers—a pair of women who lived in a homeless shelter. Tiago and several large men surrounded them, hands in the air, praying loudly. The older woman began to cry. One of the evangelists, satisfied, broke off and drifted outside. His name was Brandon, and he looked like an even better-tanned version of Pastor Rich, wearing a black baseball hat that read "Almighty" in white cursive script. He was a DJ, he said, and a traveler, but mostly, he explained, a follower of Christ. He leaned on his car, a gray Mercedes E550 convertible with a cross made of straw hanging from the rearview mirror. "Nice car," I said. Brandon stepped back and admired it. "I am so blessed, man," he said. "God gave me a Mercedes."

><

Pastor Rich likes to paraphrase the eighteenth-century revivalist John Wesley: "Preaching is simply this: Light yourself on fire and people will come from everywhere to watch you burn." And Rich is a talented preacher. He can coo and growl and seduce even better than his father and probably his father's father, who preached at backwoods tent revivals. Secular folk sometimes accuse evangelicalism of theatricality, as if that were a departure from the faith, but the traditions from which Rich descends have always embraced spectacle. The Assemblies of God, the largest Pentecostal denomination in the world and the one under which Rich Sr.—and thus, in a sense, Rich Jr.—preaches, is simultaneously rigid and almost fantastically flexible, literalist in its interpretation of Scripture yet ecstatically open to the possibility of an interventionist God.

Rich is also heir to the spiritual legacy of his father's even more famous cousin, David Wilkerson. In 1962 Wilkerson published one of the most celebrated fundamentalist memoirs of all time, *The Cross and the Switchblade*, about ministering to gangs and addicts in New York City. In book, movie, and comic-book form, *The Cross and the Switchblade* helped restore to the evangelical church some of the missionary vigor, some of the ferocity, it had lost as a result of postwar suburbanization. But Rich is equally indebted to Norman Vincent Peale, the midcentury apostle of Christian business success whose best seller *The Power of Positive Thinking* has been in print since 1952, grafting onto American evangelicalism the modern salesman's style.

Pastor Rich, who has never read either—I counted no more than a dozen books in his penthouse, and even Rich Sr. described his son's book, *Sandcastle Kings*, as "simplistic"—has through spiritual osmosis distilled the messages of both. He remains relentlessly upbeat even as he appropriates a hip-hop culture suffused with suffering and pleasure alike. It's a theology of gentrification: the gritty city as a site for "authenticity" made over to house a gospel with little mention of the cross, an urban ministry of spotless cool. He has crossed the secular divide his forebears could not. He has been to the mountain, and there he did sing "Awesome God" while hoverboarding in a conga line with Justin Bieber. You can see it on YouTube.

The scene is not without theological meaning. The meaning is: fun. Fun is at the heart of Pastor Rich's message. It's the next stage of the prosperity gospel, which holds that God wants "health and wealth" for his believers. Rich Jr. was born into this blessing. Others might have taken it for granted, but Rich did not. What, he wondered, did God want us to *do* with our prosperity? Help the poor? Sure—Rich has his people do that one Saturday morning every month. Covered. What else could you do with money and boyish good looks? You could have fun. Fun as a calling, fun as a demonstration of grace, fun as a way of living what Joel Osteen, another celebrity-pastor son of a celebrity pastor, calls "your best life now." Fun is what God wants for us.

Rich wanted to show me. He thought it would be "fun" to "shape" my story with me. On Saturday night, when I told him I was looking forward to spending time with the church's guests the next morning, Rich smiled and tilted his head quizzically. I said I'd just roam between services and talk with his flock. Chris looked pained. Rich was concerned. He did not think that sounded like the fun he wanted me to have. "I don't really know who these people are," he said. He meant he didn't know what they'd say. He must have read my face. Don't worry, he said brightly. They'd already prepped a select group of Vous insiders for me to interview. "Bro," Rich said, "let's just stage it, all right?"

There was no cynicism in his tone. *Staging it* is what Rich does. Staging it is his gospel. Consider the hair, the kicks, the teeth, that smile. Rich's followers bask in his glamour and become ever so slightly more glamorous themselves. So it has always been in the Church, the pastor as holy man setting himself on fire, catching the light and turning it toward his congregation. Rich's revelation is that for the souls he wants to reach, the light, in America now, emanates not from the Son but from the stars.

The Second Service

I was talking to a pre-approved Vous guest named Luke—"it's cool to be an attractive person!" he told me—when Chris, who'd thus far directed every interaction, was called away. I took the opportunity to wander. An older man introduced himself. "I've been watching you," he said. His name was Ted Romeo, and he was a commodities broker who'd retired, he boasted, at fifty-five. He still wore his hair slicked back finance-style. He wanted me to know he'd driven an hour from a suburb down to Miami and through what he called "the hood" surrounding José de Diego to be there. And he wanted me to know that he'd clocked me as a journalist: an outsider. He asked if I had a church. I'm Jewish, I said. What a coincidence! His wife was a Jew too. But loving Jesus was easier than being a Jew, he told me. Jewish prophets—Jeremiah, Hosea, Amos, "let justice roll down like waters"—were grumblers, interested only in what was wrong with the world. The New Testament—Jesus—was everything the Old was not. "It's about happiness!" said Romeo.

This is, of course, a simplification, since "what was wrong with the world" is what gives rise to the prophetic tradition of *chesed*, or lovingkindness, love as an action. Then, too, there was a wrinkle in Romeo's own testimony, I'd learn: While he may have in fact retired, not long beforehand a court had levied $16.4 million in fraud penalties against his two brokerages, naming him a central figure.

Romeo didn't mention this. Instead, he spoke of his appreciation for the way Rich preached without any morality at all. "I *know* I fall short," he said. Why would he want church to remind him?

We got some coffee. I started to sip. "You know what you need? You need some sugar in that." I take it black, I said. He lit up. "You like yours black? Me too! I like my coffee like I like my women." I imagined Rich's horror at this off-brand revelation. "Black and bitter," Romeo said, chortling.

That was when Chris found me. He pulled me away from my unapproved chat. "We're always going to try to control the intimacy," he said, leading me back to my designated seating and the fun story they wanted to shape with me.

><

The history of the church, when it works, when it moves souls, is that of "the word made strange," as the Anglican theologian John Milbank puts it. Not so much the old made new—that's just marketing—as the cliché turned inside out so that it's familiar and unknown at the same time, like a song that compels you to draw closer even though you've heard it countless times before.

Vous doesn't do strange. The second service, at noon, was the same as the first. Same DiCaprio, same perfectly timed winks, same pauses, as Pastor Rich considered, for the second time that day, what he was going to say next, as if he were waiting on God. Epiphany on demand.

Contrast that idea of the divine with that of Kanye in those years. Kanye's music, of which Rich was not really a fan, was infused with a questioning faith as complex as the troubled genius that would later disappear into hate, contradictions of lust and politics and fury and grief and laughter, a combination knotting and unraveling from the social gospel of "Jesus Walks" to the profane mysticism of "I Am a God." Those who hear the latter as little more than hip-hop boasting (itself a complex tradition) aren't listening for the meanings within meanings revealed through illusion and allusion.

Such convolutions are outside the obsessively curated circle of Christianity and minimalist cool preached by Rich. To him Scripture is a script; he need only read the lines with style. He cannot remember ever being lost; being *saved*, to him, is as much of a given as the Florida sunshine. The sun doesn't happen; it just is. Same as Pastor Rich's life. Nothing, he insists, has ever really happened to him at all. "If I had to preach from experience," he told me on his penthouse balcony, the sunset behind him and DawnCheré, in pink and gold, murmuring her approval, "I'd have nothing."

The Third Service

Then came the evening, and at the night service more of the same, so I left the auditorium and wandered into the courtyard. I studied the murals covering the school's surfaces, the fruit of a program gathering the best street artists of Miami to dress José de Diego—formerly known as Robert E. Lee Middle School, renamed for the Puerto Rican poet and activist—in all the light and color and eerie-splendid creativity of the surrounding art galleries from which students were excluded. There was a wall of eyes, a hundred, hundreds, heavy-lidded, dark blue, electric blue, bright and mournful. Not surveillance eyes; witness eyes, tired but still watching, holding on. The artist, Ahol Sniffs Glue, paints these eyes all over Miami and beyond. They're his signature. They're what he sells. But good art survives commodification. Something endures, an echo of the idea, a ghost of the original vision. That's what I thought I saw when I left the crowd with their hands in the air and *their* glistening eyes locked on Rich as he bent his knees and tilted his head and rocked out one more time with the same gestures, the same joy-filled smile, for the third time that day. What I saw looking back at me from the wall of eyes was the ghost of the vision. Art; gospel; witness. A cloud of witnesses, painted on a middle school wall.

Which is when it hit me: *Middle school*. This *was* the cross that was missing in Rich's church. Middle school. The crucible of American childhood. This middle school, struggling in a rising sea of disinterested wealth with a cop in the courtyard. I started pacing, revisiting the murals I'd earlier squinted at under the sun. A stag, by an artist called Nychos, galloped along the blue-and-white wall seventh graders might pass on their way from second-period math to a third-period study hall in which they'd daydream ordinary daydreams of transcendence and fear. That was the stag on the wall: it was coming out of its body, head twisted back in terror like it was looking at its hunter. The stag was still alive but witnessing its future. It was gorgeous; it was horrifying.

Across the courtyard there was an Earth goddess painted by Don Rimx, her body made of sticks, her limbs splinted, her hair green, her face scowling. She wasn't like anyone you'd ever seen on an American middle school wall, and at the same time there was a deep resemblance to the inner selves of countless children who have gleaned from the world that the adult world will not protect them, that they will have to save themselves and each other.

I finished my circuit and joined a little crowd of cool kids, Vous Crew elite, milling around outside the auditorium. To them I was just a bald dude in uninspired jeans and sensible shoes. They turned away. I felt like I was thirteen. Then a hand on my shoulder turned me around. Brandon with the Mercedes from the laundromat. He said, "Yo, what's up!" and pulled my hand in and wrapped his arm around me. Full bro hug, our hands locked in a grip that made a fist like a heart between us. Brandon said for him the night had been all about the children. He said he'd found some. I was confused. He said he'd been cruising in his Mercedes around the neighborhood, thinking about how awesome Vous is and how sad it is that none of the people who live in the neighborhood get to see that, when he came

upon a group of little boys playing. Jesus gave him a word: *Invite them.*
So he did. "I was like, 'There's candy!'"

Brandon didn't want me to get the wrong idea. "For the kids," he
clarified as if I'd been hoping for some.

"You told the parents?" I said, concerned

"Ahh." He paused, remembered. "Yeah. I saw the mom later. I
said, Wait a minute, these kids said yes too easy." One of the mothers reclaimed her children, but Brandon brought four to Vous. He
gestured around the courtyard. They were here somewhere. We tried
the nursery. The kids were "in a time of worship," so they couldn't
come out. "I have to pick them up after," Brandon said as we walked
away. "So we can definitely talk to them." Brandon seemed uncon-
cerned with or maybe unaware of even the possibility of "stranger
danger." He was guileless. He had just returned from abroad, he
said, a trip of holy wandering financed by whoever was inclined to
give him money. He made no requests; he simply befriended and
received, an odd, happy, young, beautiful man who liked talking
to anybody.

I decided to try what Chris might forbid as a "political" question.
I thought of it as the theodicy question—the question, most simply
put, of why God lets bad things happen to good people. "This is not,"
I said, "the city God wants."

Brandon nodded. It is not.

Rich often spoke of "having a heart for the city." When I'd asked
him what his city of God would look like, though, he'd been stumped.
"I don't even know!" he'd said, grinning.

Brandon had ideas. He leaned in close. "This is what Miami would
look like." He paused to let me clear my sight so I could see it too. "No
debt. No poverty. People wouldn't be so worried about their neighbor. There would be less stress. More happiness. The workload would
go way down. And things would actually get done. That's the crazy

thing!" Kids, he said, grasped this vision. Adults, not always. But we could learn.

That was when Chris found us. He did not look happy. "Are you heading into service?" he asked.

"I'm in and out," I said, "talking to Brandon . . ."

"I love Brandon," Chris said, looking at me. His voice was not loving. Brandon had not been preapproved. Then: "Um, they texted me you were trying to get to kids?"

Brandon nodded enthusiastically. Chris put a hand an inch from my arm. I tried to edge him away with my shoulder, turning back to Brandon's vision. I've been writing about American religion for years. I've been to megachurches and chapels and compounds and covens. I've met believers who say Christ was a cowboy and soldiers who etch Scripture onto their rifles and believers who think Bobby McFerrin's "Don't Worry, Be Happy" is divine revelation. And what has always made me marvel are the layers of stories beneath even the most seemingly absurd or banal surface, followers who bring to their faith depths unfathomable by their callow leaders. Maybe that's so at Vous too. But never before Vous had I encountered a church that seemed so simply and completely empty. So instead of going back into the church to again hear Rich preach about Leo, I wanted to listen, for a moment at least, to the one soul I'd met at Vous who spoke of the gospel as something more than style and good feeling.

"Everybody is taken care of," Brandon was saying, describing his Miami as City-of-God, rocking back and forth as he exulted. "Everybody sees through all the junk. Your IQ. Your credit score. Your net worth. That's what the Kingdom of God is! You see through all that."

Then the service let out, and the kids were released. Brandon took me to meet them: four little boys, ranging in age from maybe five to eight, zigzagging with energy across the darkened courtyard and balance-beaming the edges of some planters. "Whoa, guys!" said

Brandon, delighted. He stopped one of the bigger boys, wearing a Batman shirt, and asked him to tell me what he'd learned about Jesus. It was close to nine. School night. No sign of his mother. I crouched down to listen. The boy opened his mouth to speak—

"Uh-uh!" Chris sliced himself between the child and us. "Not really cool," he said. He was right. It wasn't. "We can't let you talk to these kids." It wasn't me he worried about; it was them. "We don't even know who they are." They hadn't been scripted.

I don't know how the boys got home. I walked away with Chris and then later I looked for Brandon, but I couldn't find him, so I waited for a while in the parking lot by his Mercedes while the congregation eased out the gates in their cars, heading back to their downtown condos or out to the suburbs. I waited a long time, but Brandon didn't emerge. My guess—and I can't confirm this, I'm just going on faith here—is that Chris or someone else in the Vous Crew was doing damage control, stopping Vous's one true holy fool from fucking up their message. My words, of course. Their words, the ones they'd given me in answer to every other question—*be amazing* and *dream big* and *have fun* and, murmured all the time like an amen, *so good, so good*—are cleaner than that; shiny. There wasn't a speck on them. There wasn't anything at all. I was waiting, I realized, for nothing, so I gave up and went home.

> 5 <

Whole Bottle of Red Pills

"What is 'the manosphere'?" I asked Paul Elam around three a.m. one morning. This was not a factual question. It was an existential one.

I already knew that "the manosphere" referred to an online network, vast and like the universe constantly expanding, each little twinkling star in its firmament dedicated—obviously—to men. Men and their problems. Usually with women. Some galaxies of the manosphere were dedicated to self-declared pickup artists, who want to help ordinary men trick women into having sex with them; other solar systems dealt earnestly with child custody and the Adderalization of rambunctious boys. There were constellations of MGTOWs, "Men Going Their Own Way," separatists and onanists and recluses. There were hundreds, maybe thousands, of websites and forums large and small, many openly hostile—Sluthate, Angry Harry, the

Nice Guy (he's not), the Spearhead—and many more that were brutally lewd, such as Return of Kings, published by the author of a popular series of country guides with titles such as *Bang Ukraine: How to
Sleep with Ukrainian Women, in Ukraine.*

As the flagship political site of the movement, Elam's A Voice for
Men functioned as the closest thing there was to a center, an intelligence, a superego to the bloggy manosphere id of lust and fury. Just
how big the whole thing was, nobody could say. More than fringe,
less than mainstream, but at three a.m., sitting with Elam in his
hotel room, I wasn't looking for numbers. Size didn't matter. What I
wanted to know from Elam was, *what does it all mean?*

Elam had just wrapped up a conference, "an eye-popper," he said,
his first gathering in the real world. "You can't fight titty hall," he
likes to say, but now, he thought, he was doing so. He was, he believed,
"fucking shit up." That was his slogan: "Fuck their shit up." "They"
being feminists. 6'8", 290 pounds, with the beard of John Brown
and the rumbling voice of James Earl Jones, Elam, whose name just
so happens to be "male" backwards, wanted to be a "provocateur."
Responding to a feminist critic, he once wrote, "the idea of fucking
your shit up gives me an erection." But that kind of talk is just for
show, he said. He noted that he used to be a counselor. What he was
doing, he thought, was a kind of therapy.

He wanted me to understand, so he drew a map of the manosphere,
alluding to history as he sketched, its roots in the men's liberation
movement of the 1970s and '80s and the New Age men's movement
of the '90s, "Iron John," men playing drums in the woods. The new
movement came of age online, when Elam first started posting under
the name Lester Burnham, Kevin Spacey's midlife-crisis character in
the 1999 film *American Beauty.* The movement had since fed on fact
and delusion: 9/11, perceived as insult to American manhood, and
the very long war that followed; the financial crash of 2008, and the
wages that already felt like they were falling; the strange science of

male decline—tumbling sperm counts, fewer male babies—and the rise of gender studies. Most of all, it loathed women "leaning in," women in men's locker rooms, women in combat, women with the gall to think they, too, can be funny, or president.

Elam began with two big circles next to one another. Within one he wrote "Game," "PUA," and "MRM"—"game" refers to the "techniques" used by PUAs ("pickup artists") and "MRM" stands for "men's rights movement"—and within the other, "MGTOW," who apparently merited a domain all their own. Dangling between the two spheres, he drew an oblong shaft he labeled "Dark Enlightenment," for the men who believe the problem goes beyond feminism to democracy itself. He held up the map, two big circles and a shaft. Was it—did he draw—"a dick and balls?" I asked.

"Yes," he said, chuckling, "yes, I guess it is."

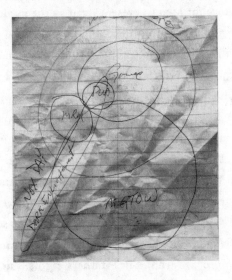

><

If you've heard of the manosphere, it may have first been in the context of Elliot Rodger, the twenty-two-year-old self-described "supreme gentleman" who on May 23, 2014, in Isla Vista, California, murdered six people. In a YouTube video he posted the day he stabbed to death three men in his apartment and opened fire on a sorority house at UC Santa Barbara, he declared the slaughter a "Day of Retribution," revenge for the world's failure to provide him "the beautiful girlfriend I deserve." Rodger was a self-declared "incel," which means involuntarily celibate, and a student of several manosphere philosophies, but his most active connection was through a forum called PUAhate. Most of its members embraced MGTOWdom after trying and failing to adopt the ways of the pickup artists—hence the "hate"—at which point their bitterness brought the angriest of them to the politics of Elam. Some of A Voice for Men's biggest web traffic followed Rodger's murder spree. Media attention surrounding the Isla Vista shootings was a two-fold gift for the group, driving new recruits to the movement and allowing A Voice for Men to present itself as the moderate middle for its opposition to mass murder.

A Voice for Men's first International Conference on Men's Issues convened a month after the killing. It was supposed to be at the Detroit Hilton Doubletree, a swank downtown hotel with $24 cocktails. But "the feminists" protested, and since the hospitality industry is pretty much in the thrall of feminism, or because feminists floated death threats, or because a member of the men's movement floated death threats so that people would understand that feminists were floating death threats even if they did not, in this instance, float any death threats—for one of these disturbing reasons, claimed A Voice for Men, the Hilton Doubletree told the first annual International Conference on Men's Issues—fathers' rights, suicide, and circumcision, aka "male genital mutilation," and also false accusations of rape, male victims of rape, and unfaithful White wives "cuckoo for cocoa penis puffs," as one speaker puts it, plus "mangina" journalists who "cherry-pick" quotes such as "cuckoo for cocoa penis puffs" out of context* to try to make men look bad—the Doubletree told these men to "go elsewhere." (The Doubletree would neither confirm nor deny this claim.)

Elsewhere was a town called St. Clair Shores, and in it a VFW, Post 1146, known as "the Bruce." As in the sign out front that declared, CRUISING AT THE BRUCE / EVERY FRIDAY NIGHT / 5–9 P.M. By "cruising" they meant muscle cars, a fact I mention because A Voice for Men was surprisingly pro-gay, or at least, *anti*-anti-gay, even if Post 1146, deaf to all that might be promised by the phrase "Cruising at the Bruce," was not. There was artillery on the lawn and a faded sign on a fence around the parking lot: WARNING. Of what, to whom, was not clear. The blacktop beyond, where conference attendees lined up to go through "security," was broken with weeds. The men didn't notice the conference's decline in circumstances. They were too excited about "security." They kept saying, "No feminist better try coming here!" Local police had dispatched four officers, and the conference attendees had deputized even more security from their own ranks. "Security" wore black polo shirts, and there were a lot of black polo shirts, but since the line was slow, Security decided to sweep us all in with a request to return for a "check." Nobody did. Only one feminist attempted entry, an activist who went by the handle "Dark Horse

* Context: a conference presentation by Terrence Popp, introduced as "infantry soldier, former professional fighter, college graduate, author, poet, warrior, comedian," a decorated combat veteran whom the conference introducer noted was "top" or "expert" with the following weapons: .50 caliber, MK-19, M-16, M203 grenade launcher, pistol, M60-MG, S.A.W. "I'm not the guy you want pissed off," said Popp, who in a presentation on veterans and suicide suggested the audience "imagine coming back from war to find out your wife—I'm trying to think of a good way to say this, but, uh, you know, went cuckoo for cocoa penis puffs"—I think Popp, who is White, meant the wife in question had sex with a Black man—"crazy for some rice crispy treats and a couple Polish sausages thrown in there. I'm just saying, the situation"— he meant *his* marriage—"was unrecoverable."

Swore." The black shirts eighty-sixed her. She set up at a nearby bar, ordered pizza, opened a tab, and invited any conference attendee who cared to talk. Feminist pizza? Not a chance. These men knew the tricks. They'd taken the red pill, they liked to say.

A red-pill moment, explained one men's rights activist (MRA), "is the day you decide nothing looks the same." It's what the movement calls the born-again experience of opening your eyes to women's *Matrix*-like control of the modern world.* For a young MRA named Max von Holtzendorff, the red-pill moment was being accused of sexual harassment by a coworker to whom he proposed sex, "being blunt and forthright, because it seemed the best way to ensure consent." For Jim Strohmeyer, a former professor, it was "six months in a box" after what he said was a false accusation of domestic violence. For Gunther Schadow, an MD/PhD, it was a "meta-study" on domestic violence that inspired him to seed a foundation with half a million dollars with which he hoped to overturn the Violence Against Women Act. For Dan Moore, whose MRA name was "Factory," the red pill was a revelation in stages. First, he said, his wife cheated on him. Then she wanted him to know it. "She'd laugh at me." His low point: lying on the floor in a fetal curl while she stood over him, mocking him. He said she had a butcher knife in her hand. (She denied this. All of it.)

For Dan Perrins, one of the security black shirts, it was the day he ended up in jail after he said he lodged a complaint against his ex, the

---

* The term "red pill" is derived from the 1999 movie *The Matrix*, in which the hero, Neo, is offered a choice of a red pill that will awaken him to the brutal truth of a world controlled by intelligent machines, or the blue pill, which will allow him to remain contentedly ignorant. "Red-pilling" has been adopted as a meme not only by MRAs but also by White nationalists, despite the film's radical commitment to genderfluid multiculturalism. "Fuck both of you," *Matrix* co-director Lilly Wachowski told Ivanka Trump and billionaire troll Elon Musk when they Tweeted their "red-pilled" status to each other in an apparent expression of contempt for Covid-19 protocols.

beginning of a legal battle that led him to a hunger strike. "I should have killed the bitch five years ago," he'd tell me. "I'd be out by now."

"Women gone insane with the power of the *pussy pass*," was how Elam described the movement's raison d'être in an essay called "When Is It OK to Punch Your Wife?" It was another one of his "provocations." Elam is White, and frequently complained about what he views as the disparagement of White men in popular culture, but he identified with Malcolm X; he believed he needed to shock society to be heard. He said his talk of "the business end of a right hook" and women who are "freaking begging" to be raped, was simply his version of Malcolm's "by any means necessary." To wit: Elam's proposal to make October "Bash a Violent Bitch Month," in which men take the women who abuse them "by the hair and smack their face against the wall till the smugness of beating on someone because you know they won't fight back drains from their nose with a few million red corpuscles."

><

Elam described such language as satire. Then again, one evening in a bar, he told me he stood by every word. A group had gathered with pitchers of beer at a place near the VFW called the Blue Goose. "It's a David-and-Goliath kind of deal," he said. He thought he was David, personally confronting the Goliath of Womanhood, his "provocations" his sling. And just as in the biblical story, it wasn't so much about killing Goliath as giving hope to his people. This, to Elam, was how his "provocations" work: "satire" that's really rage that's really a beacon, a Bat Signal: calling all angry men. "Men who've decided to check out because they can't take it anymore, guys going to live in their cars because they have nowhere to go. I get emails from people who say, 'I was suicidal until I found your website and realized I wasn't alone.'"

Factory raised his beer to Elam. "This guy saved my life," he said. It was two years previous; Factory had taken the red pill by then, but marriage, kids, and family court still proved too much. He decided to do himself in. He sent off one last email, to Elam. "Just seemed the guy I knew who'd sorta understand." Elam did; he called the police, who intervened in time.

To Elam it was clear how satire and solace, threat and solidarity, bleed into one another. It's the world that's confused, he believed, addled by feminism, and also a much older weapon in the gender war he thought had been waged against men not only since women got the vote but for centuries: feminine wiles. He referred me to the man who provided him his own red pill, which came in the form of a book, 1993's *The Myth of Male Power*. "We have long acknowledged the slavery of blacks," writes the book's author, Dr. Warren Farrell, whom Elam sees as speaking the gentler truth of his same message, a White Martin to Elam's White Malcolm. "We have yet to acknowledge the slavery of males."*

They had evidence. Men, particularly poor and working-class men, particularly men of color, are cannon fodder abroad and expendable labor at home, often trapped in jobs nobody really wants—miners, oil riggers, garbagemen—and injured at work at higher rates than women. Imprisoned at far higher rates, too, and more often the vic-

---

* Within the manosphere, Farrell passed as a gentle character. In his daylong pre-conference workshop, he asked attendees to make massage circles, to close their eyes and think of their fathers, to role-play explaining manly needs to the one woman in the session. A cover of one edition of *The Myth of Male Power* depicted its title in big red letters over a shadowy photograph of a naked woman, the "POWER" said to belong to men breaking into pieces against her buttocks. Men are slaves to lust, Farrell argues. Freedom, to Farrell, begins with men having a say over their own sexual destinies by being able to "enter the woman," as he explained to me later, with masculine "dignity" intact.

tims of violent crime. Men get hit by women nearly as often as the other way around (even if the physical damage done is decidedly one-sided). And there are almost no shelters for battered men, unless you count homeless shelters, and if you do you'd better count the men who make up the great majority of their population.

These are largely economic conditions, but conference speaker Dr. Helen Smith, in her book *Men on Strike: Why Men Are Boycotting Marriage, Fatherhood, and the American Dream—and Why It Matters,* describes the problem as "female privilege": schools, she argues, drug the boyishness out of boys, and workplaces, she claims, promote under-qualified women, leaving men dumb, doped, and too broke to afford what one of Smith's sources—echoing Elliot Rodger—describes as "an expensive bitch." To men "on strike," in Smith's parlance, women *are* the economic condition.

Which is essentially a shorter version of the solipsistic analysis of sex and money offered by Elliot Rodger in his 141-page manifesto. It's delusional, and also tragic. "Female privilege" obscures for these men and their few female allies the actual convergences of class and gender, the ways in which working-class bodies of all genders, soldiers and sex workers, miners and maids, are disposable. And their use of such terms makes it harder to hear the MRAs when they cite real numbers, such as the fact that three-quarters of the Americans who commit suicide most years are men, or that nearly as many men as women, according to a 2014 study in *The American Journal of Public Health,* report having been subject to nonconsensual sex.

The irony of the men's rights movement is that so much of its analysis is essentially a feminist one. No less a feminist theorist than the late Andrea Dworkin—a "300-plus-pound basilisk of man-hate," according to Elam, who he claimed "wanted to be raped"—critiqued the idea of men as "disposable" in her book *Right-Wing Women,* published in 1983, ten years before Warren Farrell published *The Myth of Male Power.* "Feminism," wrote Dworkin, "proposes one absolute standard of human dignity, indivisible by sex."

"Nope," says the manosphere. Or, rather, like an obnoxious child, "I can't hear you!" A number of men at the conference told me that women's studies programs teach *The SCUM Manifesto*, a 1967 screed advocating the elimination of men. That's true, I said—it's taught as an artifact. I knew, I told them, because my wife had taught it in a women's studies program. And she wasn't trying to eliminate me.

Several men looked at me sadly. "If only you knew," one said. Another hugged me. "This is a safe space," he said.

><

On the second floor of the Bruce there was a mostly empty meeting hall, robin's-egg-blue walls beneath a low-paneled ceiling, three brass seagulls next to an unused bar, and, at the back, selling swag, the women of the men's rights movement. Not girlfriends or wives. They were the Honey Badgers, their name taken from a viral You-Tube video of the actual creature, a ferocious, skunk-backed African weasel, shrugging off first a swarm of bees then the bite of a cobra in the pursuit of its prey. "Honey badger don't give a shit," says the voiceover. Such is the slogan of the Honey Badgers, who do not give a shit for the opinions of other women and their "mangina" friends.

Jessica Kenney, a doe-eyed young mom with lyrics from a metal band called Incubus tattooed beneath her right bicep, said her red-pill moment was giving birth to a boy. She began to do research. About his future. She found it in YouTube videos. This was late at night, behind the desk of a Holiday Inn Express in upstate New York. Kenney had an MBA from Syracuse, but she'd always worked jobs like this. Right now she was working two. "I used to be girl power," she said, but then she took the red pill. Late at night, behind the desk, one video leading to another. Testimonies, analyses, stats and facts. Revelations.

Reality, Kenney believed, was what might happen to her son in a world controlled by feminists. "Gynocentrism," she said. She was considering homeschooling. The feminists might deny him "opportunities," reserve every chance for girls. Kenney couldn't remember any special breaks herself, but she knew it could happen, knew now that it *was* happening, all the time, everywhere, boys shunted to the margins. As her son—he was two and a half—grew older, it would only get worse. Kenney's brow wrinkled. She feared false accusations. "For him to be punished for things that he hasn't done."

"Or even, like, sexually assaulted," interjected Kenney's comrade Alison Tieman, "and have no recourse."

Tieman went by Typhon Blue, after the Greek monster of myth with a hundred dragons' heads. She was small and sour and wise, the leader of this pack of Honey Badgers, thirty-seven years old, married to a man who, she said, was once the victim of an attempted gang rape by a mob of sixteen-year-old girls.

"It'll often happen in colleges," a Badger named Rachel Edwards said. "A guy will wake up and be like 'You weren't there before, what are you doing here?'"

Tomorrow, Typhon Blue warned, it could be my life on the line. "If a woman puts a gun to a man's head," she said, explaining the rapist-in-the-bushes threat I could face as I walked to my car that evening—"if a woman puts a gun to a man's head and says, 'I'm not even on the pill. And I have gonorrhea. I'm fucking you now.' That's not rape?"

It is, I said. That would be rape. If it happened.

It's happening right now, insisted the Badgers. A Badger named Kristal Garcia told me that "in Africa," there are "female gang-rapers" who drive around in vans, abducting men; and in Nigeria, said Kenney, a man was raped to death by six wives. "And wait," said Edwards, "do we wanna mention there's that woman who has AIDS in Africa and she's just having sex with a bunch of men? Giving them AIDS?"

I wanted to ask why all their examples came from Africa, but they left no room for questions. They said they would send me studies. Science. A whole bottle of red pills. I wrote down my email with a shaky hand. "We are giving off a lot of information," Edwards acknowledged. "It can be overwhelming."

><

I took a break on the balcony of the VFW, a blistering hot slab of concrete speckled in bird shit. In the near distance, a parking lot; beyond, Lake St. Clair. A plume of smoke spiraled up on the other side; something was burning. Kristal Garcia was telling me about her five-year-old daughter. Garcia is Black, a single mother, the daughter of a single mother. She lived with her mother, three generations of women. "Radically feminist," she said of her youth. "At eighteen, I entered the sex industry as a stripper, dominatrix, and escort." She was thirty-two now, trying to make a new career as a life coach. She had the delivery for it, soft and firm at the same time, like she was listening to you even when she was doing the talking. Her daughter's father wasn't around, but she didn't blame him. "I always tell my daughter, 'He loves you.'"

Her men's rights activism grew out of her feminism. Thinking about women's bodies. And her clients. *Their* bodies. "Penis size," she said. Viagra ads, penis-enlargement spam. She started a group called Cock Consciousness, "to empower men's bodies," which she felt weren't powerful enough. Then she found A Voice for Men. "We're not just our cocks," they told her. She changed the group's name to Loving and Supporting Men. Last year, a friend told her she was becoming a misogynist. At first, it felt horrible—"my throat constricted"—but then she began to wonder. "Feminism told me there's misogynists everywhere, the world isn't safe and I have to walk around with my keys in my hand and feel terror." But what if Garcia herself was the one feminism feared? The thought exhilarated her. "Now I'm the misogynist hiding in the bushes."

My phone buzzed with a text from a friend I'll call Ellen. Ellen lived in the Midwest, and when I told her I'd be in a Detroit suburb for the conference, she and her boyfriend, Richard, decided to tag along. They both wrote about gender; they thought it would be interesting. Ellen was twenty-six, blue-eyed, and rosy-cheeked, and one of the few women there. Men wanted to talk to her; to escape them she'd direct them to me. "T-shirt guy is REALLY excited to talk to you," she texted. I knew the shirt she meant: hand-drawn in red fabric paint, the kind kids use, a thin white tee with the legend inscribed across the narrow back of a nervous-postured wearer— FREE ROBERT MAYNARD.

He who would free one Robert Maynard was named Albert Calabrese. The Honey Badgers and I were going to lunch, so I suggested we talk there. The Honey Badgers seemed pleased. They were worried I'd spent too much time talking to women.

><

We chose a Greek restaurant called Pegasus, where the Honey Badgers grew giddy, discussing wine and Elliot Rodger. They wanted it clear that they opposed murder. If only Elliot had come to them first. They wondered if they could have helped him.

Calabrese wanted to talk about the name on his T-shirt. His vowels were smooth but distinct, rounded and clipped at the same time. Robert Maynard, he said, was a physics graduate student at the University of Arkansas, as had been Calabrese. Together they studied "early galactic evolution." His eyes flicked elsewhere. He meant to stay on the topic of Robert Maynard's freedom. "He was—" Calabrese considered how to put it. "He had a fourteen-year-old girl that he was talking to over the Internet."

Typhon Blue's gaze snapped onto Calabrese. She whispered to Garcia. They both glanced at me, then my notebook. Calabrese was off message. This was not what they wanted in a story about men's rights. MRAs would later falsely claim that I must have planted Calabrese to make them look bad. But for now it was enough that Calabrese was a man, that he had come to the conference, and that if he was there he had taken the red pill. For now they would listen.

The main difference between Robert Maynard and Albert Calabrese, Calabrese explained, was that Robert Maynard was serving ten years in prison, and Calabrese was here, with us. Why was Robert Maynard in prison? "He"—Calabrese wobbled his head, adjudicating his words—"received a naked picture of her."

Received. Passive voice, as if this were just something that happened to Maynard. Typhon Blue investigated. How did Maynard come to talk to the girl in the first place?

I'd later learn that police investigated after a complaint was filed alleging that Robert L. Maynard had sent sexually explicit photographs and messages to the girl, that he admitted to police "that it was possible" he'd done so, and that when police searched his computer they recovered forty pornographic images of children as young as nine.

Calabrese said, "He likes women. He does not *unlike* women just because they're young. He would argue, and so would I, that fourteen is a sexually mature person."

Kenney nodded, in agreement not with Calabrese's assertion about age but with his intimation that sometimes receiving child pornography might not be the recipient's fault. "There is a culture of girls who are just freely distributing pictures of themselves online. I don't think they understand what that means for somebody else."

On this point, the selfishness of adolescent girls, all concurred. One of the most popular presentations at the conference was that of Dr. Tara Palmatier, a self-declared "Shrink 4 Men," on the "specialest snowflakes that ever snowflaked." "Entitlement princesses," explained Dr. Palmatier, who had developed a formula with which to quantify them. $N=S/H$, where S=selfie, H=Hour, and N, the result, is a measurable unit of narcissism. The scientific term, she'd tell me later, is "narcissistic borderline pathology," the "feminism" she saw epitomized in girls taking pictures of themselves.

Calabrese said he didn't know "100 percent" if his friend asked an adolescent girl to send him a nude picture.

"Whether or not there was solicitation is important to know," said Typhon Blue.

"Right, right," agreed Garcia. Because if Robert Maynard just *received* the photo—

"It's something that—thankfully not to the same extent—that happened to my husband's best friend," said Kenney. She told a complicated story of a mother and a daughter, a smart phone in common, and now her husband's friend was on probation.

"The public," observed Calabrese, "does not know the difference between a pedophile and an ephebophile." Neither did I. "Somebody who likes young teens," volunteered one of the Badgers. Teens between fifteen and eighteen, I'd later learn. "There's that, and there's another word," Calabrese said. He may have meant *hebephile*—twelve to fourteen. Calabrese's cause, for which he considered Maynard a prisoner of conscience, was lowering the age of consent.

"What age?" Typhon Blue asked sharply.

"The average age of menarche," said Calabrese, "is twelve point three."

Later I'd promise Typhon Blue that I'd make clear her disagreement with Albert Calabrese. Typhon's response to "twelve point three," with as much anger and contempt as can be channeled into four letters, was: "*What?*"

"Well, the thing is, the way I see it, to be fair—"

"What age for boys?" demanded Typhon.

"I've had situations where you don't even know." Calabrese meant the age of the child.

"There's a middle ground here," said Edwards, attempting to mediate. "What happened to Robert is wrong."

Typhon Blue's husband, Jonathan, suggested that perhaps pedophilia is a problem that should be dealt with privately rather than by the state.

"Like a social worker," said Garcia.

This made Calabrese feel better. He'd come to the conference, he said, worried he'd be alone in his beliefs. Not at all. "My average conversation has gone, I would say, considerably well."

"The only part we can't agree on is age of consent," Typhon Blue said, her tone softer now.

"For me, the consent thing, it's a blurred thing." said her husband. "The whole sex thing is just a can of worms."

Yes, sighed the table.

Edwards had an idea. "Can we talk about Elliot Rodger now?"

><

Calabrese had more he wanted to say, but he wanted to do so without Typhon Blue around. After lunch, he caught my eye across the VFW lobby. He was good at that kind of communication. The sly kind. A barely perceptible nod, not a wink but a flicker. We both left the hall and made for the shore. Dead fish slapped against the crumbling concrete lining the lake's edge. The wind did nothing to dissipate the heat or the smell.

There was a point on which he disagreed with Maynard, he said.

Calabrese thought twelve point three as an age of consent is too old. He'd go with twelve. "I would rather err on the side of twelve-year-olds having sex than on the side of ruining men's lives." Unlike teenagers, he said, adults would be interested in "substance, or even a mentor-protégée relationship." Teenage boys, he said, brag.

"Maynard didn't brag?" I asked.

Calabrese laughed. "No!" Then, under his breath, "That would be silly."

Calabrese did not brag. Not really. "I'm easily googleable," he said. He was: Albert J. Calabrese Jr., a former substitute teacher in Akron, Ohio, arrested for felony sexual misconduct with a minor. "My chick wasn't a student," he claimed, by which he means not *his* student. "She asked me out." He thought it would help his case if the police knew she was more "experienced" than he was. "I was remarkably naïve." He said he didn't know he had a right to remain silent. He'd never watched a cop show. Such programs, he said, "are emotionally frustrating to me." He said he didn't want to hurt anyone. That a child would be hurt by an adult's exploitation did not seem to occur to him. His desires, he believed, were a matter of masculine dignity.

He stood on the concrete shore, cocked his black-jeaned hips, and spread his arms wide embracing the water, his back to the world. Calabrese had driven fourteen and a half hours to be here, he'd taken uppers, and he was still taking them; he was pale and dappled. Cold sweat under the hot gray sun.

›‹

I was rescued by one of the security black shirts, a tall and awkward young man whose red hair shot up in two great tufts. His name was Sage Gerard, and he was A Voice for Men's collegiate activism director. At first, I thought he'd walked down to the water to separate Calabrese from a journalist. But if that was Sage's mission, his method was the displacement of Calabrese's discourse with his own. He was relentless, running through MRA talking points on fast repeat. I made my break for the bar back up at the hall, only to realize I'd inadvertently done something terrible: I'd led Sage right to Ellen.

Sage wasn't a pickup artist. He'd drawn a cartoon about them for A Voice for Men featuring a stick-figure "nice guy" asking a stick-figure girl for a date. "Nice try, loser," says the girl. Then a stick-figure pickup artist pops up. "C'mere, skank," says the pickup artist. Stick-figure girl falls to her knees. "I want your cock," she says.

In his mind, Sage was the "nice guy." He asked Ellen what she found exciting about men's rights. What did she want to learn more about?

She told him she was surprised that she hadn't heard more about rape.

Sage said—and here I defer to Ellen's notes, which Ellen says she asked Sage if she could take: "You wanted to hear more about rape? Ooh, you're *freaky*."

Ellen: "What do you mean?"

Sage: "What do you want it to mean?"

Ellen said a friend of hers, Bryan (which is not his real name), had recently been accused of assault, and, knowing something of the circumstances, for the first time she thought the accusation might be false. She didn't know. That's what she wanted to understand.

Sage wanted to help. He asked her to come with him. They'd need someplace private. The stairwell. He had an idea. He wanted her to write a poem for her friend, a poem for men falsely accused. But Honey Badgers kept stepping over and between them. Come with me, he said. He took her to the balcony, the hot concrete. She sat down, and he pulled his chair close. Ellen told him she wasn't sure what to write.

"You do want to make an emotional impact," Sage said. He wanted her to empathize with Bryan. Many in the movement don't believe women are capable of empathy—genetically incapable—but Sage considered himself broadminded. He would teach Ellen. "He's alone," said Sage, empathizing. "He's isolated." Bryan, he said, must have "social needs." It was Ellen's job to fulfill them. "Bryan needs to know that you love him, that you're supporting him, that you will be on his side." He closed his eyes and licked his lips, waiting for Ellen to begin.

"Bryan," she said, "I hope you're not lyin'."

Sage sighed. *Women.* "Ellen, poetry doesn't have to rhyme." He'd show her. This could be a good line: "You owe her nothing but a view of your back." Sage, noted Ellen, petted her thigh. "I'm not angry at women," he explained, "but I'm angry at what they can do. You could put down your book right now and yell 'Rape!' and I would be led away in handcuffs." They thought about this. Sage said, "I hope it's OK if I hug you."

Before she could respond, he pulled her in, pulled her up out of her chair, pulled her against his chest, and held her there, rubbing her back—an embrace Ellen would later describe as "the most unconsensual hug I have ever known."

Ellen: "I still don't know what to do about the poem."

Sage loosened his grip. "I apologize for dragging you away. I wasn't going to feel OK until I talked to you." But he didn't want her to worry about him—he had a lot of women, he said, running through a list of those he'd spurned. He seemed to mean this as a reassurance: Only "desperate" men, "vulnerable" men, rape, he said, and Sage was neither. He warned her not to send mixed messages. For instance, he said, she shouldn't put her hand on a man's knee if she didn't want to have sex with him. Sage put his hand on Ellen's knee. This was not a mixed message, he wanted her to understand. She needed another hug. He needed to give it to her.

On the last night of the conference, Sage and Typhon Blue danced in a bar to "Blurred Lines." "This is our song!" cried Sage. Ellen received several marriage proposals. There was karaoke, AC/DC's "Big Balls," performed twice.* And around midnight, Ellen's boyfriend, Richard, and I joined Elam for a private after-party in his suite. Once it was determined that Ellen could come too—girls allowed—she met us there. Factory was there, too, with his girlfriend, Lori, and there was Tara Palmatier, the Shrink 4 Men, and a skinny old hippie with a thin gray ponytail and a belt buckle that said JAZZ, whom I will call Jazz. We all drank mudslides.

Elam was pleased by the entrance of another woman. "Tell me why you're here," he said, his voice soft. He fixed Ellen with his listening gaze.

"I'm interested in hard conversations," Ellen said.

She walked into that one. Factory guffawed. "This is as hard as it gets!"

"I'm curious," Elam said. "What did your friends think when you told them you were coming here?"

"To be honest?"

Elam nodded.

"I had friends who said I'd get raped."

"All right!" Elam boomed, swinging his arms together. "Let's get started!"

---

* AC/DC's "Big Balls" is deliberately dumb, the essence of which is well captured by the title. As for "Blurred Lines," by Robin Thicke, featuring TI and Pharrell Williams—quoting lyrics is costly, and I would not spare a dime for this grotesque, later denounced by Williams himself. With music that a court determined, to the tune of $7.4 million, had been lifted from Marvin Gaye, it is a collage of phrases countless rape survivors have been subjected to in the course of their assault. Fair use allows me to share one seemingly innocuous line: "I'm a nice guy." In 2021, the actor Emily Ratajkowski, who appeared in the video for the song, published a memoir titled *My Body* in which she accused Thicke of sexually assaulting her during filming.

Jazz winced.

"Get the video camera!" Factory yelled at his girlfriend. She giggled weakly.

I should be very clear here: At no point did Ellen think Elam or Factory was actually going to rape her. We knew they were joking. Just a couple of middle-aged guys joking around about rape with a young woman they'd never met before in a hotel room after midnight.

"What surprised me," Ellen said, defusing, "was how warm people were."

She'd found Elam's hinge: He launched into reminiscing about the days just past, about the love in the air. "I'm seriously choked up about it."

"I am too," said Factory. He appreciated Ellen's generous observation. He called her a "labia traitor," which he meant as a compliment.

The night wound on, with discussion of rape and "envelopment," a term for the smothering of penises, and more about the narcissism of young girls. A sore point for Factory, who had two daughters. Like young women everywhere, he said, they competed for the most extravagant rape claim. It was, he said, a status thing. When one of his daughters came home one night and told him she'd been raped, he said he asked her, "Are you fucking kidding me?" Sitting with us, he hiked his voice up to a falsetto in imitation of his child: "'Oh, I just got raped'" He laughed. There was a moment of silence. Bridge too far? "I told her if she pressed charges, I'd disown her."

Elam grinned through his beard. "That's good fathering," he said.

We moved onto the topics of cowards and pickup artists—pathetic, thought Elam, who said game comes naturally to a man who knows he's a man. The hour was getting on. We'd run out of Kahlúa. Jazz was growing a little trippy about feminism and "the end of the human race." Elam and Factory slipped out onto the balcony to share a joint, rolling their own. I followed. We looked into the darkness of St. Clair Shores and the lake beyond, three men smoking in the damp air before dawn.

When we returned to the room, Elam and Factory began to "tease" Ellen. "Your last line," Elam told me, looking at her, "should be, 'Then we got the munchies, and Paul said, *Bitch, go get me a sandwich.*'" He was joking. More satire. He would never ask a *bitch* to make him a sandwich. But seriously, he said. Seriously.

And that was when Elam drew me his diagram. The Dick & Balls. He didn't mean to, but there they were. A sign. "Yes," he said. "Yes, I guess it is." He smiled. They all smiled. We were high in the manosphere now, the great phallic oversoul, the red pills were working, the rape jokes no longer landing like bombshells, they were like the weather, ordinary as rain. We'd arrived: the dreamworld of Elam, where men are men, no matter how broken, because they can't imagine wanting simply to be human. In the manosphere they never had to. The question was never raised. That's what the manosphere meant: the solace of men, the solace of looking away.

The Trumpocene

The Second Campaign

1.

Yusif Jones, standing in front of a long row of porta potties, slid his plastic Trump mask over his face. "I'm him!" he exclaimed. He puffed up his chest in his homemade Trump shirt, a short-sleeved American flag pullover onto which he had ironed black felt letters across vertical red and white stripes:

GOT

TRUMP

?

Then he flashed the OK sign, a silver ring on his pinky. "I'm him, dude!"

The OK sign—thumb meeting index finger, three fingers splayed—has become a symbol of White power. It began as a joke; or rather, a "joke," in scare quotes, *ironic* White power, a "hoax" meant to trick liberals into believing that the raised fingers actually represent the letters *W.P.* The joke worked so well that it became real. Now, in certain circles, OK *does* mean White power—unless you say it doesn't.

Jones, a big, vein-popping, occasionally churchgoing White man burdened by his hippie mother with what he called an "Islamic" name, did not see a contradiction between his White-power display and his certainty that he was no racist. For one thing, he'd say, he was flashing it for a Black man. A self-described Black "Trumplican," proprietor of a tent full of Trump gear—T-shirts that read GOD, GUNS, AND TRUMP, and LGBT, which stands for "liberty, beer, guns and Trump," and TRUMP 45 over the image of a handgun—in the parking lot outside an arena in Bossier City, Louisiana, where some 14,000 people awaited the president's arrival still many hours distant. For another, the Trumplican appeared to like the display. "*You* can't take it!" he said, laughing and pointing at me.

Jones asked the Trumplican if he was a fan of Jesse Lee Peterson, a right-wing pastor and talk-show host who had become a MAGA man. "He's Black!" said Jones. He didn't wait for the Trumplican's answer. "You know what Jesse Lee Peterson calls Trump?" he asked. He could barely restrain himself. "The Great White Hope!" He doubled over, slapping his knee. "I love that dude." He found Peterson awesomely funny. "But it's true," Jones added, meaning the Great White Hope part. Which is how racism works at a Trump rally—signal, disavowal, repeat; the ugly words followed by the claim that it's just a joke followed by a repetition of the ugly words. Joking! Not joking. Play it again, until the ironic becomes the real.

Later, I listened to Peterson's show. Peterson called Trump "The Great White Hope," he said, because, "number one, he is White. Number two, he is of God." When Rep. Elijah Cummings, a Trump foe, died, Peterson declared on his radio show, "He dead," God's work, he believed. "That's what happens when you mess with the Great White Hope. Don't mess with God's children."

Jones only recently became one of those children. "I've been on the side of evolution my whole life," he confessed. Not so much the science end; his had been the partying wing of agnosticism. Then his fiancée persuaded him to start attending a fundamentalist church, not long before Trump was elected, and it'd given Jones a new way of looking at things. For instance, he said: the Democrats' "gay agenda."

"Oh yeah," said the Trumplican.

"Actually," said Jones, "they're pedophiles."

Jones was only the second person I'd met at the rally, so I didn't yet know just how common that perspective was. Through a season of Trump rallies across the country, I spoke with dozens of Trump supporters who believed that the Democratic establishment primarily serves as a cover for child sex trafficking. Some were familiar with QAnon, the name claimed by believers in a host of conspiracy theories centered on an alleged "deep state" coup against Trump, and his supposedly ingenious countermeasures, referred to as the coming "Storm," or "Great Awakening." Most were not. It was, they told me, simply *known*. "Perverts and murderers," said a woman in Bossier City. A youth pastor promised me that Trump knew the names of all the guilty parties and was preparing their just deserts. The president himself, in speech after speech, intimated that Judgment Day was coming. In Hershey, Pennsylvania, he spoke of "illegals" hacking and raping and bludgeoning, "relentlessly beating a wonderful, beautiful high school teenager to death with a baseball bat and chopping the body apart with a machete." And that, he added, was only what he could reveal. There was more, he said, much, much more. *Believe me.*

Such is the intimacy of Trumpism: innuendo and intimation, wink and revelation. Jones got it. To demonstrate, he popped up his Trump mask, bent over, and began sniffing the wet blacktop like a hound.

"Creepy Joe!" cried the Trumplican.

Jones bounced up and beamed as if he'd just won at charades. It was his imitation of Joe Biden, on the trail of young boys to molest. Biden as child sniffer was a popular right-wing meme, but it wasn't really Biden himself who mattered. They knew Joe was one among many. "Demons," said Jones, speaking of the Democratic Party leadership. "Not even human." Which is why it would take the Great White Hope, chosen by God, to confront them. They're too powerful for the likes of ordinary men.

Jones had tried.

"I made a mistake," he said. "I called them up." He was not just a believer in the Trumpocene's conspiracy theories, he was a soldier on their behalf, convicted in a deep-state court of law. On December 4, 2016, a man traveled from North Carolina to a Washington, DC, pizzeria called Comet Ping Pong, the basement of which, according to the Pizzagate conspiracy theory, was the heart of a Democratic child-sex-trafficking ring. The man was there to save the children, which he attempted to do by opening fire with an AR-15. Inspired, Jones decided to do his part. Three days after the assault, according to testimony he later gave, Jones called another pizzeria down the street. "Honest mistake!" he explained to me. He thought it was the child-sex-trafficking one. "I'm coming to finish what the other guy didn't," he told them. "I'm coming there to save the kids, and then I'm going to shoot you and everyone in the place." He did not think to block his number.

This is what amazed him now: Caller ID. "They didn't even have a recording!" After spending forty days and forty nights in jail, he said (thirty-three, actually), Jones decided to plead guilty to one count of interstate threatening communications. Now, though, he claimed he hadn't actually threatened to shoot, but he couldn't risk prison because of his lawn-service business. Also, his pets. "So I said fuck it, I'll take the guilty plea, because at least what I'm pleading guilty to is good. Even my preacher said that. He said, 'You did a good thing.'"

The Trumplican agreed. "It's good," he said.

"It's real!" said Jones, eyes wide.

The *real* of which he spoke—"I was on Yahoo News," Jones said, holding up the page on his phone—is that of the reality TV from which his leader sprang. *The Apprentice, Celebrity Apprentice*. A reality set free from context or history, shimmering with feeling, millions of individual truths—Jones's, Jesse Lee Peterson's, the Ping Pong shooter's—all streaming toward one great "fact": Trump.

Jones disappeared behind his mask. The clock was ticking past noon. The president would be here in less than seven hours. It was time to get in line.

2.

In 2016, I attended Trump rallies around the country to witness the role played by religion. Back then, the candidate was taken as living proof of what's known as the prosperity gospel, not so much concerned with saving society as it is with getting right with God by getting rich. Show your faith in His blessings, as revealed in the opulent lives of His anointed preachers, and good fortune will trickle down. Like Trump, the prosperity gospel is transactional. Quid pro quo, a deal with God: affluence (or the dream of it to come) in return for unquestioning belief.

And yet even the belief part of that trade is situational, a fake-it-till-you-make-it faith by which appearance counts as much as reality. That was as true of Trump's evangelical coalition of the willing as it was of his fortune. In 2016, most were back-benchers, such as Lance Wallnau. Trumpologists point to the 2011 White House Correspondents' Dinner, at which President Obama mocked Trump's conspiracy-mongering birtherism, as the beginning of Trump's forever campaign. But in the bestselling book Wallnau spun from his marketing catchphrase for Trump, *God's Chaos Candidate,* he offered a different—if just as racist—origin story:

> While watching the evening news with his wife, Melania, [Trump] witnessed the escalating violence and riots happening in Baltimore. In that moment, Melania turned to Trump and said, "If you run now, you will be president."
>
> "What?" Trump was legitimately shocked by this sudden declaration. "I thought you said I was too bright and brash to get elected?" She turned back to the plasma screen and said, "Something has changed. They are ready for you now."

They are ready for you now. Enough Americans were, in 2016, when, whatever Russian interference that may have occurred aside, the Trump campaign channeled a convergence of conservatisms. It was the coming together of the populist economic Right and the so-called Alt-Right, the resurgence of Reagan's men and the rise of a new generation; the money of the elite and the electoral volume of the masses, all brought together under a white flag not of surrender but of supremacy, felt if not said. The coin of the realm in this new age was perhaps the commemorative golden one Wallnau put on sale for $45, a "point of contact" between believers and God to pray for Trump's reelection, featuring images of Trump and the biblical King Cyrus, a gentile who became God's tool. So, too, declared Wallnau, was Trump God's vessel: "the self-made man who can 'get it done,' enters the arena, and through the pressure of circumstance becomes the God-shaped man God enables to do what he could never do in his own strength."

But that was then. God's chaos candidate became the Chosen One, a claim Trump and his lieutenants made with the same joking/not joking simultaneity he brought at his rallies to the idea of a permanent presidency. He was trolling us, but as with the OK sign for White power, the irony had grown earnest, the joke had been born again as sincere, or, at least, "sincere."

Such was the deal Trump struck with Christian nationalism. And a good deal—the kind that pays—is not only transactional, it's transformative. With some minor exceptions, the establishment Christian Right embraced the gospel of Trump, and it prospered: Trump's administration stocked top to bottom with its apostles, the movement mightier even "post-Trump" than it was under George W. Bush or Reagan. Trump, meanwhile, fused his penchant for self-pity with the paranoia that runs like a third rail through Christian conservatism, the thrilling promise of "spiritual war" with dark and hidden powers.

In 2016, the Trump faith was Make America Great Again, the prospect of the restoration of a mythic (read: White) past. By the second campaign the new religion was a secret one, its enemy invisible and everywhere: the deep state, the pedos and the FBI, Democrat-ruled sanctuary cities and the "illegals" they sent forth to pillage the heartland. MAGA became KAG, Keep America Great—which required not a new prosperity, which Trump's legions believed he had delivered, but the eradication of America's enemies, which are within. "If you do not bring forth what is within you," as the Gospel of Thomas puts it, "what you do not bring forth will destroy you."

The Gospel of Thomas—the doubting one—does not, of course, reside with Matthew, Mark, Luke, and John in the King James. But then, Trump didn't read the Bible. He didn't need to. Rule books are for losers. *Reading* is for losers. The gospel of Trump, like that of Thomas—noncanonical, antiestablishment—is Gnostic, a form of exclusive knowledge reserved for the faithful, a "truth" you must have the eyes to see.

Gnosticism, which dates at least to the second century CE, is the path Christianity did not take, most of its texts destroyed as heretical, most of its ideas forgotten until the 1945 discovery in Egypt of thirteen ancient books in a sealed clay jar. Or maybe not so much forgotten as bastardized over the centuries into countless conspiracy theories, the deep-seated belief that there exist truths *they*—there is always a *they* in all these ersatz Gnosticisms, from the bishops and bureaucrats of the early Church to the modern media peddling fake news—do not want *us,* the people, to perceive. There's something almost democratic in the modern American distortion of Gnosticism. "Recognize what is before your eyes," the Gospel of Thomas advises, "and that which is hidden will be revealed." One needs no diplomas to know truth, no "data" contrived by "experts." Knowledge lies not in scholarship or information but within, "the gut," as Trump had long maintained, or "right here," as he said at one of his coronavirus briefings, tapping his temple to show us "the metric" by which he would know when it was safe for us to go outside, when we could gather again by the thousands to adore him.

3.

In Bossier City, the line wound through a parking lot, a sluggish ser-pent that moved only in hiccups and burps. Nobody seemed to mind. Two young women in front of me, who had taken off work to travel from Arkansas in bedazzled red-white-and-blue Trump gear, passed the time bragging about their firsthand knowledge of the Clintons. They held my place so I could take a snapshot of a man who wore a T-shirt depicting Bill and Hillary—him with a handgun, her, leather-gloved, flexing a garrote—over the words CLINTONS: THEY CAN'T SUICIDE US ALL. "They say," confided one of the women, "that the Clintons may have suicided my uncle." He had been a prominent conservative lawyer in their town, and he had died at a restaurant, choking on steak. Or had he? *They* called such killings—caused by the Clintons, for reasons upon which one could only speculate—"Arkan-cide."

Inside, on the arena floor, a crowd had gathered before the stage to stand for hours—no sitting permitted—rather than wait in the stands. I struck up a conversation with a middle-aged couple in matching black long-sleeved shirts declaring in white block letters, TRUMP'S TWEETS MATTER. They were missionaries. The husband, Pastor Sean Jones, wore a red MAGA hat and a biblically full beard, and his face looked weathered, wary, and wise. Wedged between his legs was a black hat that read GOD WINS, a reference to a seminal QAnon post. He'd been gifted the shirt and the hat by another pastor, who, like Pastor Sean, traveled from rally to rally. Pastor Sean's gift for his fellow Trumpers, in turn, was a small New Testament enhanced with the U.S. Constitution, a document he believed was "God-breathed." He said he had distributed thousands.

Trump was still hours distant, but the arena was nearing capacity, the playlist on rotation like a plane that can't land, much of it the same as '16, Queen, the Stones, and Pavarotti. The crowd liked it that way. They liked hearing the same songs over and over, knowing all the words.

In 2016, the mood at Trump's rallies was electric but heavy, a mix of dread and ecstasy, anger and the possibility of "winning"— winning so much, Trump promised, that we would get tired of winning. Since then he had won; and won and won and won. The energy now was victorious, and even darker. Not potential but kinetic, synchronized. "You can feel it," said Pastor Sean's wife. Sean nodded. "Likeminded." Even I know the verse to which he referred. Philippians 2:2: "Fulfill ye my joy, that ye be likeminded, having the same love, being of one accord, of one mind." One mind, 14,000 hats, most of them red, like Pastor Sean's.

But if the arena was a safe space for Trump's people, the world outside was more frightening than ever. "Secret murders everywhere," said Pastor Sean, his voice a growl. "Pedophiles, and evil." He believed God had chosen Trump for this battle. That which those who were blind to God's clues called crude and divisive, Pastor Sean took as proof of Trump's anointing. He was God's champion, a fighter, a "counterpuncher," as Trump described himself. The prefix was essential to the old manly myth, "I don't start fights, but I finish them." An odd fit on Trump, this claim of stoic reserve, which was why, in the mythos, Trump sometimes had to smirk and throw the first punch, after all. It was a matter, to the believers, of almost mystical timing; Trump alone knew when to jab and when to weave and when to roundhouse. All of which had put Trump's life in danger, said Pastor Sean. "He knows too much."

"About the Democrats?"

Pastor Sean nodded. Pastor Sean was not like some of these people—he waved at the crowd—so deluded as to believe that most Democrats are *conscious* servants of Satan. Sean, himself a victim of SRA—satanic ritual abuse—knew that there are those who do the devil's work without realizing whom they serve. To him the great virtue of Trump was clarity. At this late hour, he said, we could not help but see through a glass darkly—"1 Corinthians 1:13." But even in this dim tide a brightness grew, and we saw illuminated not the glory but the horror: the American carnage, the vastness of the forces arrayed against God. Democrats, CNN, "all of it," Pastor Sean grumbled, flicking a finger at the caged-in media pen. "Lot of movie stars too," he added. He scanned the crowd. "De Niro," he muttered, low enough that I had to lean in to hear him. Before he could explain, the music stopped; it was time to pledge allegiance. To the flag, and to the president for which it now stood, one man, under God.

I made my way over to the source of the TRUMP'S TWEETS MATTER T-shirts: a cluster of men close to the stage, sharing strips of beef jerky from a red Solo cup. The shirts were the work of one among them, a black-hatted man known as the Trumped-Up Cowboy. The Cowboy, holding court, was not entertaining strangers at the moment, so a former youth pastor in his entourage, Dave Thompson, agreed to speak to me. He handed me his card: "God Wins/Prayer Warrior," and on the back a Bible verse, 2 Chronicles 7:14, in which God promises "my people" to "heal their land."

Like Pastor Sean, Pastor Dave followed Trump across the country. He led prayer meetings outside the president's rallies every day, at 7:14, a.m. and p.m. A real estate broker, Pastor Dave felt a "spiritual drawing" to devote his life to Trump. He'd started at a rally in his home state of Texas, where he befriended some superfans: Richard, from New York, who had been to sixty-eight or sixty-nine rallies, and

Rick, from Ohio, who had been to seventeen. Attending rallies, Dave realized, was a calling.

He followed Richard and Rick to a rally in Minneapolis, at which Trump debuted his impression of texts between former FBI agents Peter Strzok and Lisa Page. Strzok was one of the top agents assigned to the investigation of Russian influence within Trump's 2016 campaign. In texts to Page, with whom he was having an affair, the couple spoke of "stopping" Trump. To Trump and his followers, this fact invalidated any criticism of his backchannel communications with the Russian government. But it was the reality-show aspect of the texts that Trump relished and that delighted Pastor Dave. "Oh, I love you so much," Trump moaned, pretending to be Page. "I love you, Peter!" Then he became Strzok, working up to a climax: "I love you too, Lisa! Lisa! Lisa! Oh God! I love you, Lisa!"

At a rally in Mississippi, Pastor Dave met the Cowboy, who had taken under his wing a group of boys from Kentucky. Pastor Dave and the Cowboy began traveling the Trump trail together, serving as chaperones for the kids, who became known as the Trumped-Up Teens. The Cowboy personally paid for the boys' airfare and put them up in tents in parking lots outside the arenas. "Look," Dave said, gesturing toward the stage. Near the front stood the boys, sixteen years old, maybe seventeen, eight of them wearing matching shirts from the Cowboy. Dave read the shirts aloud: "Trump's. Tweets. Matter." The Cowboy, Dave said, found the boys in the woods. (Or maybe, he said later, it was actually at a Trump rally in Lexington.) Now he flew the boys to rallies to spread the word.

"The tweets?" I asked.

"Yes. They matter. They mean things." He pointed. There: one of their shirts. And there, up in the seats. Another shirt. And there, and there, and there, as if repetition itself was proof.

"It's not a joke?" I asked, since the shirts were also a mockery of Black Lives Matter.

"No!" Dave wasn't offended. "It's like—" He looked for a word.

"Scripture?"

"Yes," he said with a youth pastor's approving grin. "Like Scripture." Every tweet, every misspelling, every typo, every strange capitalization—especially the capitalizations, said Dave—had meaning. "The truth is right there in what the media think are his mistakes. He doesn't make mistakes." The message of that which in the tweets fools mistook for error, Dave thought, was: Study the layers. "Trump is known as a five-dimension chess player." And he was sending us clues. "Look," he said, again pointing at the Kentucky boys. Phil Collins was playing, "In the Air Tonight," and the boys leaned hard over the barrier, straining toward the stage, grinning as it approached: the drum solo, eight boys drumming air, *ba-dum-dum-dum-dum,* like a body tumbling down a flight of stairs.

4.

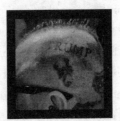

"Look upon me, you who reflect upon me," declares the divine voice of perhaps the most famous Gnostic text, a poem called "The Thunder, Perfect Mind." So it was in the arenas of Trump, thousands of red hats just like his, the hats that at each rally he threw to the crowd, giving of himself. Such were the miracles of Trump, adored for his golden tower, his golden faucets, his generosity. He who has taken the most also gives the most.

"The Thunder," too, presents the divine as a series of contradictions:

I am the honored one and the scorned one.

I am the whore and the holy one. . . .

You who tell the truth about me, lie about me,

And you who have lied about me, tell the truth about me. . . .

I am the strength and I am fear. . . .

I am the one who is disgraced and the great one. . . .

I, I am godless,

And I am the one whose God is great. . . .

I am the control and the uncontrollable.

I am the union and the dissolution.

Nonbelievers roll their eyes over the apparent hypocrisy of Trump as a tribune of family values, the dopiness of the rubes who considered him a moral leader. Nonbelievers, in other words, miss the point. They lack gnosis. Very few believers denied Trump's sordid past. Some turned to the old Christian ready-made of redemption: Their man was lost, but now he was found. Others loved him precisely *because* he was a sinner—if a man of such vast, crass, and open appetites can embody the nation, then you, too, student of porn, monster-truck lover, ultimate fighter in your dreams and games, could claim an anointing. "I am the substance," "The Thunder" continues, "and the one who has no substance." Indeed.

The Gnostics might have especially appreciated the most absurd Trumpian paradox: He sat at the heart of power even as he proclaimed himself an outsider. He was, by virtue of decades of what we might call executive drift—our slow but steady abandonment of checks and balances, our embrace of the "unitary executive"— literally the "greatest," so long as we detach "great" from its modern conflation with "good." Great, in the ancient sense, means *big*, existentially large. "I am the one whom they call the Law," declares "The Thunder," "and you have called me Lawlessness." Yes. Both. The power and the pique, at the same time.

Trump was for his followers what Gnostics called "The Depth," or, perhaps more aptly, "The Abyss." Gnostics believed that what other Christians considered God was a "demiurge"—fake news, a front, an entity deluded into believing itself the source of power because it had constructed the material world. In the gospel of Trump, that was the bureaucracy of government. Cut the red tape, drain the swamp, deregulate—let the Trump within you be Trump—and the true depth of the divine is revealed.

But if Trump was the Depth, what to make of the deep state? The Gnostics had a term for that, too, for the bishops and deacons, the elites of the church they loathed as corrupt. They called such people "waterless canals." Democrats and RINOs ("Republicans in name only"): waterless canals. Barack Obama, Joe Biden: waterless canals. All those who Trump said betrayed Trump, those whom the believers insisted he invited into his sphere with the secret purpose of exposing them—the chiefs of staff and cabinet secretaries he fired or forced to resign—revealed: waterless canals.

5.

Two weeks after the rally in Bossier City, I traveled to the BB&T Center in Sunrise, Florida, for another gathering of the faithful. I began the morning with a trio of tailgating bros in the parking lot, one of whom wore red-white-and-blue footie pajamas despite the heat. When they offered to smoke me up I broke away and joined a pack of Proud Boys—trying to blend in despite the fact that I was shorter, older, and much less tattooed—but they started talking about getting their hands on some journalists, so I peeled away, hitching onto a conversation with a Biker for Trump collecting signatures for the campaign. Signatures for what? I asked. "Just names," he said.

His name was Ed Himmelman. Beneath his MAGA cap he wore his white beard in two braids adorned with red, white, and blue beads. His camouflage vest declared him a member of the Last Militia, founded in Ohio in 2009 to champion an America "where men can wear knives and guns." The Second Amendment, in Ed's book, was second only, to, well, the First. Freedom of religion—or, as Ed thought of it, religion as freedom. So it had been in Ed's life, which was a far rougher proposition before he came to the Lord. When he wasn't in camouflage, he wore a monk's brown robe. "I've taken my vows," Ed said. Just as Trump had. "God is using him," Ed explained.

It was time to enter the arena. Inside, close to the stage, a man gave me his business card. JFK35.com, it reads—his private collection of Kennedy paraphernalia, including one of JFK's sweaters, his cufflinks, and a perfect duplicate of the 1961 Lincoln limo in which he was killed. Many I met at the rallies said they had been Democrats once, back when the Democratic Party stood for something besides open borders and pedophilia. The joy of a Trump rally wasn't partisan; it was the convert's conviction that they have entered the light, undiluted and pure.

The purest believer I met in Sunrise was Diane G, who asked me not to use her last name, for fear of Democrat retaliation. Diane G's hair was platinum and long, her jeans white, her skin very tan. Her ice-blue eyes were so large she seemed to sparkle when she smiled. "I'm in the electrical world," she said. She meant she once owned a successful lighting-design firm; she pointed at the great banks of stage lights—there, and there, and there, admiring the arrangement, glorying in Trump's illumination. She was born into spectacle, a

"PK," a preacher's kid, raised in the Church of the Foursquare Gospel, a Pentecostal denomination founded in 1923 by a preacher named Aimee Semple McPherson with the belief that church should above all be entertaining. McPherson once delivered a sermon dressed as a motorcycle cop, complete with a motorcycle onstage. Likewise it was Trump's showmanship that won Diane, his 2015 descent to the people by way of his golden escalator, the way in which, in 2016, he seemed to fill TV screens with power. She wanted to look away. "I was a Never Trumper!" She couldn't. She looked, and then she saw.

Was it something he said? A policy, a position?

No. "My faith helped me see him." The Holy Ghost gave her what some Christians call the gift of discernment, an idea rooted in the Book of Acts that just as some are gifted the ability to speak in tongues, languages not their own, others are gifted the ability to discern spirits, to perceive wickedness within what might seem righteous, and holiness within what might, to the undiscerning, be mistaken for profane. She learned discernment the hard way. Disillusionment in her church, about which she could not speak—"this is church now!" she said, spinning in a circle on the arena floor to Aerosmith's "Dream On"—and heartbreak in Haiti, where she said she had inherited from her father a home for abused children. She raised money for school fees and sneakers and backpacks, but after the 2010 earthquake, she learned firsthand the deception of so many who promise aid. "It's deep," she said, ticking off offenders: various agencies, the UN, and most of all Bill and Hillary Clinton.

Before the earthquake, they pushed "the American plan," an aid program that drove Haitians off their land. Even Bill Clinton acknowledged it was a "devil's bargain." After the earthquake, it was worse: epic mismanagement of disaster relief by Clinton loyalists, serious allegations of corruption. But Diane lacked the language of structural critique. She had only the blunt terms of her faith. *Good* and *evil* and *spiritual war*. The Clintons' mistakes could not be errors, or even hubris; they were the deepest of sins. They were evildoers. Thus the logic and theology of the Democratic Party's dissolving margin: the arrogance of good intentions, followed by incompetence, leading to the conclusion that the system must have been rigged all along.

Enter the businessman. "Trump is not my god," said Diane. "But God put him there." God put him in power and planted a seed of faith in his heart. If you knew how to look, you could watch it grow. "It's amazing," Diane shouted. She took hold of my arm, squeezing. "It gets bigger and bigger!"

As her faith in Trump grew, so too her certainty that what she had witnessed abroad had been not just wrong but supernaturally wicked. Rape, pillaging, ritual sacrifice; the old racist myths of Haiti that have lurked in the White American mind since the first U.S. invasion, in 1915, or maybe since 1791 when Haiti became the first Black nation to free itself from slavery. To Diane, it was all happening right now, pressing against the inside of her skull, which she held with the tips of her fingers. It was too terrible to speak of. She turned away, to the happiness of a small circle of new friends she'd made at the rally, a whole family decked out in Trumpwear. But she kept coming back. "The truth and the lies," she said. I didn't know what she meant. She turned away again, returned again, her eyes watery. "I'm going to say it," she decided. But she couldn't. She walked off. Her friends were worried. She came back. *"They eat the children."* The Clintons, she meant. She shook with tears. Her friends nodded.

Later I asked several of them if they shared Diane's concern. Some said no, they didn't think there was cannibalism afoot at the present time. Just pedophilia. Some said "Arkan-cide." But in the moment, there at the rally, there was only fellow feeling for Diane, a red-white-and-blue bedazzled woman beside her draping an arm gently across her sister-in-Trump's quivering shoulders.

6.

After the rally, in the far reaches of the parking lot, Diane invited me to sit with her in her white Cadillac SUV. Beside us a mini jumbotron, attended by a group of Black Trump supporters, displayed rapid-fire images of Trump, his giant face glowing in the night. Music throbbed, blue, green, purple light pulsed into the Caddy. Diane's face was in shadow. She wanted to know if I'd received the message. If I had *discerned*. "You listened to him tonight and you kept in mind what I said, and you realized he talks to us in codes, right? Now you get it?"

Maybe I did. "The Great Awakening?" I said, referring to a Qmeme she was searching for on her phone, tying Trump's ascendancy to the religious revival that preceded the American Revolution.

"Exactly!" Diane said, proud of me. She pointed to the kabbalistic discipline of alphanumeric codes known as gematria, in which numbers and letters are treated as interchangeable. "The numbers tell us certain things," she said. His stats, his recitations of data meant not so much as fact as a kind of numerical psalm, a song of endless winning. "And the capital letters"—the tweets, just as Pastor Dave had told me in Louisiana. "Anything capitalized," Diane said, "we add up as a number." Such codes are a baseline of conspiracy theories going back centuries. To Diane and other Qbelievers, this did not disprove the system; it was evidence of how deep ran the struggle. "Two thousand years," said Diane. Christianity, roughly speaking.

"It's a lot to take in," I stammered. "Maybe I'm reading too much into it—"

"I thought that!" Diane had once been where I was. Which is why she believed God had put me in her white Cadillac. "You're gonna get red-pilled one way or the other from me!" Maybe she sensed my concern. "You need to! For your spiritual health. You better get your life right with God, *now*." Her voice rose. "It's all about God!" she shouted. "All about spiritual warfare. Trump will tell you that. Over and over and over."

"But he didn't talk a lot about God—"

"*You're not listening.*" The knowledge was waiting for me, she whispered, moved again nearly to tears: *awaken*.

It was time to proceed down what Diane called the "rabbit holes." These were like secret pathways to spiritual truths. She had a long riff, for instance, about how Disney draws on satanic influences to control the minds of America's youth (an increasingly mainstream view within right-wing media criticism), and a discussion of Operation Paperclip, the post–World War II program by which the U.S. government really did secretly import Nazi war criminals to work on biological weapons, and, yes, the possibility of mind control. That actually happened. And the connection Diane drew between Disney and these secret Nazis, while not true, wasn't as farfetched as one might think. Walt Disney admired Mussolini and in 1938 quietly hosted Nazi filmmaker Leni Riefenstahl, a month after Kristallnacht. Disney did not team up with Nazis to cook up mind-control methods encoded into cartoons, but the roots of Diane's "logic" weren't hard to find.

But I digress, which is what happens when you start thinking along these lines. A digression can inform one's main inquiry. For Diane, every branching path led to a new maze she felt it her duty to explore, as a "digital soldier" in the service of Trump. For instance, what *really* happened in Las Vegas on October 1, 2017, when, according to the *official* story, a lone gunman named Stephen Paddock shot and killed fifty-nine concertgoers at a country music festival? According to Diane, this was part of a plan to kill Trump. She said he'd been scheduled to speak in Vegas just days after.

Whose plan? Saudi Arabia's.

"I didn't know that."

Diane rolled her eyes. *"I know that,"* she said. "I'm *telling* you."

Later, as I listened to my recording of our conversation, I found myself thinking, I can't use any of this. It's too much. This doesn't represent anything but one woman's delusions. Then I googled the Las Vegas shooting. And—Diane was far from alone. The belief that the Vegas massacre was the work of a nefarious "they" is actually much closer to the world most of us inhabit than the outer reaches of QAnon. It began with the conspiracy broadcaster Alex Jones, then gathered force via a fifty-one-page PowerPoint document by a retired senior CIA officer and a man named Rich Higgins, Trump's former director of strategic planning for the National Security Council, who would later be given op-ed space for his ideas in the *Wall Street Journal*. The theory noted that the Islamic State claimed credit for Paddock's attack. (In fact, Paddock's views were far closer to Diane's, riddled with conspiracies and a desire for an American "awakening.") Also, that a man on the same floor as the shooter had reportedly eaten Turkish kebab; and that this man was known to have supported transgender rights on his Facebook page. Which added up in the Right's fever-dream "intel" to an ISIS–Antifa attack on American soil. From Jones to Higgins and then to Fox News's most popular host, Tucker Carlson, who, several months after the shooting, invited a GOP congressman and retired Army National Guard brigadier general named Scott Perry (later closely linked to the January 6 insurrection) onto his show to promulgate what Rep. Perry described as "credible evidence of a possible terrorist nexus."

Which may seem to you insane. It is also "mainstream." Carlson's show reaches a viewership almost inconceivably greater than any possible readership of this account. Add to that Jones's *Infowars* empire, and countless tweets, posts, and threads online—not to mention the conspiratorial anti-Muslim musings of Trump himself, and the widespread Republican belief that the few hundred or thousand black-bandanaed weekend street fights of Antifa actually constituted an armed paramilitary wing of the Democratic Party—and what you got was this: Diane was not fringe. She might have been closer to the new center of American life than you are.

We'd stepped out of her Cadillac so she could smoke. Everybody had gone. We stood alone beneath the flat, hot Florida night, ambered by streetlights. Smoke rattling out of her lungs, Diane looked older now than she had inside the arena. It was hard on the body, the truth. Diane said her red-pill moment correlated roughly with a heart attack she'd had a few years ago. "I have a heart thing myself," I told her. I knew how it makes you feel as if you're seeing the nature of things for the first time, the death as well as the life within each of us.

My damaged heart, hers? Diane did not believe in coincidences. "You were meant to run into me tonight," she said. She knew I didn't believe her. Yet. "I used to think he was just an arrogant fuck," she said of Trump. She got it. She understood how he came across if you couldn't read the codes.

I started to ask why Trump didn't just give a speech revealing all that he had been secretly shown by God. But then I caught myself. If the gospel of Trump was a gift to the initiated, its value lay precisely in its exclusivity. Let the elites and the ivory-tower fools wallow in their "expertise."

"Diane, are you familiar with the concept of Gnosticism?"

It wasn't cold, but she shivered. "Yes! Very much." She seemed to appraise me differently.

"Like secret knowledge," I said—and also not like it.

Diane nodded. She saw the connection. "It's not that," she said of Trump's gospel, "but it is." She was speaking in the aphoristic language of one of those ancient Gnostic codices.

"Why," I asked, "do the numbers matter?" The endless gematria, the counting of letters, every date an echo of another.

"They"—the big *they*—"think dates have power. Numbers."

"But Diane, they don't."

Her eyes went wide. She grinned. *"Exactly."*

7.

There was a point in every rally when Trump confronted the enemy directly. Not Hillary Clinton or Joe Biden or Mexican immigrants but a small group of people penned in a metal cage on the arena floor. They were "very bad people" and "scum" and "liars." Why did Trump permit them in the arena? To teach us. "Look at them!" he'd cry, pointing. His people would turn to the cage to scream, a ritual that in every rally came early and then often. If I had thought to bring a sound-level meter to the rallies, I could give you a precise rendering in decibels of the ascending passions of the Trumpocene: God, guns, and, loudest of all, hating CNN and the very idea of media—mediation, someone who might know more than you—that it's made to stand for. A cartoon Trump pissing on the CNN logo was a popular T-shirt at rallies; another read: "Rope. Tree. Journalist. Some assembly required."

"Does *anybody* think the media is honest?" Trump asked the crowd at a rally I attended in Hershey, Pennsylvania.

"No!" they cried.

"Does anybody think they're totally corrupt and dishonest?"

"Yes!" they cried. A woman next to me leaned back on her heels, lower lip tucked under her teeth, eyes closed, arms stretched, her two middle fingers raised.

Journalists were the true enemy within. "Illegals," in the mind's eye of the believers, were easily identifiable by color, and implicitly subhuman and thus unable to truly plot America's destruction. They were not the enemy itself but rather its pawns, the hordes that "the media" ushered toward our borders. But even though "the media" may be on our televisions, it was not always easy to see. The enemy was cunning; it attempted to blend. It always had. In tsarist Russia and Nazi Germany, it was the Jews; in Cold War America, it was communists; after the collapse of the Soviet Union, the American Right rallied for a while around hating the gays. All had in common the ability to pass. Now it was the journalists. They moved among us unseen; your own child could become one.

So it was in Hershey, where I—a writer, a Jew, no less, got my ticket and entered with the crowd and finally, at last, donned the red hat. So many around me were wearing camouflage, why shouldn't I? In part it was a practical decision, made in the parking lot, after hours in line. It was cold and it was raining and I am bald. When a vendor came by pushing a cart, I forked over $20. It also felt prudent. The crowd in Hershey—self-declared "sweetest place on Earth," where the streetlights are shaped like giant Hershey Kisses—felt meaner than in Louisiana or Florida. There seemed to be fewer families and more knots of young men chanting *Trump! Trump! Trump!*, punctuating the name with raised fists.

Inside I found a spot not far from the stage. Sometimes Trump rambled; sometimes he owned the crowd. When Trump was on, he worked his hands like a bellows, in and out, counting "the lies," the deceptions, each instance of disrespect to Trump projected into the lives of his followers, conflated with all the personal wrongs they had suffered. He spoke for them. Through him, they *became* him, each man and woman remade as *Trump, Trump, Trump.* "They spied on our campaign!" Who spied? *Who* didn't matter, it was the verb that counted. *Spied.* "They hid it! Hid it so nobody could see it!" Hid what? *What* didn't matter, it was the verb, *hid,* and the response, Trump spreading his hands wide: *Trump! Trump! Trump!*

Don't be fooled by his fractured syntax. His sentences were not so much broken as syncretic, fusing with the thoughts of his followers. There was comedy: the Lisa Page routine, a full skit about windmills that, its verbatim text from one performance given line breaks, could almost be read as a bad Gnostic poem:

Tremendous fumes.
Gases are spewing
into the atmosphere.
You know we have a world
right?
The world
is tiny
compared to the universe.
So tremendous, tremendous
amount of fumes.

There were numbers: 131 records, 182 judges, one-eighth of an inch, 250 years, 160,000 new jobs. What did these numbers mean? Trump. The numbers were Trump numbers, good numbers, the best numbers, just as the enemies were Trump enemies, bad enemies, the worst enemies. "Say it!" Trump growled, as if he were holding one by the throat, choking a confession out of him: "Say it, you crooked bastard!" The crowd screamed. Say what? *Crooked. Bastard.* "I'd like to *force* him to say it!" The crowd wanted to watch.

Trump's timing, so puzzling to those who expect somber gravitas, was that of a Borscht Belt comedian. Only, he tweaked the Jewish comic formula of funny-because-it's-sad, sad-because-it's-funny. With Trump, it was funny because it was mean.

Time for a "joke," again with numbers. "Five years," Trump said. He paused, smirked, letting the crowd fill it in; it was their joke too. "Nine years, thirteen years, seventeen years, twenty-one years, twenty-five years, twenty-nine years." Then the punch line: "When I leave office."

The crowd roared. "Now," Trump said, pointing to his cage full of reporters, "I'm only doing that to drive them totally crazy. That drives them crazy. Even joking about it!" Joking. "I don't know, should we give it a shot? Maybe we'll give it a shot." Maybe. "I'm only kidding. Media, I'm only kidding." Not joking. It worked: His "joke" would be the only part of the rally that made the evening news, none of the violent dream that followed. If Trump said it was a joke, reporters reported that claim. They wanted to believe that some norms still held. Some feared that if they acknowledged just how far beyond norms he'd gone, they'd be normalizing the new American spectrum, one in which dictatorship had become not just a hyperbolic charge thrown around by each party's most heated partisans but an actual idea. A joke or maybe a possibility, sooner rather than later.

Then, in Hershey, without transition, because none was needed, suddenly Trump was not joking at all. "Deadly sanctuary cities," he announced, as if that were what he'd been talking about all along. "Demonstrating their sneering contempt, scorn and disdain for every American." How? "These jurisdictions deliberately release dangerous, violent, criminal aliens out of their jails and directly onto your streets, where they are free to offend, where they are free to kill, where they are free to rape." Trump's bellows hands shifted, horizontal to vertical; now he was chopping. "Brutalized," *chop!* "Murdered," *chop!* "Hacking," *chop!* "Ripping out, in two cases, their hearts." "Innocent American" hearts. "Relentlessly beating a wonderful"—he lowered his voice, slow-pouring the image into our minds—"beautiful high school teenager"—

we could see her as he did, as blond as his own beloved Ivanka—"to death, with a *baseball bat*." It wasn't a joke, it was a horror movie. "*And chopping the body apart with a machete!*" A machete—even the knives were alien. Why did this happen? Because *they* wanted it to happen, Democrats who gave "safe haven to those who commit violent sex crimes."

More: "These are only the cases we know about." There were dark truths, hidden. Philadelphia, he said, and the crowd less than 100 miles away in Hershey, Pennsylvania, booed. "One of the very worst sanctuaries anywhere in America. Philadelphia." A man's voice somewhere ahead of me cried out, "Fuuuck!" More. Like a liturgy, a horrible psalm of repetition. "Illegal alien" and "rape" and "sexual assault of a child" and "alien," and "unlawful contact with a minor" and more "rape" and "indecent exposure" and "sex crimes" and "animal"; "*released by Philadelphia to wander free in your communities!*" It was happening right now. "As we speak, a criminal illegal alien with three prior deportations is roaming free in Pennsylvania because he was released by the city of Philadelphia! The city of"—he smiled, joking, not joking, shaking his head, wait for it, the punch line, his thumb and finger pinching together, the OK-sign-that-is-not-a-sign because it's just the way Trump moves—"*the City of Brotherly Love!*"

8.

"There's a lot of drops," Pastor Dave told me by phone after we met in Bossier City. By "drops" he meant clues. The pandemic was in full and terrible blossom, and tens of thousands of Americans had already died from a virus that Trump had attempted to laugh off. His rallies temporarily suspended, he'd stumbled on daily televised coronavirus briefings as a form of mass spectacle, a way to continue attacking the media and dismissing the experts and disseminating secret codes. The two-hour performances weren't meant to inform or comfort or unite. They were Trump's rallies for what would prove to be an all-too-brief era of social distancing. The president's most devoted followers continued to parse his words, his gestures, even the color of his ties for hidden meaning.

"Think of it as many layers," Dave explained. "He's sending messages." The venue may have changed, but the pattern remained: Trump, the press, the invisible enemies. Codes within codes. Red tie, pink tie. Stripes? Consider the implications. Don't blink. "If you watch," Dave said, "he'll do the air Q with his hands, a circle with a slash at the bottom."

Did Trump really mean to slide in such an obvious tell? Wouldn't that give it away?

"Take it as a whole," Dave said. All of it—virus, rapists, child murderers. How *they* conspired against Trump.

Weren't *they* winning?

Not at all. This was the plan. "He wants to discipline us," Dave said. *He*, in this instance, meant not Trump but his father: God. Like Trump, Covid-19 was an instrument of His will, and He had allowed the virus as a punishment for our "corporate" sin. *Corporate* as in *corpus*, the body, the nation as one flesh and its failure, as a nation, to fully embrace Him and his messenger, Trump. But there was good news. God had given us a chance to redeem ourselves: "We could use this as an opportunity to purge. To get rid of the dross and hold on to the pure."

A purge. A promise. "Take it as a whole," Dave repeated, advising me to watch the televised Covid briefings for every detail—the way those on the stage next to Trump tapped their legs, perhaps a spiritual Morse code, the way they blinked. Open your eyes. The awakening will be great, the greatest, and the rallies would return.

Only the truly initiated—Dave, Diane, QAnon—knew the name of "The Storm" that was coming, but nearly all of Trump's devotees could read the signs, red flares over blue seas: A CNN crew arrested on camera, live, in Minneapolis; in New York, a viral video of a riot cop flashing the OK symbol; and in Washington, following a tear-gas processional, the president of the United States marching through the sterile aftermath to hold aloft a Bible, upside down—a sign? A signal?—its red ribbon dangling along his wrist like a snake's tongue.

What did it mean?

"Pray over it," said Dave, of that which was given for our witness. "Let it settle."

Tick-Tock

The Forever Campaign

She saw shadows. She always had. She was spiritual. Not Christian—she'd left that behind when she'd left Waco, in her early twenties. She got into Wicca, "super witchy," said a friend. "She was fun, happy, a little wild. Just a normal girl." I'll call her Evelyn, because she's a hostage now, a captive of the beliefs that swarm any public mention of her real name. Not that she's special. She's not notorious. There are Evelyns everywhere.

This Evelyn was in Austin. She was thirty, she liked to party, she had a broad mountain-girl face and forest-colored eyes and her long brown hair ran to honey at the ends. She worked when she could; sometimes she stripped. She had a boyfriend who took care of her. She'd never had much luck holding a job. When she lost one she'd go home. That's how it was: back and forth between Waco, her family, and Austin, her friends. Right to Left, red to blue. She was bright—a good listener, says one friend, a liberal lawyer whom Evelyn called "Freedom Fighter." She was gullible, says another friend, the one who introduced Evelyn to QAnon not long into the pandemic. Not because she believed in it, or thought Evelyn would, but because they were both bored, locked down, stuck at home, staring at screens. "For shits and giggles," said Evelyn's friend.

Which is how Evelyn came to believe that the shadows that she'd seen within Wicca as the nuances of life might be—no, *were*—actually the satanic forces of which QAnon warned. Q, she learned—an anonymous figure on a message board—was in fact a government "insider." He revealed President Trump's decades-old plan to destroy the deep state—the satanic forces. "It's been going on for centuries," she wrote to her friend Freedom Fighter. Q communicated through cryptic "drops." She thought this wise. Q could transmit only to those willing to discern. Evelyn discerned. She "followed the white rabbit." She "went down the rabbit hole." She drank more, her mind raced, her hair grew wild. Her skin became ashen, except when it flushed with color. She could feel her blood moving in strange ways.

Evelyn came to believe that the darkness to which she'd always been sensitive was not part of the light but at war with it. That the shadows had become flesh and that the flesh had become politics and that the love of Trump she had come to embrace because she loved her Trump-loving family—because she chose her mother, her father, over her liberal beliefs—demanded the hatred of Trump's true enemies: the "cabal." Child-sacrificing elites, not just pedophiles but cannibals, harvesters of children's adrenal glands for an evil concoction one part Botox and two parts blood libel.

Do I need to say none of this is true? Would it matter?

On the morning of August 12, 2020, Evelyn decided it was time to #SaveTheChildren, as the hashtag that's been co-opted by Q puts it. By then she had been awake, a friend believes, for three days. There was just so much information. So many links. She got into her little red two-door Pontiac Fiero. It was older than she was. She'd been drinking—she'd later test at twice the limit—but that didn't slow her. She had done her research. YouTube and tweets and podcasts. The algorithms fed her. She fed the algorithms, making memes. She'd text her findings to her friends. One tried to warn her: "You're being used."

"I'm seeing things," she answered.

"Three a.m., four a.m., five a.m.," said the friend who had introduced Evelyn to QAnon. Evelyn didn't realize her friend thought Q was funny. Her friend didn't know Evelyn was taking it seriously. "One hundred percent," said the friend now, "like the Bible, like it was gold." When she realized what was happening, the friend tried to talk Evelyn down.

"*Go to sleep*," she begged.

"I can't," Evelyn said. "I'm not sleeping till Trump does."

She believed her president was working tirelessly to prepare for the Storm, the salvation of democracy by way of a mass roundup and execution of the cabalists.

At 9:22 that morning, Evelyn found one. It was obvious—the cabalist was driving a white van, the kind used by kidnappers in movies. (The kind used by caterers in real life.) Evelyn saw a child in the van. (The caterer's daughter.) Red light. The caterer stopped; Evelyn jumped out, screaming; the caterer hit the gas. Evelyn kept hunting. Soon she saw another shadow: a young Latinx woman driving a red Dodge Caravan. The driver was a student, nineteen. "I was on my way to school to register for classes," she told me. She asked me not to use her real name, because she was still worried. She knew there are more Evelyns. She knew what happens online.

The student saw the little red car zoom right up her bumper. She sped up. The little red car pulled around and veered, crashing, into the Caravan. Then it came around the other side. The student tried to turn in to a police station. The red car rammed from behind.

The student saw a police cruiser in a supermarket parking lot. She squealed in, honking. The red car followed. "She kept ramming into me." Eight times. Maybe more. "A lot of times." The student shook and shook. "Half my body went numb."

><

Had Evelyn not crashed into a concrete pylon, she might have committed murder. She was trying. And if she'd done so, she might be as infamous as Kyle Rittenhouse, the White seventeen-year-old who brought his gun to a Black Lives Matter protest in Kenosha, Wisconsin, where he killed two protesters, and whose original defense attorney declared Rittenhouse had fired the first shot of the "Second American Revolution."* Instead, Evelyn is just a woman who went too far—or, from the point of view of QAnon, not far enough. "Q is I," she wrote her friend after being released on bail. "Q is you . . . Q is us." That Evelyn might have spiraled into some different sort of chaos had Trump and Q not been there to feed her delusion is not a reassurance. Because Trump *was* there, and he saw shadows too.

There are no turning points when the world is spinning out of control. The Trump interview with Fox News host Laura Ingraham that aired toward the end of what much of the media called 2020's "protest summer" did not so much mark a new low as erase altogether the meaning of pre-Trump terms such as "new low." There is only the abyss. We're all in it together, and Trump is down here too.

"Biden," he says, slumped in a chair across from Ingraham in the White House's blue-carpeted, blue-draped Brady Press Briefing Room, "Biden is, I don't even like to mention Biden"—fact-check: he did—"because he's not controlling anything." This was Trump boil-

---

* Rittenhouse was acquitted, after which Trump invited him and his mother to Mar-a-Lago.

erplate. He began calling Biden a "puppet" of unnamed powers in 2019. Ingraham attempts to normalize. The media of which Trump approved didn't just parrot his words, it laundered them. Ingraham asks who's "pulling the strings." She proposes "Obama's people," invoking the specter of a Black president and signaling, whether she means to or not, to QAnon, followers who know that "Obama's people" means "pedophiles." It's the kind of *yes, and* message that'd usually elicit a smirk from Trump, whose style is that of an insult comic.

Not this time. He tilts forward, his hands uncharacteristically clasped between his knees, and breaks eye contact, glancing away. His voice gathers texture. "People that you've never heard of, people that are in the dark shadows, people—"

"Dark shadows," says Ingraham. "What is that?" It's not a question, it's a redirect.

"No," Trump says, as if he knows how he sounds. "People that you haven't heard of," he repeats. In the past when Trump spoke of Biden's puppeteers, he wanted you to think you knew who he meant. "Reasonable" Republicans understood it was Democratic Party leaders. Racists heard him calling out Rep. Alexandria Ocasio-Cortez and "the Squad" of progressive lawmakers, impertinent women of color. And the deeper read was George Soros, maybe the Rothschilds, Jewish financiers real and imagined.

But something different is happening with Ingraham. He is not insinuating that she knows who he's talking about—he is insisting she does not. It's none of the usual suspects. Nobody and everybody, nameless and everywhere. When he glances away it is as if only he can see them, an intimate moment not between Trump and Ingraham but between Trump and his own mind. We're witnessing a man cross a line. Not one of transgression—to him, such borders mean nothing—but of belief.

"There are people that are on the streets," he says. "There are people that are controlling the streets." The "invisible enemy" he's spoken of before, the one QAnon calls "Clinton" or "Comey" or "Podesta." But those are names. This foe has no name. He speaks of an airplane "in a certain city," one full of "thugs" in "dark uniforms." Indistinguishable; like a virus. This happened, he says, then: "They're on a plane." *Present tense.* "This is all happening." Right now. It has the dream logic of a nursery rhyme. On the streets, in the air, dark shadows everywhere.

What Trump is describing is no more nor less exotic than the evangelical concept of spiritual war, the conflict thought to be raging always, around us and within, between believers and "principalities" and "powers," according to Ephesians; or demons, in the contemporary vernacular. QAnon translated the concept from King James into Trumpish, but Trump is no more reading Q drops than undead John-John, JFK Jr., believed to be Trump's secret collaborator-in-hiding—the king and the prince—is writing them. For once, there is nothing contrived about Trump's answer. He's not saying what he thinks MAGA wants to hear. *Dark shadows* is, in fact, the wrong answer, as Ingraham tries to signal. But he can't hear her.

Trump once flirted with and fed morsels to evangelicalism's spiritual warriors and the rabbit-holers of Q. That was when they were distinct constituencies. But they had been merging, the theology of Q possessing evangelicalism, the organization of the Christian Right incarnating Q's digital power. Together they became a base; and Trump's identity. He was no longer a con artist. Now he was his own mark, like an email scammer who clicks on his own malware. He was not selling a dream, he was dreaming it. The difference between him and his believers was that he had the power to make the dream real, for them, for him, for us. To summon into being the "American carnage" he nightmared at his inauguration, the cities he said were desolate set ablaze, the killers in the street recast as heroes, with paramilitary backup, fear a daily given, the plague risen up from legend to fill the land with ghosts. This was his dream. We were all nightmaring it together.

›‹

When Trump's press secretary, Kayleigh McEnany, was asked to explain Trump's defense of QAnon, she insisted that neither she nor the president knew a thing about it. But at the close of the interview, apropos of nothing, she said, "There's a lot of children in this country who have died on the streets of Democrat cities. We're focused on capturing criminals." What was she talking about? Maybe she meant gun violence in Chicago, a favorite Trump topic, or the American womanhood he described falling prey to "illegals," human "animals." But I heard Q. I heard #SaveTheChildren. Was she signaling, I wondered? A very Q question.

I thought of *Praying Medic,* one of the most popular Q podcasts, to which I'd started listening. "This information is real; distractions are necessary," says the Medic, explaining the need for Q's cryptic constructions. So real it demands the poetry of dreams, not the dull prose of politics. "Double meanings," like loop-the-loops, kairos—sacred time—disguised as chronos, "tick tock," as QAnon says. Consider the third of November, a date seemingly promised by Q in October 2017 to deliver indictments against the cabal, around which "public riots" (versus the private kind?) would be organized in an attempt to prevent their arrests. November 3, 2017, came and went without a perp walk or broken windows. But who knows *which* November 3 Q meant, asks the Medic. I see the answer before he says it—there are riots now, and November is coming. Tick-tock. I thought of Rittenhouse's first shot the week before Trump's dark shadows, and his lawyer's "Second American Revolution," and the limp plastic bag beneath the streetlight that Rittenhouse's supporters claimed was a Molotov cocktail, requiring him to use deadly force; and of Michael Reinoehl, the Portland antifascist protester, who days later said *his* kill shot—he lay in wait for an armed member of a group called Patriot Prayer—"felt like the beginning of a war." I thought

of "retribution," Trump's term for the police killing, three days after that, of Reinoehl. "That's the way it has to be," Trump explained. Tit-tat, tick-tock. I thought of Michael R. Caputo, the Trump aide who on Facebook warned of Joe Biden's death squads and called for supporters to stock ammunition and also spoke of shadows: "Shadows on the ceiling in my apartment, there alone, shadows are so long." And of Trump, always Trump. Covid-sick, pawing at the window of his airtight limousine outside Walter Reed, driven by Secret Service agents in pale gowns. Unmasked, on the White House portico, returned from the hospital, breathing disease, visibly gasping. He tells us he feels better than he has in twenty years. The drugs, I thought, the steroids. But what if it's true? What if he is growing stronger? Not electorally—more unbound? Walking deeper into his own shadow, drawing us after?

I shook it off; insane. But what about McEnany? I started listening to another Q-related podcast, this one a debunking, *QAnon Anonymous*. Its hosts also heard echoes in McEnany's words. It was on this podcast that I learned of the woman I'm calling Evelyn. When I called one of the hosts, Julian Feeld, to ask how he'd found her, he said a listener had seen the attack in the local Waco news. The report mentioned nothing about QAnon. But the listener wondered if there was more. Feeld didn't wonder, he just knew there had to be. He knew because he'd been listening even longer. In his voice I hear what sounds like pleasure, a kind of frightened delight in piecing together the puzzle of QAnon's shattered mind. The Praying Medic sounds like this too. It is a mix of amiable and urgent, seemingly at odds with the history of conspiracy-mongering. Neither man grabs you by the lapels. They do not demand your attention. They don't have to. If you love Trump, you're receiving the signal. If you fear him, fear he'll never really be gone now no matter the outcome, that he's a chronic condition or maybe a terminal one, then you're hearing it too.

"Blood makes noise," declares a speaker at a #SaveTheChildren rally in Los Angeles recorded by Feeld. (This is something some people do now, attend other people's rallies to record, to document, to decipher. I am one of these people.) It is a gathering of the unexpected: White hipsters, Black men, Latinx women, mothers concerned for their children. The speaker says the blood of the children is spilled by the cabal into the earth, where it's soaked up by the roots of trees—she doesn't need to mention Thomas Jefferson, "the tree of liberty," for patriots to hear the echo—which then grow fruit, which "we" eat. "Their blood is now inside us!" she crows. Is this a victory? The crowd cheers. "And we cry out with"—I hear it; can you?—"the voice of the children!"

This is the nightmare: We are both the children and the cannibals. We are victims and killers, the innocence and the revenge. Do I need to say that none of this is true? *Yes.* We are none of us innocent, none of us martyrs. Such words are for faith. Democracy is a practice. It may not be real yet, but it is not a dream. It's something you do, something we could make, in this life. The real one.

III

Goodnight, Irene
On Survival

⟩⟨

> 8 <

The Undertow

Although no one believed in civil war, the air reeked of it . . .
—Henry Adams, *The Education of Henry Adams*, recalling 1860

1. The Capitol, January 6, 2021

We watched her die before we knew her name. We watched almost in real time or soon after, her death looped and memed before the fight for the Capitol was over. A shaky video gives us a crowd throbbing against two wooden, windowed doors, one reinforced glass pane spiderwebbing, three Capitol police officers, oddly passive, standing between the crowd and members of Congress on the other side. We don't yet know to look for her, but she's there, on the screen, the only woman. She's up front ("a firecracker," her friends will say), scream-ing at cops. ("Joking," her defenders will claim.) There's a knife in her pocket. She shouts: "Just open the door!" It's barricaded, tables and chairs. "Break it down!" chants the crowd. A young man wearing a tight black T-shirt and a $325 black Canada Goose Aviator fur hat, shouts "HEEYYY!" He stretches out his arms, each a delta of pulsing veins—he has already punched the glass, hard—and opens his palms. Calming? No, gathering. "Fuck the blue!" shouts the crowd. A tall White man wearing a yellow "Don't Tread on Me" flag tied like a bib beneath his red MAGA hat hands Goose a heavy black helmet with which to batter the glass.[1]

Goose lines the helmet with his furry hat to cushion his fist. The three cops slide out of the way. ("Escape route," one will later tell investigators; they thought they were going to be killed.) "Go! Go! Get this shit!" the videographer shouts. They get that shit—pounding the reinforced glass.

"Gun!" the videographer yells. Two hands emerge from behind a pillar on the other side, aiming.

Fourteen seconds left. Does she hear them shout "gun"? Can she make out the warnings that Michael Byrd, a plainclothes lieu-tenant in the Capitol Police, will say he delivers? That the man stand-ing beside her will say "she didn't heed"? "Please," Byrd will say he shouted. "Stop! Get back!" She doesn't. He aims. "Center mass," he'll say.

There are more videos. There she is, bobbing up and down, strain-

---

1　Canada Goose is Zachary Jordan Alam. He's twenty-nine years old, a University of Virginia grad, the son of a Pakistani immigrant. His father is a biologist who works for the government. The man with the Gadsden-flag bib is Christopher Ray Grider. He is thirty-nine, co-owner with his wife of a vineyard in Texas named Kissing Tree, for the hackberry tree they climbed together as high school freshmen. After he is contacted by law enforcement, his wife, Crystal, will get rid of her husband's red hat and his yellow rattlesnake flag.

ing. Her long smooth face, her dark golden hair, her golden skin. She has come to this moment—seven seconds now, more cops flowing up the stairs, rifles at the ready—from Ocean Beach, California, where she lived in a bungalow, beneath avocado and lime trees. Little woman, 5′2″, 115 pounds, her mother will say. A hundred and ten, according to Rep. Paul Gosar, an Arizona Republican who will make her name into a martyr song, "#onemoreinthenameoflove," recasting U2's anthem for Martin Luther King Jr., as a tribute to her. She's thirty-five; or in her "twenties," one witness will say; or "sixteen, supposedly," according to a pastor, each middle-aged man aging the dead woman backward, into the imagined innocence of girlhood.[2]

Goose smashes the glass.

"Go!" she shouts. She's boosted up, crouching on the windowsill with her red-white-and-blue backpack like some absurd American bird.[3]

The gunshot sounds like a cannon. Glock 22, .40 caliber. Big gun. One boom.

She falls back. Her body unfurls. Her hands fly up, open and

2 *Martyr*—the word—is derived from an ancient Greek term for witness. In early Christianity it came to mean one who bears witness with the sacrifice of their life. The insurrectionist pastor who declares her "sixteen, supposedly," Ren Schuffman of Freedom Fellowship in Mustang, Oklahoma, is yet a different kind of "witness": that of social media, one who bears memes. "Sixteen," says Pastor Schuffman in a video he makes outside the Capitol shortly after the shooting. He says "sixteen" four times. Then he finds a man who really did witness her die. "About sixteen?" suggests the pastor. "I don't know exactly how old," the witness answers. Pastor Schuffman persists. "Okay, but young?" He needs her to be young. The witness cooperates: "She was young." Then Schuffman prays—for the witness. For this bearded, camouflaged, middle-aged man, true protagonist of the martyr myth in which the dead woman is merely deus ex machina.

3 What's in the backpack? According to the District of Columbia Department of Forensic Services: "clothing, stickers, US currency, a face mask," a California driver's license and four credit cards with the name of her first husband—publicly she went by that of her second—"gloves. sunglasses, a wallet, and cigarettes."

empty, raised to her temples. As if rather than a bullet it's an unsettling thought that's passing through her.

Nobody attempts to catch her.

"#Sayhername," the patriots will tweet, delighting in their twisting of a campaign created for Black women killed by police. It's grotesque. But the dead are the dead, no matter what they died doing, so, yes, her name: Ashli Babbitt. She was not a hashtag. When she was a girl in rural Lakeside, California, she'd ride her horse to the 7-Eleven. She was a fast talker, a scrapper. "She just did boy things," her brother Roger will say. Her nickname on her high school water polo team was "The Enforcer." She joined the Air Force at seventeen. Two wars, eight deployments, fourteen years. Her favorite movie was *The Big Lebowski*. Her thing was the shaka, the "hang loose" hand symbol, extended thumb and pinky. She did not climb the ranks, but she did marry, and then divorce, and in between she voted for Barack Obama, and she fell in love with a Marine named Aaron Babbitt. There was some trouble with his ex, who in 2016 claimed Ashli rammed her car three times, but Ashli was acquitted and anyway, maybe love is like that sometimes, at least for Ashli in 2016, since that was when she fell hard for Donald J. Trump. "#Love," she wrote beside his name that Halloween, in the first of more than 8,000 tweets. "She was all in," says Aaron Babbitt, who did not share her devotion.[4] She believed the

---

4 Aaron Babbitt is sort of a lunk, the quiet type, a big, bearded body builder who before his wife was killed only passively shared her politics. He saw "politics" as her thing. "It's not my scene," he'd tell TMZ. He loved her for how intense she was. He says they didn't have the kind of relationship where he'd ever try to stop her. He says if he'd been there, maybe he could've saved her. In the raw video of an interview he'd give to a right-wing documentarian—the family won't respond to my inquiries—you see him running through his mind all the things he could have said the morning of January 5. He saw her last while she was taking a shower. She said, "You don't want me to go, do you?" He kissed her. Told her he'd pick her up Friday, would bring her favorite burrito to the airport. Then she was gone. Then he gets a call. January 6. He turns on the TV. "I knew it was her immediately, by the clothes, the hair, the face."

election was stolen. She believed Trump was "one of gods [*sic*] greatest warriors." She thought she'd be his "boots on the ground." She wanted to be "the storm." She had a husband and together they had a girlfriend. She had four younger brothers and parents who loved her, and in the end, she left them all. To save America, or to commit an act of terror; to step into the breach, or to die like a traitor. Ashli had olive eyes. Strong shoulders. An earnest face. Gone, now, like her 8,000 tweets. Like the ashes her family sifted into the ocean. What's left is a meme, "Ashli Babbitt," on Twitter and Fox and Newsmax and Telegram. Two words in the mouth of the man for whom she died, who did not bother to say her name for six months after that death, until the day it proved useful. To him.[5]

She's still bleeding. "Flashlight! Flashlight!" someone shouts. One

---

He tells himself the blood isn't hers. He starts calling hospitals. Gets his family calling hospitals. He wants to turn the TV off. They keep showing it, "over and over and over again," her body falling, but as long as he keeps it on she might be alive, she's falling but not yet fallen, and they keep showing her die until he collapses on the kitchen floor.

Does he deserve sympathy? Do you join those who deem her killing uncomplicated—"play stupid games, win stupid prizes," as one *Washington Post* commenter put it? Or celebrate it—"super glad she is dead" was a popular response; or who mock it, such as the cut-up who created an account called "Dead Cunt Ashli Babbitt"; or those who embrace the authoritarian "justice" of the insurrectionists themselves, such as the commenter who observed "that bullet cost a lot less than a trial, so as a taxpayer I'm grateful"? Do you see her as a terrorist or a dupe? Fascism's fool? Was the policeman's bullet legitimate deadly force? The inevitable punctuation point of the Big Lie? Both? Neither?

5 "Who shot Ashli Babbitt?" Trump asked in a one-sentence statement July 1, the day his business was indicted for tax fraud. Soon it became part of his repertoire: "The person that shot Ashli Babbitt, boom, right in the head, why isn't that being studied?" he asked. She was not shot in the head, but for Trump the story worked better if she had been. "Who shot Ashli Babbitt?" he asked a Fox News host. "Why are they keeping that secret?" They weren't. But for Trump, the story worked better if they were, and nobody there would contradict him.

of the videographers has a flashlight. The beam makes her beach-tanned skin pale. Her blood is bright. The blue of the Trump flag tied round her neck, like a cravat, is nearly luminous. Her eyes are open. Her lips move. One man, tapping furiously at his phone, think he hears her last words: "It's cool."

Her face disappears into the blaze of the flashlight's glare. Police push her comrades back. "She needs fucking help!" the videographer screams. He is filming a policeman's leg. Another voice says, "She's gone!" Another shouts, "We gotta get EMS here"—oblivious to the fact that it is his presence, and that of the hundreds with him, the patriots—the rioters—the insurrectionists—who make that impossible.

"Get the fuck back!" screams a cop in another video. "We can't save her if—" But they won't get back. The police try to radio for help, but there are too many cops on the air, radioing for help, and none of them can hear one another. "Make a hole!" shouts a videographer, urging men to move aside for medics to come through, but only enough shift out of the way for a gray-bearded man wearing a "Camp Auschwitz" hoodie to slip away from the scene.

"Dog, someone just died," yet another videographer says to a man beside him.

"Yeah," says the witness who remains. "I can't believe I seen it."

2. Sacramento, California, six months later

Nisenen land[6]

6 Later, somewhere in the desert of Nevada or the salt flats of Utah, on my long drive home to Vermont from Sacramento, I remembered how when I first came west, at nineteen years old, I brought with me Dee Brown's account of American genocide, *Bury My Heart at Wounded Knee*. I read it as an account of original sin, something that happened very long ago. It was not so long ago. Nothing in America is. In 2021, Ashli Babbitt invoked 1776; news anchors compared the invasion of the Capitol to the War of 1812. Sacramento, the oldest incorporated city in California, dates back only to 1849. In 1887, Chief Charley Cully of the Nisenan people obtained an allotment under the Dawes Act, which broke up communally held Indigenous land into private property. Chief Cully, "owner" of seventy-five acres of his people's once-vast country, hoped to build from it a home for his people.

It worked, sort of. In 1913, Woodrow Wilson created a Nisenan reservation by executive order. In 1964, the U.S. government "terminated" that recognition. Also in '64: the Gulf of Tonkin Resolution, granting Lyndon Johnson the power to pursue a war against North Vietnam, though it would not be called a war. There was never a declaration of war against the Nisenan people, either. The Wikipedia page for Sacramento says: "These Native American people left little evidence of their existence."

The Justice for Ashli Babbitt Rally opened with a prayer, asking God to bless Ashli's family, sitting in a row of white "Justice 4 Ashli" T-shirts, and to work on the hearts of the "opposition," which, whether I liked it or not, was me. Ashli's mother, Mikki Witthoeft, had already told me that morning that she wouldn't talk to me. "Media," she'd growled. "Goddamned media," she'd clarify when she took the podium, naming the enemy she held most responsible for her daughter's death.

Leading the prayer was a "patriot" pastor called JP. He looked like an especially dangerous mushroom. JP wore a big black floppy sun hat, mirrored shades, a stars-and-stripes gaiter, green half gloves, and utility-belted jeans that puddled around his ankles. His black T-shirt featured in golden letters a "battle verse" popular with patriots, Joshua 1:9. "Be strong and courageous," the Lord instructs Joshua as he readies to storm Jericho and, at God's inexplicable command, to slaughter all—"man and woman, young and old"—within.

We were on the west side of the California State Capitol, designed to echo the Capitol in Washington, but carved out of

---

Here is a website created by the Nisenan: www.nisenan.org. Around the corner from the rally for Ashli Babbitt I'm in Sacramento to attend, there's a memorial for the Californians who served in Vietnam, erected in 1988. Here's a picture:

The Nisenan have neither memorial nor territory. This land? It's hot. Stolen. Recently. Armed robbery. Somewhere in the desert of Nevada or Utah, this White reporter, dizzy from the collapse of American time made manifest on January 6, 2021, will come to understand land acknowledgments as recognitions of the real: facts, evidence, particularly important to any story about what America is or was—great or genocidal—or might become.

soft, yellow stone as if from pale butter. Police outnumbered the crowd, observing from heavy-hooved draft horses, standing by their bikes, skulking behind every giant red incense cedar. There was a column of armored officers from the Highway Patrol. But there were also other forces. The rally had been called by a new group named Saviors of Liberty, hatched three weeks earlier in a pickup truck by a couple of White dudes drinking beer and pondering all that was wrong in the world and how they might fix it by assembling a supergroup of right-wing fraternal organizations. They'd need new T-shirts. Lady Liberty bleached white on a black tee, looking in apparent sorrow on a red-and-black American flag, vertical so that its stripes appeared to bleed. Packed within these T-shirts was a cadre of muscle-bound men, some bulked up by bulletproof plates, many flexing studded leather gloves. Many were Proud Boys. "No colors," one would say on an insider's livestream, part of a plan to go incognito post-insurrection. At least one man working security didn't get the message. His T-shirt featured the crossed butcher cleavers of the White nationalist American Guard (formerly known as the Soldiers of Odin), borrowed from Daniel Day-Lewis's depiction of "Bill the Butcher" in Martin Scorsese's *The Gangs of New York*—a "traditionalist" identity derived from Hollywood and Marvel *Thor* comics.

A rally organizer keeping a lower profile was a woman named Chelsea Knight, an administrator of Placer County for Trump and a co-administrator with her husband, Victor Knight, of a Telegram chat group called 1488,[7] which surely had nothing to do with the

*7 I know about the Knights because such identifications have become so routine at clashes of fascists and Antifa that the event can't really be said to have concluded until post-rally Twitter threads unspool. Fascists and Antifa meet in the streets and bring their photographers. Afterward, scholars among them study the images, cross-reference with social media, and make identifications. Then they publish them with screenshots, such as an image posted by Victor Knight on 1488

"fourteen words" embraced by White supremacists—prattle about protecting White children—and the number 88, as in the eighth letter of the alphabet, *H*, which times two in the idiot math of American fascism equals "Heil Hitler." That was more Victor's thing than Chelsea's. He was the one with an SS Totenkopf skull tattooed on his left fist. ("L-O-V-E" was spelled out across the fingers of his other hand). Victor was there, too, and that plus the 90-up heat on the sunblasted concrete of the plaza, plus a promise of disruption from local Antifa may have explained the low civilian turnout. An old White man in cowboy boots and cowboy hat amened in the front row and another, who boasted he was at the Capitol on January 6, patrolled on a Segway, trailing a flapping Old Glory. Most of the crowd huddled back in the shade, propping up flags. A Second Amendment activist ranted against Critical Race Theory. The connection to Ashli was vague. An indicted January 6 insurrectionist, Jorge Riley, said schools are making our kids gay. "Tell it, George!" shouted the old cowboy.

Then Antifa arrived. A column of mostly black-clad, black-masked protesters coming around the bend from a rally on the other side of the Capitol, for what should have been the twenty-eighth birthday of Breonna Taylor, a Black woman shot dead in her home by police on March 13, 2020. The Saviors in their studded gloves were ready. A man in a skull mask took a shot at the tallest Antifa, a beanpole draped in black but for his fists and the pale white skin around his eyes. Some of the Saviors seemed to recognize him. They

---

of a man wearing a skull mask like one Victor wears and Hammerwaffen "fashwave" sunglasses similar to those Victor wears, gripping a giant pistol labeled WHITE IDENTITY, beneath the legend JEWS DON'T FEAR ELECTIONS—meaning, they fear guns.

called him "Nosferatu," after the eponymous vampire of the classic 1922 horror film.

He was skinny compared to the Saviors, but he knew how to take a punch; it bounced off his head, and you could almost hear him smile beneath his mask as he leaned right back in and declared, "That's a pussy-ass move right there."

"You wanna play ball?" a right-wing livestreamer named Josh Fulfer screamed for his 60,000 followers. At the insurrection, he was among the first to announce Ashli's death. "The lamb of God," he said then. He was here today with a woman and a baby. "This is what we're fighting for, guys," he'd declare, filming the pink-cheeked infant between skirmishes.

The Saviors had Antifa surrounded. Another Savior threw a punch. Bike cops observed. An Antifa protester took a swipe. Cops charged—at Antifa. An Antifa cried out.

"Shut up, fatass!" Fulfer bellowed.

"Fuck yourself, faggot," she shouted.

The police withdrew. She moved in. A Savior bumped her with his tactical vest; like a battleship, she bumped back.

"Get that fucking camera out of my face," said the Savior, reaching over her shoulder at an Antifa videographer behind her.

"What about that camera?" she said, reaching past him toward a videographer on his side. The Savior slammed her, cops charged her again, and the Saviors gloated behind their thin blue line.

"These cops want to let us go at 'em," said the man next to me. It was one of the speakers, Jorge Riley, the indicted J6er.

"They don't have any worries about what the outcome would be," said a ripped Savior.

Riley smiled. He wore a black leather vest over a black tee and his long black hair in a ponytail. "I'm a French-speaking Native American Jew," he liked to say. "For Jesus," he'd add after a beat, waiting for a laugh. Sometimes he spoke in the third person: "a veteran"—101st Airborne—"who doesn't like guns, even though he was a sniper." He said he was Iroquois and Blackfoot. He'd invaded the Capitol with three white feathers braided into his hair, three streaks of black paint running down each cheek like mascara tears. His "war paint" had worn away, but Riley kept charging. "Does this mean I took my land back?" he'd posted. In a video, he says: "I may or may not have rubbed my butt on Nasty Pelosi's desk." This was as close as Jorge Riley came to coy.

Figure Eight

Screenshot of "Statement of Facts," *United States of America v. Jorge Aaron Riley.*

Before January 6, Riley had held several positions in the local Republican establishment. Two days after the insurrection he posted his address on Facebook: "Come take my life. I'm right here. You will all die." The FBI, he said, didn't get it. The "joke," the invitation, the threat, was for Antifa. He nodded with a crooked grin at the protesters. "I got six charges," he boasted. (Three.) "It's all over the internet." He said he liked cops, except the cop who shot Ashli.

"You feel like the cops are on your side?" I asked.

"Obviously!" He swung his arms open like a ringmaster. "They're here protecting me." He turned to a woman beside him and asked for the name of the officer who killed George Floyd. Derek Chauvin. "And they only prosecuted him," continued Riley, "because these people"—the protesters—"threw a fit." A White cop's knee on a Black man's neck for nine minutes? "Somebody doing their job." A Black cop's split-second shot at a White woman leading a mob? Riley agreed with one of the other rally speakers: "assassination."

Such is the seesaw reality of January 6. "No cops were hurt," Riley said. More than 150 were. Five would die. In a video made at the Capitol, Riley claimed that after one battle involving pepper spray and a fire extinguisher, he and his comrades hugged it out with the police. Delusion? No—Riley's smirk bespoke self-awareness. Disinformation? Too obvious for his taste. More like lucid dreaming: a deliberately surreal assault. I thought of a Telegram message one of the Proud Boy organizers sent on January 6: "I want to see thousands of normies burn that city to ash today." It wasn't their own crimes that thrilled them, it was the prospect of drawing the many into their boogaloo vision, their civil-war dreams. The city still stands. But in my mind—in the imagination of anyone who even now marvels at how close we came, how close we still are—it burns. The coup was a bust. The psyop? Victory.

Now, in Sacramento, the speaker at the podium, a former TV host named Jamie Allman, who was taken off the air of a St. Louis ABC affiliate after he tweeted his desire to "ram a hot poker up the ass" of a Parkland shooting survivor, declared January 6 "one of the most beautiful days I've seen in America."[8]

In the back of the crowd, protesters challenged patriots to define "Nazi."

"Somebody who wants border security," said one.

"We love America," said another.

"If Ashli Babbitt were here," continued Allman—*if*, the eternal conditional of martyr mythology—"I guarantee you she'd be out there"—on the edge of the fascist/antifascist rumble—"talking to those people."

"Scum!" a patriot screamed.

"Traitors!" an Antifa screamed.

"Wuhan!" answered a patriot.

"Ashli Babbitt," Allman said, "does not want you to be afraid, ever again." Present tense. Ashli Babbitt lives, in the hallucinatory. Then Allman said the patriots would one day return to Washington, to remember her. Ashli Babbitt dies, in perpetuity.

"I suffered," said Riley. "But I didn't pay the price Ashli did." He thought this was for a reason. "I'm like the guy from *300*, right? I lived to be able to tell her story."

At the podium, Allman: "What her death does, when we compare it to Crispus Attucks, is—it *calls* for a revolution!"

---

8 "Parkland," I write, as if that will mean much to a reader a year from now. The 2018 school shooting in Parkland, Florida, where a young Trump supporter who had expressed interest online in killing Blacks, Jews, and immigrants murdered seventeen people, was one of twenty-four such shootings resulting in death or injury that year. "Parkland" for a while became synonymous with the horror, but like "Sandy Hook" before it—2012, twenty-seven dead—and "Columbine" before that—1999, seventeen dead—"Parkland" will soon enough fade, just as "January 6," may, by the time you read this, be relegated to a footnote within an ongoing time-line of such "patriotism."

"It *calls*"—emphasis Allman's. The myth of history was calling the patriots. The "Spirit of 1776" (Attucks, a Black Wampanoag man, was killed in 1770), and *300*, the 2006 CGI blood opera in which three hundred Spartan warriors slaughter uncountable foes until all but one Spartan fall to an overwhelming Persian horde. Attucks, the first man to die in one war, and the fictional Spartan warrior who was the only survivor in a film, the source material of which is a comic book. Sacrifice stripped of history. Salvation through sadism. "Trial by combat," as Rudy Giuliani promised from the stage on January 6, hours before the mob made it real. "The first Patriot Martyr of the Second American Revolution," an Oath Keeper posted on January 6 before anyone knew who the martyr was, only that hers was the mythical victimhood of a White woman, killed by a Black man, they could now claim.

><

Now came the mother: Michelle Witthoeft, Mikki with an *i*, for independence, which is why she named her firstborn Ashli-with-an-i. Mikki adrift in her oversized Ashli T-shirt, wrists ringed by many red plastic Justice 4 Ashli bands, her brilliant white hair pulled back severely. A doleful woman, her proud, lupine face that of her daughter's but whittled by grief. She hid her eyes behind sunglasses, giant black lenses, white-rimmed.

As she began, an Antifa chant of "BLACK LIVES MATTER" ricocheted off the Capitol behind her, at the entrance to which this morning she'd erected a banner: Ashli's big grin on the left, Ashli flashing a shaka sign on the right.

"I miss her every day," said the mother. "There are things I want to tell her." Her voice wobbled. "Questions I want to ask." She paused, then let it in: the fury. "My daughter was publicly executed!" She gathered herself, torn between rage and her desire for dignity. "Everybody knows Breonna Taylor," she said. From the back: "BLACK LIVES MATTER!" "Everybody knows George Floyd," Ashli's mother said. The two women sitting next to me, Jorge Riley's girlfriend, Kelli Morgan, in a sun hat with a leopard-print band, and a friend in cutoff jeans bedazzled red-white-and-blue across her back pockets—she said her name was "Freedom"—screamed, "Criminals!"

"Why don't people know who Ashli Babbitt is?" asked Ashli's mother.

"The criminal frickin' media!" affirmed Freedom.

"Exactly," said the mother. Why wouldn't the media say her daughter's name? (They did, but the mother thought they said it wrong, as if her daughter had not died a hero.)

Antifa: BLACK LIVES MATTER!

"Let your representatives know," pleaded the mother, her voice wavering. "Over, and over, and over." (Know what? She didn't say.)

Antifa: NO MORE NAZ-EES!

The mother stopped. Pulled the microphone close: "ASH-LI BAB-BITT!" The same up-down, up-down cadence as "Black Lives Matter."

She shouted it again. "ASH-LI BAB-BIT!"

The crowd cheered. Kelli and Freedom hollered. They came for the rage, and now at last, four syllables like four fingers squeezing into a fist, it was here.

"That's right!" cried Mikki. "There's no shame in what happened January sixth."

Antifa: BLACK LIVES MAT-TER!

To which the patriots finally had a reply they thought equal: ASH-LI BAB-BITT!

One White woman.

White

Space

164 › The Undertow

><

The skirmishers skirmished on, more shoving than punching, a gray-bearded man wearing a Space Force hat leaping into his best karate stance at the approach of a Black woman. "She was in my space!" Space Force cried. I ping-ponged between the front of the rally and the back, the rhetoric and the action. Ashli's mother told the crowd to be proud Americans. Kelli and Freedom cheered. "Be proud *White* Americans!" said Ashli's mom. Kelli and Freedom shrieked. Ashli's mother went on to list other races she felt should be proud Americans, too, but she was hard to hear over Kelli and Freedom screaming.

Toward the back, a livestreamer named Julius was providing commentary. "She's right, she's right," he told his camera. He mimicked an imaginary Leftist responding in a nasal whine: "'slavery, slavery, slavery.'" Julius was Black; he wore a Saviors T-shirt with bleached-white Lady Liberty. "No one got time for all a that," he said.

Julius was not alone as a man of color in the crowd—there was also Jorge Riley, and the Second Amendment speaker, a Black man. I met nearly as many self-identified Latino people as White ones. They wanted it known that not all patriots were as pale as liberals imagined. This was true. And yet, Kelli and Freedom shrieked for Whiteness, I think, not because they were blind but because they wanted to be. They wanted to believe in what historian Anthea Butler, author of *White Evangelical Racism*, describes as an implicit "promise of Whiteness" offered to people of color willing to collaborate with White supremacy. This bait-and-switch—the promise of Whiteness is by definition unfulfillable—may be the next American contribution to fascism.[9] It would not be the first. As documented in historian

---

9 In 2008 I published a history of an elite Christian nationalist movement called *The Family*. Even though the Family's leaders have long expressed admiration for the organizing prowess of Hitler, I argued that this predilection didn't merit labeling

James Q. Whitman's *Hitler's American Model*, Hitler looked to American westward expansion, the way, as he said with admiration, that the U.S. "gunned down the millions of redskins," as inspiration for his eastern ambitions. Nazis admired American eugenics as much as *The Great Gatsby*'s Tom Buchanan, who said, "it's all scientific stuff, it's been proved." But they deemed the "one-drop rule"—the notion that even "one drop" of Black "blood" made a person ineligible for full citizenship—too extreme. So it is now: the purification project of the old fascism has also "been proved" too extreme to be practical for a nation in which the Rightist ascendency can contend for the loyalty of a third of Latinx voters. This time, White supremacy welcomes all. Or, at least, a sufficient veneer of "all" to reassure its more timid adherents that border walls and "Muslim bans" and "kung flu" and "Black crime" and "replacement theory" somehow do not add up to the dreaded *r*-word, which anyway these days, in the new authoritarian imagination, only happens in "reverse," against White people.

Such victims feel themselves drawn together not by Whiteness but by that of which it is made. By their belief in a strongman and their desire for an iron-fisted God and their love of the way guns make them feel inside and their grief over Covid-19 and their denial of Covid-19 and their loathing of "systemic" as descriptive of that which they can't see, can't hold in their hands and weigh, and their

---

with what I then called "The 'F' Word"—fascism. I meant no defense; rather, that Christian nationalism is a different sort of authoritarianism. I believed that within the United States, Christian nationalism's ostensible commitment to some kind of idea of Christ prevented the movement from ever going all in on the cult of personality necessary to foment true fascism. I was wrong. One by one in recent years, objections to describing militant Trumpism as fascist have fallen away. In addition to "the personality" of Trump, the movement his presidency quickened now cultivates paramilitaries and glorifies violence as a means of purification, thrives on othering its enemies, declares itself persecuted for "Whiteness," diagnoses the nation as decadent, and embraces the revisionist myth of a MAGA past—as exemplified in its dream of adding Trump's likeness to Mount Rushmore.

certainty that countless children are being taken, stolen and raped, or if not in body then in spirit, "indoctrinated" to "hate themselves." They are angry about their own bodies, about how other people's bodies make them feel, about eating too much because they're afraid they won't have enough, about not having enough, about others having more. They are drawn together by their love of "fairness," which is how it used to be, they're certain they remember, or, if they're too young, they've been told. Or maybe they've all just seen it in a movie, a Western or a space opera or a revenge fantasy, the forever frontier that is equal parts *Little House on the Prairie* and *The Punisher*. Make America Great Again: the solace of tautology, a loop, a return; a story the end of which has already been written, in the past.

And yet, "slavery, slavery, slavery," murmurs the actual past. So they insist otherwise, they imagine otherwise. An imagination that draws curtains carefully around its stage, that looks inward. That curdles. "It gets to be too much, sometimes," Julius lamented.

It does.

At the podium now was John Pierce, Esq., a ruddy-faced Harvard man in a pink Brooks Brothers shirt who boasted a roster of past and present clients representing nearly the full range of right-wing concerns: many January 6 defendants, Rudy Giuliani, lesser-known Trump minions, Proud Boys, and—the name for which the crowd gave a rouse—Kyle Rittenhouse, the babyfaced MAGA icon who'd be acquitted after killing two men at a Black Lives Matter protest. Ashli, said Pierce, "was all of us. Just like me and you; perhaps she was even more." Even more like "us" than we are ourselves. Yes, I thought, considering the range of the gathering, the grief at the podium and the violent glee in the street. It was this spectrum to which Ashli had been drawn, this which she became. The rally was her portrait, her marble, her bronze. "Generations from now," Pierce declared, "when this once again is a free land, Americans will remember one name from that very fateful day on January 6." Trump? No. Ashli, aka the "us" for whom she stands.

Martyrdom is a magic trick, a sleight of hand and soul by which the dead, who have no say in the matter, substitute as the center of the story for those who survive to tell it. "She did not die in vain!" cried Pierce. Her death was a "warning." Of what? *Slavery, slavery, slavery*—"our" liberties stolen, "the worst political divide in our nation since the Civil War." A subtle move, that, just like the speakers who conflated the insurrection with Martin Luther King Jr.'s March on Washington. To a "color-blind" crowd, the implicit equation was one of themselves with the formerly enslaved. Black becomes White, White becomes the oppressed. Just as White people took the land from Indigenous people and then named themselves their victims, so, too, has Whiteness always been a means of claiming the suffering it inflicts on others as its own. White grievance, White justification, the nation not so much fallen as falling, forever in peril, forever in need of redemption, all these forevers overlapping to create the image of an "innocence" that never was. There are open White supremacists on the Right. Some were brawling at the back. But it is the rhetoric of color-blindness that produces the vision of Whiteness without Blackness— as if race could mean anything without an Other. Whiteness wants the Other, needs it, makes it by means of law and whip and fable: think *The Perils of Pauline*, *The Hazards of Helen*, images of White women tied to railroad tracks, here comes the big black engine; think *The Birth of a Nation*, the White virgin who flees the desire of a Black man—

—by leaping to her death off a cliff, foreplay to the film's real consummation, the lynching that follows in her name.

But it's different now. Isn't it? "We live in very bad times," preached Pierce in Sacramento, "in the eternal battle between freedom and tyranny." [10] But all is not lost, he said—literally, he said, "all is not lost"—for God so loved the world he sent us an "angel like Ashli Babbitt," to "remind us" that freedom "comes at a cost," and that the price is "blood."

Whose?

At the back of the rally, Nosferatu was down. A Black woman in a Raiders T-shirt tried to slap a Savior and disappeared beneath a pile of thick White men. Julius told 1488's Chelsea Knight, who was holding a flag with an image of an AR-15, that he wished he'd brought a deck of cards. To defuse the situation. "Man," he mused, "if I had my cards with me!" He was a magician. "Everybody likes to see a card trick, I'm telling you."

Here's some magic: White woman breaks into a building and tries to crawl through a smashed-out window and gets killed—and then lives forever.

Ashli Babbitt was processed, made productive, almost immediately after her death, transformed right away into yet another flag, like a new tarot card in the deck of fascism, where it joined the Gadsden, the coiled snake on yellow, and the Blue Lives Matter—an American flag drained of color but for a blue bar across the middle, created as a rebuttal to Black Lives Matter—and the "America Rising"—red gothic script above a skull glaring out of the Stars-and-Stripes in monochrome. All flew in Sacramento, or, at least, hung limp in the heat. Vexillology, the study of flags, is a theatrical discipline. The flags on display—like those of January 6, most famously the Confed-

---

10 Eternal, indeed: D. W. Griffith's *The Birth of a Nation*, the 1915 template for so much of Hollywood's dramatic conventions—and in turn the racial imagination of men such as Pierce—features scenes of Black people stuffing ballot boxes and White men denied the vote not so different from the 2020 election coverage of Fox News. In the film, a beneficiary of this stolen election is a mixed-race tyrant, Silas Lynch, even his name evidence of the old inversion by which racism projects its crimes onto its victims.

erate Battle Flag—were those of imaginary nations, fascisms, plural, nostalgic and aspirational, the Right's bitter utopianism.

Ashli's flag is black, in its middle a white silhouette of Ashli in front of a red Capitol framed within a shield. It's surrounded by six white stars, for the six states then falsely alleged stolen from Trump, and there's a blue star on the White woman's neck, for the shot that made her legend, which actually hit her in her shoulder. A crown radiates from her flowing hair, like that of Liberty or a saint. Ashli's flag multiplies. In another, her face develops beatific features. Some flags trade her blue star for a thick red drop of blood. The six stars no longer work once it becomes known that the whole country had been stolen, so the six became four, "for the 4 Martyrs that were killed at the capital," reads a post on Telegram from "The Western Chauvinist," referring to Ashli and three other insurrectionists. Roseanne Boyland, trampled by the mob; Kevin D. Greeson, heart attack; and Ben Philips, inventor of the Trumparoo, a kangaroo stuffy dressed as Trump, who died of a stroke.

Memes and theories, memes as theories. "Who Killed Ashli Babbitt?" written in the cartoonish style of the 1988 film *Who Framed Roger Rabbit?* Ashli compared to George Floyd, by those who acknowledge Floyd was murdered and say they simply want "equal justice" for the White woman; and by those who say Floyd deserved what he got, and from this conclude Ashli's innocence, as if Floyd's murder, six months before hers, was somehow payback for her death by the gun of a Black cop. On social media there's an image of an oil painting of Ashli falling, her MAGA cap flying (she did not wear one), an American flag fluttering (the flag she wore like a cape bore only Trump's name). The simplest memes and saddest for those who actually cared for her, show a younger, less angry Ashli in her uniform, with SAY HER NAME in block letters, the wrenching of that phrase from its Black context erased through repetition until her earnest partisans came to believe hers was, in a sense, the first murder of the revolution. Crispus Attucks born again as a White woman. Woman is become warrior (read: male), even as warrior is victim, stabbed in the back by liberalism. An account on the right-wing social media site Parler depicts Ashli as an armored, avenging angel; a Twitter account called We Are Ashli Babbitt features an avatar of Blind Justice holding scales above the words "in her other hand, is a sword." The banner on this account features Malcolm X, claiming his militance for the White woman's memory, as if "by any means necessary" was a battle cry for a White-supremacist coup attempt. At one rally for Ashli—Sacramento's was the first of many—Proud Boys distributed a "challenge coin" featuring a variation of the first Ashli flag, her face still white, her hair now golden, and the Capitol aflame, VENGEANCE in white faux-gothic lettering.

In Sacramento, a young pastor-in-training who stood with the Saviors but said he opposed fighting rejected the Malcolm path. "We're the MLKs, not the Malcolm X's," Thomas Kurozovich, a slender White man with tight brown curls parted down the middle, told me. We were talking to another would-be peacemaker, Richard—no last names, he said—a giant tall and wide, draped in a nearly dress-length T-shirt split vertically between the American flag and a silhouette of Christ. Today is for Ashli, he said. "It's kind of sacred, you know?" He invited Thomas and me to a meeting at his church, Glad Tidings, in Yuba City, later in the evening.

"You're, like, the fourth person who's invited me there," Thomas marveled.

Not a coincidence, Richard said. "There's a lot more going on here than you can see." Spiritually, he meant. "Come to church if you want to find out what all this means."

"'All this,' as in, life?" I asked, not wanting to undertake a long drive for standard-grade evangelism.

"No, as in Ashli Babbitt! If you want to know why Ashli Babbitt died and why she lives in our heart. What it means to have an *American* heart."

Did I? I lingered at the Capitol. Too long for a group of Saviors decked out full commando. One pushed his chest into my notebook. His buddies gathered. I was surrounded—until a big guy wearing a blue T-shirt depicting Snoopy napping and the words "Red, White, and Chill," said, "He's cool! I vetted him." I'd told him I liked his shirt. "I vetted him twice, actually," said Snoopy. By which he meant, I can only guess, that he'd gathered I'm a White man and a Snoopy fan. Good enough! The commando smiled. "Just checking," he said.[11]

---

11 I mock because I can. We're blood, after all—I *am* a White man. Or, at least, half, according to a neighbor of mine, Nazi Ralph, who dings me 50 percent for my Jewish father. Ralph's a real-deal Nazi—swastika tattoos, meth eyes, and an open-carry loaded Glock 9 he says he'll use to take care of me should I cross any of his invisible lines. But all this makes him arguably more marginal to the greater project of Whiteness than a White man like me: educated, Ivied, granted the real estate of paper and ink by a mainstream publisher. I enjoy the White male privilege that allows me to emerge from a potential scrum with the Proud Boys unscathed, to sit with Nazi Ralph and his loaded 9 while he rants White power, to mock the menace for the entertainment of my readers.

3. The Church of the Insurrection, later that night

Nisenan land

Vessels, Church of Glad Tidings

Double-vetted, I drove an hour north, through flat land and orange groves, to the Church of Glad Tidings in Yuba City. "Yuba-dooba-doo!" as Glad Tidings' cherub-cheeked Pastor Dave Bryan called it, or sometimes "Foreversville." From the beginning of the pandemic, Pastor Dave refused for his church any Covid precautions. Instead, "we advertised we will be open every night." Every night for a month he led his flock in prayer. The state said "lockdown"; he said "*revival*." The church never closed its doors. "No one else had the courage," he said, and for that Glad Tidings graduated from a local profile to a national one. Leading lights of the Right came to address the flock. Gen. Michael Flynn, Trump's first national security advisor,[12] gave a sermon that went viral—the church presented him with a customized AR-15 onstage. "Maybe I'll find somebody in Washington, DC," he declared, holding the weapon. Less noticed was the custom gun presented by the church to Pastor Dave. Inscribed, noted Pastor Dave as he pointed the rifle to the heavens, with what he called "The Hebrew battle cry." "*Rak chazak amats*," he read, quoting the same verse the patriot pastor who'd opened Ashli's rally had worn on his T-shirt, Joshua 1:9, God's encouragement to Joshua as he prepares to conquer Jericho and kill anything that moves.

Glad Tidings sat by railroad tracks that cut through agricultural fields. Kids lined up outside in the dry and dusty air to ride Train to Glory, an elaborate golf cart made to look like a locomotive. Inside, the first thing I noticed was the pulpit: It was made of swords. A red-hilted shaft of steel plunged into the stage, intersected midpoint by

---

12 January 22–February 13, 2017. He soon pled guilty to lying to the FBI about communications with the Russians. On July 4, 2020, Flynn publicly pledged his loyalty to the QAnon conspiracy theory that holds that the U.S. government is secretly controlled by Satan-worshipping cannibalistic pedophiles. That November, Trump pardoned him, Flynn proposed that Trump impose martial law, and Trump floated Flynn as the director of the FBI.

two black-hilted blades to form an upside-down triangle. Racked like rifles beside the swords were three tall shofars, the ram's-horn trumpets used in Judaism, pornographically long. "Shofar, so good," Pastor Dave would say when a member of his flock blew his own.

I saw no crosses. "They miss the point," said Pastor Dave. He compared the cross, the crucifix, the method by which Jesus is believed, by those who believe, to have died for our sins, to the tender dove: weak-tea figuration that fails to convey the great breadth of ass kicked by Christ once he was risen.

Dave's own fighting days were past. His hair was still thick and dark, but his goatee was gray and long, fraying at its edges. He favored cowboy boots and tight shirts beneath lively patterned button-downs, worn open the better to display his jumbo belt buckles. And yet even now, he said, he was a spiritual warrior. "I am an exorcist," he explained, "used to all things weird and wonderful."

"Like in *The Exorcist*?" I asked.

"Exactly," he said. He smiled. "So that'll stretch your brain all sorts of ways."

Where once Pastor Dave's ministry mostly involved driving out cancers and lifting the yoke of addiction, now his attention was turned toward the enemy incarnate: mask mandators, vaccinators, election stealers. Servants of Satan, no kidding. Also, journalists. It may have been the fact that I'd come from the Ashli rally that redeemed me.

I spotted Thomas the street pastor. He asked if I'd read Psalm 91, Scripture invoked by snake handlers: "thou shalt tread upon the lion and the adder." "Covid's like snakes or strychnine," he said "'No plague shall take you.'" It was a gloss on Psalm 91's tenth verse. "This is a spirit-filled church." His voice was gentle. He gestured across the sanctuary. Capacity 900, nobody masked.

The worship band began to play in front of three giant screens projecting the lyrics to contemporary hymns over a slideshow backdrop of mountain vistas and waterfalls. It wasn't Yuba City, just a generic "creation," a divine anywhere rather than the local landscape of drought and fire, migrant worker and strip mall. An associate pastor took the stage to tell us about upcoming events, women's groups, and "the militia new recruit meeting."

Then came Pastor Dave to bring on the guest speaker. But first, a confession. "I have tried to be faithful," Pastor Dave said. But he had strayed. Not from his marriage—from Trump. It was not supposed to be like this. He meant the prophecies. Within conservative Pentecostal circles, Trump's 2020 victory had been widely foretold, by way of vision and dream. Its theft had not. But God helps those who help themselves. On January 6, God's people did just that. "We were able to take the castle," Pastor Dave said—the Capitol—and yet that glory, too, melted into air. "And then suddenly it is, well, quiet." He seemed embarrassed. "Frustrated." His buttered-toast voice sounded like it was going to crumble. The election was stolen and then the revolution defeated with just the one shot that killed Ashli. "Why the heck," he wondered, "would we ever vote again for anybody?" But Pastor Dave brought his dark questions to the Lord, and the Lord answered—"supernatural," he said—through that night's special guest, David Straight. "He goes from deep rabbit hole to deep rabbit hole to"—there were no other words for the depths illuminated by Straight, so Pastor Dave tripled down on the ones he had—"*deep rabbit hole.*"

Down we went. Straight was no typical evangelist. He didn't so much take the stage as drift toward its center. A large-shouldered man in an anonymous outfit of blue denim and black slacks, at ease in the space among others his broad-beamed back afforded. He combed his graying hair back loosely slicked, but he was not slick. He had no notes. Nothing prepared. He would speak, or not speak, as the spirit led. He paced, not speaking, one hand in a pocket. "I'm one of those guys you probably don't know," he murmured. He looked

away. His voice was a rumination. "I've always worked in the shadows, and"—a pause just long enough to let us know he didn't care if
we believed him—"I've done a lot of things. I travel all over the world
and"—that pause—"I've done a lot of missions." He had worked "in
intelligence." He had "guarded presidents." He had served President
Trump under three executive orders. He was out here, he said, in the
churches, because President Trump "looked at me right in the eye
and said, 'I've done everything I can. It's up to you to be hard on your
people.'" Us. "He says, 'Get 'em to stand. Give 'em power. Show them
how to have power.'" He had worked through the U.S. Judge Advocate General's Corps, JAG, and as leader of a top-secret team under
Melania. Just a month previous, the team arrested ninety-five child
traffickers.

The congregation cheered. "Booyah!" somebody hollered.

"Under President Trump," he continued, "we arrested fifteen
thousand."

"Glory to God!"

"Dominoes are falling," said Straight.

"C'mon!" shouted Pastor Dave, urging them to topple.

That none of this was true seemed to occur to no one. Melania's
secret child-trafficking response team? It made sense to the faithful. Fifteen thousand arrests they'd never heard of? Black ops, like
a thief in the night. Straight would say so himself: "I was taught to
be on the move, to keep moving, to go silently into the night and get
things done."

But now the lines had been drawn. It was all coming out. The
hour, finally, really was nigh.

"Audit the vote?" he said. "All of it, everywhere." *Amen!* Their belief
in this statement confirmed for them that which had preceded it.
Then Straight cemented the authenticity of his claim. He named a
state senator in Pennsylvania leading the fight there. He said, Wisconsin. He said, Arizona. It was a fantasy of undoing, of rolling back

time. But it was not fully delusional. The audit in Maricopa County, for instance, was absurd, yes, and also real. This is how you construct an alternate reality, the juxtaposition of the verifiable and the absurd, each vouching for the other.

"There's more than that," said Straight. "Last year"—the pause, which we'd learned now to listen for, a promise of deeper things— "some journalists won the lottery." Wait for it. "Thirty of 'em." He was telling a joke. "Got to go down to Guantánamo Bay. And"—here came the funny—"they're a little stuck down there." Cheering, laughter, amens. The joke was justice, the media behind bars. And it got better. President Trump—for he was still president, not only did he never lose, he never left office—had set aside, for the rest of the journalists soon to be rounded up, the entirety of Guam as "Gitmo 2.0" and Tierra del Fuego as "Gitmo 3.0."

"Word up, Lord!" called a believer.

Would it have helped if I raised my hand—know-it-all—and said that Guam, according to numerous reputable sources (on my phone) was already home to roughly 170,000 U.S. citizens? That Tierra del Fuego was an archipelago split between Argentina and Chile? No. Fake news. Americans in Guam? That was as believable as Joe Biden winning California.

So it went. Hillary, we learned, had secretly already been executed. What, you've seen her since? Green screens. Big Tech trickery, the name we give witchcraft in the twenty-first century. And there are, in fact, *two* United States, the one that "lives in our hearts" and the wicked one, which is actually a corporation. "Two governments exist side by side," observed Straight. Trump was not only still president of the real one, he was the nineteenth president, because most of the others since Lincoln, including Honest Abe, were illegal. ("The nineteenth?" someone near me wondered. Would Straight lose them here? It did say "45" right on Trump's hat. But no—Straight was in the Word, a spiritual condition almost like speaking in tongues, based not on reason but on trust, the people's faith that there is meaning especially in that which may at first seem strange.) Trump, Straight cooed, "is the commander in chief of the military right now, today." Which meant, he said, that "he has not turned over the football." The nuclear codes; the God power. *Amen.*

Such were the spiritual "truths" of the Trumpocene, which did not end January 20, 2021. The politics of the fringe may not be rational, but they're cunning, surrounding the center and moving inward, until suddenly there they are, at the heart of things: the QAnon Shaman, who on January 6 wore horns into the Senate Chamber to leave a menacing note for the vice president, or a congresswoman, Marjorie Taylor Greene, who has called for Democrats' execution; Ashli Babbitt, who died empty-handed, or Lauren Boebert, a Colorado congresswoman who open carries; the "zip-tie guy," seen at the insurrection leaping over Senate chamber seats with a handful of wrist restraints for hostages, or a senator, handsome young Josh Hawley, who raised his fist in solidarity.

Straight, like adherents of the QAnon conspiracy theory and its spin-offs, called what was happening now a "Great Awakening," and such was the inward tide of the first one, too, in the eighteenth century, when an equally unsettling man named Jonathan Edwards thrilled and confused his congregation with talk of sinners in the hand of an angry God, dangled over hellfire "much as one holds a spider or some loathsome insect." Straight was no Edwards, but the revival of which he and the martyr Ashli were part—"#TheGreat-Awakening," as Ashli tweeted—was not so much aberration as the continuity of feverish dreams twisting through the American mind since the beginning.

Straight didn't mention Ashli, but I understood why Big Richard at the rally had urged me to come hear him. I really was learning why she died. Not the trajectory of the bullet or the thought process of the man who pulled the trigger or the election lie that stoked the mob. I was learning the dream. "All I dream about and pray for," as she wrote; "it is all connected," "the pedos" and the "enslaved." "You can't sell your soul to the devil without a price." The math was simple, "2+2=4," equals, somehow, "DEATH BY FIRING SQUAD" for any politician insufficiently MAGA. She had come to care deeply for the 800,000 children she incorrectly believed stolen every year, and near the end she posted videos in which she spoke with hurtling indignation about immigration and drugs and homelessness.[13] She experienced her anger as love: channeled it all into belief; embraced the authority of her president-redeemer. It was the word *authority* that mattered. Ashli embraced *authority*, full-stop, as the fundamental frame for knowing the world.

Straight spoke at length on maritime law, about how legally we were all vessels, and thus subject to the same regulations as ports and pursers, the ship's officer in charge of money. *Purser; person.* It was all right there for those with ears to hear. With each term he introduced he revealed a secret etymology—"*deep* rabbit holes"—reassuring us at the same time that the winding path on which Straight had been sent by Trump to lead us would restore to us, We the People, command of our own ships, our vessels, our bodies. No longer would we be unlawfully taken or boarded, neither by taxes nor vaccines. But first we had to return to the beginning: our own. We learned how, by signing our birth certificates—government documents—our own mothers unwittingly condemned us to slavery. Yes, slavery. It all went back to the Fourteenth Amendment. You may believe that's the one that ensured the rights of formerly enslaved people through "equal protection of the laws." That's what *they* want you to think. "It's not

13 800,000 comes from the National Center for Missing and Exploited Children, which notes also that most are found within hours, most are family disputes, and that close to 99 percent of the children are returned home safely. The number abducted by strangers is in the low hundreds.

your fault," Straight said. You got fake news. You got critical race theory. You believed what you were told, which is why you do not know that the Fourteenth Amendment made *you*—the great White "you"— a slave, no longer free under the natural law of God as breathed into the Constitution but instead dominated by the "laws" bureaucrats make for bankers.

What Straight was doing was not so simple as rhetorically waving a Confederate flag, even if it amounted to much the same grievance-switching as perpetrated by the myth of the Lost Cause—White people as the true victims of the structures built for the sake of White power. Straight swaddled that myth in universalism, providing not a smirking veneer but cozy layers of deniability. In his telling, the problem with the Fourteenth Amendment, ratified in 1868, wasn't what it did for Black people. It was the aftermath of the Civil War, Reconstruction, 1865–77—during which the federal government sought, unevenly, to enforce those equal protections—which is for the modern Right the root of "big government." That is, "control." People you cannot see, in places to which you haven't been, having a say in how you live your life.

"See," preached Straight, "in Genesis 1:26 through 28 God gave *me*, man, dominion over the land, the air, and the water and everything therein. And this is *law*." And the law, Straight argued, "says what it says and doesn't say what it doesn't say." *Amens* rippled through the sanctuary, appreciation for the literalism that set you free. The law, said Straight, tells us that we are not "citizens" but *kings*. "God is our king of kings. He ain't the king of slaves."

The people nodded. They were impressed by what they believed was his discernment. In the New Testament this phrase, "king of kings," is meant to set God above the rulers of the world, whose authority Scripture famously lets stand. ("Render therefore unto Caesar the things that are Caesar's," Jesus advises.) But were one to present such a quibble, it would be only a different breed of literal-mindedness, deaf to the metaphors of others. There was world-building in Straight's rhetoric, same as the imaginary past summed up in Ashli Babbitt's use of a date, 1776, and its spirit, the year itself like the Holy Ghost. It's dialectical: thesis, antithesis, synthesis. There was the gospel of the Father, which Christians call the Old Testament, and the gospel of the Son, which they call the New, and now came a gospel of 1776, apotheosis of revenge and redemption. "We chant 1776 because it reminds us of revolting against our government," said another insurrectionist. The night of January 5, insurrection eve, a user on a forum called TheDonald.win posted a snapshot of a weapons cache they declared ready to go, "blocks away from the Capitol"; the poster called themselves "2021is1776," one word crushing centuries into the now. The word *revolution* itself is like that, too, as much a term of physics or metaphysics as of politics and war, a term for a kind of return, full circle, back to the beginning.

Chronologically, it's impossible, but maybe that's the point. The permanent revolution of the American frontier imagination, suggests historian Greg Grandin in *The End of the Myth*, is an attempt to break "through history"—like climbing through a broken window. It wasn't so much the fists and flagpoles that did the breaking on January 6 as it was the myths that propel them. The insurrectionists call such stories "research," and believe each soul must google their own.

"Real history," as David Straight said. He went to the primary sources, "the letters and journals" of the founders, the original text of the laws and the Constitution and the Bible, which he claimed—incorrectly—the Constitution was based on. Straight told Glad Tidings that an undefined *they* tried to destroy the true Constitution—literally, claimed *they* burned all but one copy. This is not true, but it reveals something about the construction of intellectual authority within the insurrectionist Right. It is based on a ragged democratization of knowledge, a protestant rejection of academic expertise, the idea that unmediated truth is available to us all through the invisible archive of chat groups and YouTube and Parler. That is, social media, the most mediated human interaction we have yet conceived.

They're not completely wrong—the turn toward primary sources is in one sense a democratization. Imagine you're Ashli Babbitt, inclined toward knowledge of the world, alert to the way such knowing can shape your life. At seventeen you join the Air Force because you know about 9/11. You're posted around the globe. You learn things. You're curious. Online you find answers. You read the Constitution, you read the Declaration. You don't ask for permission to enter the invisible archive. You don't need to. Your mind is free. You don't ask permission to enter the Capitol. You don't need to. Your body is free. 1776, 2021. You've broken through history. You've broken through the glass. The powerful flee before you. The People are behind you. You are the revolution. Your body itself is the primary source—but it's the context that kills you.

In the beginning, preached Straight, "the free men of America were busy being kings, settling on the land" (empty, in this telling); "clearing the land" (cultivated for centuries); "planting their gardens, their crops" (many introduced to them by Indigenous people); "raisin' the kids, loggin', huntin', trappin'." Straight stopped to let the congregation imagine—or, as they believed, *remember*—this Eden. As history it was bunk, as politics, fascist kitsch. But as desire? Longing? The wish to be free, to live in the moment, unmediated, no more rent or mortgage, to enter the myth, the invisible archive, as the hero of your own story?

MASK FREE AUTONOMOUS ZONE, read a red-white-and-blue poster on the front door of the pool-cleaning business Ashli Babbitt ran with her husband and her brother,

Better known as

AMERICA.

Through these doors, the only thing

that should be touching your lips

is an ice-cold beer or some pizza,

a burrito or a burger or maybe some donuts!

We shake hands like men,

fist bump like homies,

we smile, laugh, shout,

and have a damn good time!

><

The night aged. I stepped out at times, but Straight was always there, beamed by screen into the lobby. On-screen, Straight was talking about Child Protective Services, which in the Q-inflected cosmos of the Right is a key element of the government's plan to deprive parents of their right to do as they please with their offspring. "You put a bullet in the forehead of anyone who comes for them," Straight advised.

I spoke to a young woman named Madison, supervising a group of tween girls. She was a student at Chico State. She said a lot of what Straight taught went over her head, but "it gets you to think, for sure."

Like the news of Hillary Clinton being executed?

"Yeah!" she said brightly. "It's interesting!"

In the sanctuary, Straight brought nearly three hours of teaching to a close with a challenge for us: "Learn," he whispered, "*learn.*"

Thomas the street pastor and I stood to stretch. Big Richard spotted us. "There you are!" He wanted to introduce us to Pastor Dave. Maybe Dave would allow that some of what we'd heard went beyond the realm of the verifiable?

"Some of it was very new," he agreed. "But I was inspired." What Straight had said about child trafficking had especially resonated. He ran through more of Straight's lessons, "the illegality of income tax" and the legal difference, according to the hidden, true laws of the real America, "between private property and real estate." Dave's wife was a realtor, he said, so he'd found this especially important, because—

"Your wife's also a dog breeder!" Big Richard interrupted.

Dave lurched to a stop. "Yeah. She is." He nodded curtly.

Richard mistook his pastor's annoyed half-smile for approval. "Creation of a whole new breed!" he said. "Right out of this church! The sheepadoodle."

Facts matter. "The *mini* sheepadoodle," Dave corrected. "It is amazing," he admitted. "The home of a whole brand-new thing. God gave her an idea."

An associate pastor rebuked Richard. Why had Richard brought this up, he hissed.

"Because he's a writer!" Richard whispered.

Richard had helped me, so I wanted to help him. "You know what a good detail is," I offered. We shared a fellowship of laughter and canine awe. "It's magnificent," said Dave. He and his wife sold the puppies for $3,000 per—living, super-cute juxtapositions of the verifiable and the absurd.

"Anyway," Pastor Dave said. He moved on to Hillary's execution. He'd found this news a balm for the wound of the failed coup. "All the good, the patriots, the people who really care, they made a huge surge to do the right thing. And then we were told to all go home. It's over." The real message of Straight's hours on the stage, he believed: It wasn't. Which may have been the one true lesson of the evening.

We moved outside. Close to midnight, freight trains rolling. Pastor Dave did not normally talk to the media, he said. But he was talking to me. It was the hour of deeper truths. "I love the cross, but sometimes symbolism demeans that which it was meant to represent." Now was the time for war, spiritual or otherwise. The resurrection, of Christ, yes, and also the real America, rising from the grave, its symbol not the cross but, said Dave, "the empty tomb." Like the end of Mel Gibson's gory 2004 film *Passion of the Christ*, when Christ's death shroud collapses, the body disappeared, and then beside it the living Savior is there, naked and ripped as mournful strings give way to the *da-da-da-dum-dum* of a military drum and buff Jesus marches to war.

At the crossing, a whistle blew. What are the odds, I asked Pastor Dave, that I'd fly across the country to attend a rally for Ashli and find myself at this church out in the country, learning the theology of Ashli's cause? "Is it just coincidence?"

Everyone laughed. "There is no such thing as 'coincidence,'" Pastor Dave said. Ashli, me, the Capitol, Sacramento: we were a constellation drawn by the Creator. "Did you know that in the language of Scripture there's no word for coincidence in either the Old Testament or the New?"

"Amazing," Thomas whispered.

"Coincidence," explained Dave, "is just a spectacular thing, that God remains anonymous." For instance: Covid-19. He told me Scripture teaches that what your enemies—here he meant China, which he thought had intentionally created the disease, and Dr. Fauci, who had tried to spread it—intend as evil against you, God will make good. Is that not the whole point of the risen Christ? The meaning of every martyr?

But what about the dead who don't rise? Not Jesus, not Ashli—all those already gone, killed by Covid?

"This will blow your mind," Dave said. Covid was real and the dead were many, but there was a "good part": the godless churches, the ones with crosses instead of swords, had closed their doors.

"Clearing the field?"

"Yeah!" The good part was that God had spoken: "an announcement that those who truly want to represent me, please stand up." Dave, meanwhile, wanted to speak of trials and executions for those who don't. This, too, he thought, was the good part: that now we knew who was standing, and who was not, and who, in the coming freedom, would dangle.

4. Inland

Or maybe here's the good part: There *is* a word for coincidence in the Bible, a friend told me. Seth Sanders is a professor of ancient languages and religion at the University of California at Davis, and the author of *The Invention of Hebrew*. "The root קרה and associated noun מקרה are fairly frequently used, and mean to encounter by chance,"

Seth wrote me. He added a dig at Dave: "this is not something that someone well-versed in Hebrew would say. It's something that someone who maybe took a class or two in order to bolster their authority but doesn't remember much and or doesn't care what the Bible really says in its original languages would say."

It's satisfying when an expert flattens a false claim. That's how so many of us believe we'll resist the undertow of civil war, fact-checking our way back to solid ground. But much like the cross for Pastor Dave, such corrections miss the point. You can't fact-check a myth.

How to say then, that Ashli Babbitt is not a martyr? There's the word itself, *martyr*, which means "witness," one's life given as testament to some larger truth. The story for which she put herself in front of the gun, that the election was stolen? Verifiably false. Count, recount and do it again, Georgia or Michigan or Arizona, and the outcome is the same. But what if she died as a witness not to fact but to dream? The solace of the surreal, the comfort of chaos, the great relief of all the "issues" falling away, like a body letting go, falling backward, into the Foreversville of conflict itself as the cause for which one fights. The topic—the border, guns, election "integrity," pedophiles—does not matter. Only the fight. "It's cool." How do you disprove *that*?

From Yuba City, I turned inward. I decided that instead of flying I'd rent a car and drive back east, haunted by Ashli, martyr of the full 360-degree revolution: empire's expansion inverted, moving no longer outward but in. Toward the center. The ouroboros of Whiteness, the serpent that having consumed all else starts on its own flesh.

I drove over Donner Pass the next night, listening to talk radio rise and fall according to the ridgeline, the mountain static. "First-time caller," defending the AR-15, "it's our heritage." Deeper than that, thought the host—such guns are practically our DNA. Every little boy, he said, has a certain sound in his "repertoire": *buda-buda-*

buda! he thrummed his lips and his tongue, imitating the sound of an assault rifle. He liked the sound so much he couldn't stop. *Buda-buda-buda* filled the airwaves. I flipped the dial. Kenny Loggins, "Danger Zone."

"Be safe," Aaron Babbitt texted Ashli as she prepared to take off for Washington the day before the insurrection. "I cannot lose you." So writes the one left at home. Ashli was headed toward the front. She responded not as wife or lover but as soldier: "Tons of trump supporters on my plane!!!!"

"Nobody knows who shot her," a patriot named Julie Osburn told me when we talked beside a playground outside Reno, a stamp of green in the endless beige.[14] I noted that we did know who shot Ashli, Lt. Michael Byrd. This did not alter her opinion. "God has us," she said. All of it—Ashli, the broken window, and the bullet, and also the coverup that followed, the way they kept the shooter's name a secret (it's true, they did), which in turn taught patriots yet another lesson—"God's plan."

"The narrative," Aaron Babbitt told Jamie Allman for his "1776" series of videos, "that this is all set up and preplanned? This is completely false." He and Ashli were on vacation in Mexico for Christmas 2020. "She just said, 'I think I want to go see the president.'" He thought it was a whim. January 1, though, she bought a ticket. "She had no clear plans."

Near Lovelock, Nevada,[15] a desert town split by the highway between a mine and a prison, I pulled over to study a compound built around the ruins of a smelter. Militia? Meth lab? Zombies? I walked closer. In the wind ("there's something strange happening with the wind," Julie Osburn had told me) the rust-red steel lace of the smelter seemed to sing. It sounded like voices, then like

14 Wašišiw ʔítdeh land.

15 Northern Paiute land.

footsteps, then like a shotgun being pumped for action. "The only good thing about a shotgun, that sound," a clerk named Brian at Scorpius Tactical, supplier of fine militia gear, told me near Reno. His store specialized in custom AR-15s. A shotgun, he said, can no longer meet your self-defense needs. He asked me to peer down an AR's barrel. "You can't see the craftsmanship with your naked eye," he said, "but you'll understand." They sold iron targets, too, for shooting in the desert. That's what people do here, he said. Shoot the desert. Shoot old ruins. For fun? For training, he said. "Given how things have gone this past year." Another customer volunteered that his father had killed two home invaders once, while he and his siblings slept unawares. Brian told me he'd moved to Nevada from Louisiana, after going two months without power, following "bad weather." Two months of "AR-15 time." There was a lot of bad weather these days. He mentioned the McCloskeys. I nodded. That couple in Missouri, invited to speak at the Republican Convention after their armed response to a Black Lives Matter march past their suburban lawn, he a pudgy old Clyde in a pink polo with his AR-15, she an aging Bonnie with her little silver handgun.

"Just the projection," said Brian. Of force. Good for sales. He said he could retrieve one of his own rifles—he had many—from his safe and establish three points of contact—shoulder, grip, trigger finger—in less than five seconds. "I'm prepared."

There were no zombies at the compound.

Brian was in nursing school.

I spoke to another customer, a skinny young dude in black shorts and American-flag socks and a camo hat that read BATTLE BORN, Nevada's motto, but I didn't take good notes. All I have that means anything is "constantly threatened."

><

Ashli was posting videos. In her kitchen, driving to work, her voice an outraged squeak that swings low every few words. Indignation. "There's riots, there's arrests, there's rapes, there's drugs," she says, sitting at her breakfast table. "I—I am so tired of it!" she says, at the wheel of her car, looking back and forth between the camera in her phone and the road. "Where is everybody?" she demands. "Huh? Huh?" Her lips curl like the mouth of a vase. Driving to work, she rants about migrant caravans. She's fifteen minutes from the border. "Thousands of people on the other side." They're coming. Nobody's doing anything. She's posting a lot of social media. She's a digital soldier. She was a real soldier. She's going to take it IRL.

Sometime in 2020, a man will tell Ashli's local CBS affiliate, he had to stop doing business with her. She didn't want to talk about pools anymore, she wanted to talk about Trump. About his enemies.

"A lot of it," the man told CBS8 San Diego, "didn't make any sense."

She was not, though, by anybody's account, "crazy." Maybe her ideas were, but she wasn't. She was mad.

But—so what? White rage, like "White tears" is yet another name for the method by which Whiteness seduces some White people into claiming other people's grief as their own. To which many quite reasonably say, *Get over yourself.* And yet, while sorrow and anger are shaped by race, they are not products of it alone. How much of Ashli's anger was rooted in her experience as a woman? As, seemingly, queer in practice if not in name? How much had been formed by her Air Force career—dead-ended, according to some accounts, by her insistence on speaking up for others? Did her failed first marriage play a role? How much was linked to her struggling business's debt, a court judgment against it for $71,000 on an ill-considered short-term loan charging interest she calculated at 169 percent?

Given the choices she made at the end about how to channel all this anger, it's fair to say none of these questions matter. Her pain may have been real, but she chose to pass it on, as publicly as possible. But that makes understanding the direction of her anger, if not its roots, essential. Not how it was constructed—there are always more tributaries than can be counted—but how it was aimed. The anger that dislodged her from one dream—"She was happy," her brother Roger told CNN, she "talked about how she lived in a beautiful place, this was the American dream"—and propelled her into another, the red dream, cascading into the Capitol, down the hallway and—almost—through that window.

Her death did not end her anger. Her death itself became the dream of others. Consider Garrett Miller, of Dallas, Texas. You won't remember his name, but you may have heard of his arrest: When the FBI came to his door, they found him wearing a T-shirt declaring, I WAS THERE, WASHINGTON, D.C., JANUARY 6, 2021. The prosecution's charging memo, which includes a collection of his social-media posts, isn't as amusing. He'd become obsessed with Ashli. "A beautiful soul," he wrote. "They murdered a child." At first, he hoped that killing Rep. Alexandria Ocasio-Cortez might balance the scales. Then he found out about Lt. Michael Byrd, the Black officer who shot Ashli. Online, Miller debated execution methods. He concluded that the rope would be the most Christian for a "prize" such as Byrd. It would maintain the patriots' innocence in the coming civil war, since "liberal history tellers" would not be able to say that patriots had started the shooting. "She fought fir me," he wrote, "now I fight fir her." *Sic.*

Just talk? "Aspirational chatter," as the FBI put it, defending its inaction before January 6? Miller says he had a gun at the Capitol. At his house, along with body armor and more guns, states the charging memo, "the FBI recovered numerous ropes."

It felt drier here, inland. "Record heatwave," warned the radio. The Christian stations were serene. The sky darkened. Smoke, not rain. I was driving through fire, detoured onto leaner roads. Some-

where I paused to watch flames lick over a ridge. What was it that
that burned? Wildflowers? The smoke wasn't just black and orange
but green and sometimes purple. The sun peered through, copper,
like a far-away penny.

"It was an incredible thing," a Nevada patriot named Matt Virden
told me over the phone. He meant the moment Ashli was killed. He
was there, but outside when a man who said he'd been inside, *with
her,* staggered from the building. Virden told me he could see it, the
death, the meaning: "the ghost on his face."

I wanted to meet Virden in Reno, from which he'd traveled to the
Capitol, but I was already east of the city and its great or maybe just
midsized casinos with their red-tinted doors and their Roman foun-
tains and their many-pixeled fantasias, in which I'd spent the night,
listening to the never-ending jingles and the dull clinking payouts of
the slots, reading the sliver-thin *Reno Gazette,* a kind of ghost paper,
like a ghost town, gutted of news, drifting off between what classi-
fieds remained. Virden returned my call later. The FBI had been to
visit. He hoped they wouldn't return. If they did it was God's plan.
Spiritual war is moving, onto the material plane. IRL. No more
hiding.

But his calls to me kept being interrupted. His kids, he was a
young father, and his job. He worked for *his* father, a doctor, selling
his father's invention, pellets implanted beneath your skin to raise
and lower your hormones. Testosterone. Estrogen. And his own
health concerns interrupted. Once, while we were texting, heatstroke
came over him. "Super hot." Dry heaves. "Luckily, I had been fast-

ing." He started losing his vision. "In my eyeballs." So he drove to the ER. Turned out to be nothing. He didn't take chances—he'd had an aortic replacement, his chest cut right open. I told him I got it. With me, heart disease at a relatively young age. Through this—the unreliability of our most essential organ—we recognized one another.

The news at the Capitol, he said—they'd shot a girl—"spread like wildfire. Before you knew it, everybody was aware of it. This is a different situation now." The megaphones spoke now not of 1776 but of Ashli, though they did not yet know her name. She was still bleeding. Virden thought there were a couple thousand there, on the Capitol steps. He claimed five hundred circled up and held hands. (Consider these spiritual numbers, not necessarily physical fact. Virden said with his own eyes he saw more than a million souls. Ashli, striding toward her death, made a breathless selfie video putting it at 3 million.) Anyway, they prayed. He couldn't remember the words. "Everybody bowed their heads and had incredible reverence for what had happened and what was going on." The shooting, the blood, the battle. To Virden, it was peaceful. The love. Hand in hand. The spirit. 1776. The dead girl.

My friend Phil had given me a book to read, a novel by his daughter, Ivy Pochoda, called *These Women*. I'd brought it with me. It kept me company in the desert, at night, when I wasn't driving. A California story. About how women are killed and how we tell stories about these killings. "Here are the ways a body can come apart," writes Pochoda. "It can drown or be drowned and turn the color of a deep-sea creature that has never seen the light of day. It can get trapped between the dirty, barnacled rocks and bang on them for a day or more before someone takes it away. By then it will barely seem a body at all, but rather an obscene organism, a swollen alien form."

Which reminded me as I drove of some good writing advice: Remember the bodies. But what were the bodies in this story? The bodies of the believers. The body of Christ. The body politic. The body of "the nation." How does *that* body "come apart"? The answer is in the question I'd learned to ask the believers: "Do you think there'll be a civil war?" They all said "*Yes.*" Most thought it was coming, soon, and some said it was already here. Some said Ashli Babbitt was the first casualty; others noted January 6 as one more date in a calendar crowded with the death days of modern martyrs. All the blond daughters of the Angel Families, the term used by the Right for those whose loved ones have been murdered by "illegals"; every cop ever killed even close to the line of duty (except at the Capitol); Vicki Weaver, shot to death at Ruby Ridge by an FBI sniper as she cradled her ten-month-old baby when the government came to take her husband, Randy, away for the simple act of selling two sawed-off shotguns to an informant with whom he'd discussed joining forces in the coming battle against a federal government he believed secretly controlled by Jews.

Vicki Weaver as seen from a U.S. Marshal's
surveillance position.

Most of the believers expressed some form of sorrow for what had become, in their imaginations, the *fact* of this coming war; some grew red in the cheek. "The spirit of 1776," they said. You could almost hear the blood throb faster in their veins.

But what do any of us—Americans, native-born—really know about civil war? Beyond what we've read or watched in movies or seen in the news of other nations? When I asked, *civil war*, when the believers answered, *civil war*, we were speaking in metaphors we could barely comprehend. We were describing a feeling that frightened or exhilarated us: a body coming apart.

In Logan, Utah, Eastern Shoshone and Shoshone-Bannock land, I stopped to visit an old friend, Andrew. We'd been best friends as children, best men at each other's weddings, and we hadn't seen each other in the seventeen years since. He was a present-centered man. "I don't really do the past," he said. He was a scientist, he studied soil, the actual land; also a cyclist, extreme. As I drove cross-country west to east, he was preparing to participate in a race—one he thought he might win—up its spine. South to north, border to border, 2,700 miles of mostly unpaved trail in the same two weeks it'd take me to drive. I was on the horizontal, he was on the vertical when we crossed paths. "How do you do it?" I asked.

"Focus," he said. "I don't *try* to think."

Thoughts came to him in their own time. He pushed his body but waited for his mind. Thoughts came in the form of flora—at Utah State he taught a course in plant identification. On a hike into the canyon by his home he showed me a bright yellow flower called dyer's woad, from which a blue dye can be extracted, once so valuable it sparked wars. Or thoughts came as fauna. "Antelope, wild horses. Bears. Too many bears." Sometimes he carried bear spray in place of a water bottle. Once, up north, a grizzly charged. A trucker offered him shelter in his cab. "You have to take care," Andrew said.

Twenty years ago, he and I had driven west for the first time together, saw the Rocky Mountains rise from the plains as we came over the horizon at dawn. I'd return east, but Andrew ping-ponged until finally he settled in Utah. For years, he lived among homes color-coded on a neighborhood map not by faith but by the intensity of one's commitment to God. Andrew's house alone was a little black square, a mark of no faith at all. It used to bother him. Now, he said, "Mormons are nice." Just an observation. A fact. That was their contract with God, he thought, the deal they make for living on land both beautiful and severe.

Andrew was renovating his house, so I airbnbed a second-floor apartment downtown, hot, stuffy. I turned on a ceiling fan in the bedroom and propped a box fan in the window to drown out the ceiling fan's noise, which reminded me of the singing smelter near Lovelock. Neither were enough, so I slept uncovered on polyester sheets, the blinds open in case a breeze were to come through town. It did not, but early a siren woke me. Only I thought it was my eldest child, two thousand miles east, a nightmare, the wail in the night. I was up, immediately, damp with sweat, I was ready—then I saw a fire truck pass by outside and fell back into dreamless sleep. Since coming west I'd been sleeping without dreams. An hour later I was awoken again. This time by the wind, arrived at last and banging one of the windows in the kitchen. I let it bang, and lay in bed, waiting to know what to do.

I had a name an hour south. Scott Sneddon, an Air Force veteran and the founder of a local militia called American Patriot III, as in the 3 percent of the population patriots believe fought in the Revolutionary War. Three: a number to them not dispiriting but inspiring. If true it would mean 3 percent of a people can overthrow a regime. But it's not true. A better estimate is that around 25 percent of the colonists participated in the revolution. What 3 percent can do, though—the tactics we typically describe as terrorism, violence in service of a meme—is frightening.

I found Sneddon's phone number online. He was also a realtor. He advertised with a big, dough-faced smile, pointing at you, the customer, with hands like happy six-shooters. When I called, he said, sure, he'd be glad to meet. After the bad press around January 6, he felt it important to show the bright side of the militia movement. In Utah, he said, it's "nice. Community." Thinking of the black square on my friend's neighborhood map, I asked what *community* meant to him. Community, said Sneddon, is about being prepared to take care of your own.

"Prepared?" I asked.

"For whatever happens."

"Preppers?"

"Yeah!" he said, pleased that I followed.

"Doomsday?"

Could be, he allowed. He liked "nicer" terms. "Love," he said, "is about being ready."

5. It's Bigger Than You Expect

When I got to Layton (Eastern Shoshone and Goshute land), I called Sneddon. He seemed embarrassed. There was something he hadn't mentioned: That day he was convening a memorial for his recently deceased father. He'd thought he could "squeeze" me in. But he found himself overwhelmed by mourning relations. "It's bigger than you expect," he said. Grief, I think he meant. It is. [16]

At the edge of town, I stopped for a beer at an American Legion post that looked like a log cabin. On its door were two faded plastic wreaths tacked over a sign.

WARNING
Security
Camera

16 I wondered if I should press him. That's what journalists do. We're worse than the media haters can imagine. We leave a message and when we don't get an answer, we leave another and sometimes we just knock on a door on the other side of which, we know, is fear, or grief, or anger that does not want our questions. Our measuring gaze. But we want it. Their fear, their grief, their anger. Our measuring gaze. So we soothe, we cajole. We seek "access." *Open, sesame. Give us your story.* Every journalist, the guilty ones, at least, knows what Janet Malcolm wrote in *The Journalist and the Murderer*: "Every journalist who is not too stupid or full of himself to notice what is going on knows that what he does is morally indefensible. He is a kind of confidence man, preying on people's vanity, ignorance, or loneliness, gaining their trust and betraying them without remorse." Since we know what Malcolm wrote we think our readers do too. Some do. Sneddon didn't. Was he lying about his father's memorial? Had he simply thought better of talking to a reporter? He should have. But I thought he was telling the truth, and I didn't have the stomach anymore—I should say the heart—for that kind of story, so I offered my condolences and hung up. I wanted to follow rather than to find, to let the strange wind of the singing smelter set my course.

Besides, I had a destination outside the narrative: Golden, Colorado, to distribute the ashes of my stepmother, dead of cancer just weeks after Ashli, and as I approached Golden I found my grief looming larger than I'd known it would. It's bigger than you expect.

One wreath was white and purple, the other red and sliding off a wicker brace that encircled a POW-MIA logo, the black silhouette of a downcast man, only one word visible: FORGOTTEN. Martyrs of another age. Inside looked like a hunting lodge on the Fourth of July, red-white-and-blue oilcloth, a patriotic pinwheel at each round table, all empty. Every barstool but one was taken. A TV droned. Men snoozed, folding themselves round beers gone flat and warm. It was two thirty. I sat at the empty stool at the end, kitty-corner to a white-bearded man in a Navy ballcap who was working his way through a giant mug of coffee and a stack of newspapers. He muttered. Column inches advanced. Bad news? Of course. I told him I was following the ghost of Ashli Babbitt across the country. I said it just like that. "Yuh-huh," he said. He acknowledged that he knew the name, but his wide-framed glasses remained fixed on the paper.

"Fake news?" I asked.

He put the paper down and examined me. Then he picked it up and held it between two fingers, like a tissue. "*No* news," he said. "The problem's right there." He gestured to the man beside me, lost in his phone. "We gave it all to those things, and we let our newspapers shrink till they're almost nothing, and then we wonder why we don't know anything." Which is how, he said, speaking of Ashli and the collapse of which she was a symbol, you get to Washington, January 6–wise. "We did it to ourselves."

This was not what I was expecting. The man's name was—he made sure I wrote first and last down correctly and then told me not to use either. "I would prefer you put 'The Man I Met in the American Legion Post in Layton, Utah,'" he said. "I don't want some son of a bitch bombing my house."

"Put 'Post 87,'" said the bartender, an old woman with the most beautiful teeth, and a wide, gently earnest smile. Her name was—she told it to me, said I could use it, but The Man I Met in the American Legion overruled her. "She doesn't need her name in there. You put her name in there, people'll figure out she's here, and people don't need to know that." She smiled and acquiesced.

The Man's views were not, he explained, typical. He was a Republican, but not a Trumper. "And the Trumpers right now have control."

Then, as if answering himself, in a softer tone he agreed: "Yeah. That's too bad."

The Man went on in his stronger voice: "There won't be any way for the parties to come together to think about the country."

"So what happens?" The Man's softer self asked himself, sounding sad.

"I don't know what happens," The Man's bitter self answered himself. He sounded sad too.

As he talked, the TV played a slow, soft piano melody. It was an ad for a bank, but there were no words. Just the music. I recognized it: "Gymnopédie No. 1," by the nineteenth-century French composer Erik Satie. I knew it because it's like a lullaby, almost elegiac, and after my son was born I'd sit with him for hours in a rocking chair playing Satie's Gymnopédies and Gnossiennes, thinking, as many parents do these days, about the world into which I'd helped bring him. You might know this melody that became a part of The Man's words too. It's used in movies and commercials. A cliché. A beautiful one.

"I don't bitch about paying taxes," said The Man. He sounded puzzled. He accepted the price of society. He was grateful. He was a veteran. He had been overseas. He was thinking about infrastructure. Not policy; the texture of things. "I don't particularly like streets that are made of mud and asphalt combined. I don't like the idea that the power goes out whenever it feels like it."

Then, the other side of the argument: "We lose power here," the softer, sadder self observed.

"Yeah," his more certain self said, "it's usually a fire or a storm."

He thought about hospitals. About how in small towns and now small cities they were closing. He considered the empty buildings. He contemplated water. "I like the idea of good water," he said. "And we're going to be shutting off the water here, probably. Just to stay alive. The drought."

Another old man drifted into our corner. Built like an elf, chipmunk cheeks and a beard whittled to a point beneath a black cowboy hat crested by a pin of a golden bald eagle, spreading its wings across an American flag. He jabbed with his beard in my direction. "He ain't givin' us nothin'?" he asked The Man, his voice like dry paste. I started to explain. "Just givin' you a hard time," he said. He felt a need to intervene lest The Man misrepresent Post 87 as a den of socialism. He didn't mind if I used his name. Tom Woodring, veteran, Air Force, the full twenty. His concern, he said, was the past. History. "Why," he asked, "are they teaching the White kids that they're the slave to the Black? That they shouldna been born?" The thought made him hot.

"I never heard that," murmured the bartender.

Neither had The Man. He turned on Tom. "And she's a school bus driver, last thirty years," he snapped, speaking for the bartender.

"It was on the news," said Tom.

"Have you ever seen anything good on the news?" The Man demanded. TV news, he meant, is a racket. "They want to sell one side."

Tom could get behind that. "They're running the country!" The "country," by his account, was a story. "If they don't like to hear you, they cut you off. If you don't want it told, they put it out there. I know what's going on." Example: "Why did they kill a woman with no guns?" Ashli. "Why won't the news tell us who killed her? And she was in the military!"

The Man interrupted. His quiet voice, but not gentle now: "What were the circumstances?"

"That's the question!" said Tom.

"No, no, no. The facts."

Tom and I told the story together. Me: "She was inside the Capitol when—"

Tom: "Inside the Capitol. They shot her—"

Me: "—she was climbing through a broken window—"

The Man summarized, incredulous: "She was climbing through a broken window, in the Capitol, when there's a riot going on, and there's congressmen, and they had no idea whether she had a gun, and she was coming through the window? I'd a blown her away in a heartbeat."

"Yeah," said Tom. But he meant "no." The Man pivoted to face him. Tom, about as tall standing as The Man was seated, brought his Stetson brim to brim with The Man's Navy ballcap. "What about those guys that tore down that guy's fence?"

The Man looked confused.

Tom shouted, "Got in his yard and him and his wife came with guns to chase them off"—Tom mimed aiming two pistols, one in each hand like a gunfighter—"and they went to jail, not the fucking convict!"

"Around here?" I asked. The Man shrugged, as confused as I was.

"Another state!" said Tom, embarrassed that he didn't have the details.

I made a guess: "St. Louis?" St. Louis, Tom agreed. Ah—the McCloskeys. Who did not go to jail. By "convict" Tom meant "Black protesters," who he felt should have been imprisoned. Who were in the street, not the yard. But what about Ashli? Did she not cross that line?

No—that's different. "She was already in the building!" It's not trespassing, he insisted, if you're already inside. "She wasn't breaking in, she was going in a window that's *inside* the building. And it's already broken." He mimed climbing through the window, a hand on each side of the frame, lifting a foot off the ground. "She didn't break it. It was already broken by somebody else who went through." (They hadn't.) He stepped out of his imaginary window and then climbed back in, peering at me to see if I grasped the demonstration. The facts: his old man body, the window, right there, in the space he'd opened between him and The Man. He became Ashli, looking around. "What's going on?" Tom-as-Ashli asked, like a curious little girl. "I want to know what's happening." He poked his head out, smiling with innocent wonder, a girl who had wandered into the Capitol, where there was so very much to see.

Then Tom slashed away the window with a chop of his hand. He became the shooter: quick draw, invisible six-guns: "BOOM-BOOM!" he shouted. Dreaming the death, thrilled by his own alarm. His shoulders collapsed. He sighed, decades of disappointment easing out of his frame, and he looked down at the poor fallen girl. "Now you know," he whispered.

The Man was indignant. "We're supposed to be a country of laws." He scowled. He and Tom had both served. How could Tom forget his oath? "In this country we solve problems with the ballot box," he declared. Ashli Babbitt was a traitor. They all were. "If I could have a selective machine gun"—The Man cradled an invisible one in his arms. *Buda-buda-buda.* "I'd a blasted every goddamn one of them to hell and back."

><

I spent the next couple hundred miles after the Legion attempting to adjudicate in my mind Tom's and The Man's trial by mime. Which side was I on? The Man's, until his imaginary killing spree. But there was a thread of truth in Tom's performance too. The Department of Justice said only that it could not prove that Lt. Byrd did not *believe* he was acting in self-defense. That awkward double negative is a contortion of the law considered exceptionally friendly to officers who use force in the line of duty. It's worth noting what else the Justice Department declared: "evidence that an officer acted out of fear, mistake, panic, misperception, negligence, or even poor judgment cannot establish the high level of intent" needed to press charges. Byrd thought shots had been fired. This wasn't true. He acted out of "misperception" based on the panic of whoever it was who said over the radio that shooting had begun. The first and only shot was Byrd's, determined by the Justice Department not to be a correct one but rather an error it deemed reasonable.

"She was not brandishing a weapon. There was no lunging. She was shot right in an open window," Ashli's family's attorney, Terrell Roberts, told me. "An 'imminent threat' has to be realistic." Of course, it was Roberts's job to see it that way. So I called Seth Stoughton—a former police officer, a law professor at the University of South Carolina, and a key expert witness for the prosecution in the trial of Derek Chauvin. An imminent threat, he explained, has three components: ability to do damage; opportunity to do so; and intention. Intention we can't know, but we might reasonably side with Lt. Byrd in believing Ashli was dangerous. Ability, though—did she have the means to do harm? Let's grant that, too, in the form of the knife in her pocket. Which leaves opportunity—if Ashli had drawn her knife, who could she have stabbed? Stoughton: "I'm not sure I look at that position she's in"—wedged in the window—"and say she can imminently kill or injure someone."

Then there's the scene of the killing, on federal property. The Constitution reserves most of the power to make criminal law for the states. Crimes on federal property are typically prosecuted according to the laws of the surrounding state. But the Capitol is surrounded by the District of Columbia, which lacks the same status. So Byrd was exonerated not according to homicide law applicable to nearly every other shooting in the United States but rather a civil rights statute, 18 U.S.C. § 242, that would have required that the government prove Byrd "willfully" deprived Ashli of her constitutional rights, "with a bad purpose." Short of a declaration from Byrd of murderous intent, this standard would make a conviction—of Byrd, or most other police officers charged with its violation—nearly impossible. Which was why the 2021 George Floyd Justice in Policing Act would have struck the word *willfully* from 18 U.S.C. § 242. But the same Republicans who asked, "Who killed Ashli Babbitt?" had no qualms about killing the George Floyd Act, an apparent contradiction that seems like evidence of hypocrisy only if you mistakenly believe that the question of who killed Ashli was ever meant to be answered. The believers stoked their own paranoia by arriving at no fixed point. They said it was Byrd or simply "a Black man," they said he was a bad cop or not a cop at all but a member of Mike Pence's "private" security team, which did not exist, or that he was an agent of the deep state. They said, in short, that the bogeyman killed Ashli. The enemy, the particulars of which do not matter.

6. Rifle, Colorado

Núu-agha-tʉvʉ-pʉ land

I came into the mountains at the so-called golden hour, through cliffs the color of sand and grace. Wildfire smoke made the whole Western Slope seem becalmed, as if through the particles the sun breathed soft light. Time layered in stone, olive, rust, and dusky violet. I was listening to Christian radio. A preacher from Wisconsin. An amiable voice, beneath its surface a sense of fracture. Ochre, if I had to give the preacher's voice a color.

"Quite a few years ago," the preacher mused, "we went to the coast. I was studying on the beach while my three teenage boys were out in the ocean." His three boys frolicked in the waves; the preacher considered God's word. Sound sifted away—until the preacher heard his wife screaming. "She said, 'Honey.'" He had shorn the memory of alarm. "'Do you hear the boys hollering for help?'" In his telling she asks as if she is simply curious. *Do you hear our children drowning?* "I looked up. And listened. I said, 'Well, it kind of seems like they are.'" He dropped his Bible in the sand, he sprinted to the water. "Only problem, I was wearing blue jeans. Have you ever tried to swim in blue jeans?" His legs were heavy. The water carried his boys away. "The undercurrent," said the preacher. The undertow. "I was drowning myself," he observed.

And then—I don't know. The radio signal stayed strong, the preacher kept talking, his voice carrying me up into darker canyons too steep for the setting sun. Evidently, he survived. His three boys? He never did mention. The story, which we may imagine as beginning in fact, had been made into parable, the meaning of real things smoothed like sea glass. Myth carries people away. The preacher spoke more about the weight of his jeans. "The weight of our lives." The weight, he said, is anything that distracts us from God. His *sovereignty*. His authority. That was all that mattered, even more than his three boys. The "weight" that drags you down could be anything. "It may be a love." Even for your children. "Lay it aside," he rumbled. There is no saving this world.

When I first came west at nineteen, I had my own religion. I thought that the mountains were the Earth's secrets rising to be seen, by me, as if geology were revelation. This is a widespread misperception. Over the years, I came to think of them instead as indifferent, not made for me or anybody, not made at all. There is no intention.

But now, driving, I saw them as tender. Maybe it was the haze. These mountains still grow but as they do their peaks soften and drift down to the plains. They rise, they subside. I thought of Andrew, my friend, who would be soon riding his bicycle up this spine across which I drove. His mind would be clear. "I don't really do the past." Neither do the mountains. I imagined them sleeping. But they were never awake. Or always awake, always sleeping, rising, sinking. How does a body come apart? How does democracy dissolve? It subsides.

I drove down a riverine valley into the town of Rifle. Riparian green punctured by factories and grain elevators, the spike of a steeple at the edge of town. Shredded tire on the road and two men by a broken blue pickup, hood raised, drinking beer and watching the sun's last smoke-filtered light, purple and violent, shot through with the palest of pink hues. Dead deer down by the water, its body half-open.

I was hoping to eat dinner at a restaurant I'd heard about called Shooters. Like Hooters, but with guns. Waitresses in cutoffs, each of them armed. It was the creation of a congresswoman named Lauren Boebert, and she carried too. "I am the militia," she'd declared. There's a photograph of her flanked by two servers in their Daisy Dukes and cowboy boots, armed with eight guns between the three of them. Boebert looks back over her shoulder, not at the viewer, but down at the assault rifle the buttstock of which she is framing—no other way to put this, one must respect self-presentation—with her ass.

"Buttstock," though, is only the correct term if it's a rifle. This gun may actually be a very elaborate pistol. "For an AR-15 to be that short and still have a buttstock," a gun enthusiast friend told me, "it would need to be registered with ATF as a 'short-barrel rifle'"—subject to much greater regulation. "The 'pistol brace' she has in place of a stock is meant to be clamped around your forearm to stabilize the weapon if you fire it like a pistol." My friend called it a "photo-op gun"—lacking a sight, he said, "you could point it at something and maybe hit it, but definitely couldn't hit anything at a distance that would require adjusting aim for vertical drop or wind."

Perhaps accuracy was not Boebert's chief concern. Responses to another viral image of Boebert, Zooming into a congressional committee hearing, made much of the crossed AR-15s she chose as her background but took no note of her short bookshelf, which featured multiple copies of a volume called *Dressed to Kill*. I bought a copy. Above the title are the words "You Don't Have to Take It Anymore Because You Are . . ." The subtitle is: *A Biblical Approach to Spiritual Warfare and Armor*. The gun, the book, Boebert in her cutoffs. Boebert's Twitter banner brings it all together: a blue-jean crotch shot of a Glock on her hip, crossed hands holding a virginally white "45" cap in front of her fly, a kind of Morse-code militant eroticism.

On January 6, Boebert tweeted, "Today is 1776." As the mob grew, she shouted on the House floor, "Madame Speaker! I have constituents outside this building right now!" A viral rumor claimed she shared House Speaker Nancy Pelosi's location. This was not true. She just tweeted that the Speaker had left the chamber. In case anyone was interested. "*Naaaaancy!*" the insurrectionists called as they filled the corridors. "Where are *yoooo*, Nancy?"

But I hadn't come to Shooters to meet Boebert. Her story was a stunted one: long gun, short bookshelf. I was here for the atmosphere. Dinner was a bust. They were winding down when I arrived after eight, and the only waitress remaining was an older Latinx

woman who spoke limited English, which was surprising, since Boebert's views on immigration and English were exactly what you'd
imagine. She didn't even carry a gun. But when I returned the next
day for lunch, the place was packed with thick-boned ranchers and
their children, some carrying—the ranchers, not the children, though
that would come in due time—and builders, construction workers on
break. There were three tall white crosses at the entrance, and a life-
size cardboard Trump, and an image of Trump cut into an American
flag made of steel, and a map of America on which was tacked play
money—what looked like a $20, featuring Trump; a $1,000 bill, featuring Trump—and a picture of John Wayne. There was a woodcut of
"We the People" above an AR-15. A woodcut of a Blue Lives Matter
flag bracketed by AR-15s. A wooden sign that listed "Top Ten Reasons Why Men Prefer Guns Over Women." (Number 1: "You can buy
a silencer for a gun!") The waitresses by day were young and looked
White. The guns riding their hips were huge. I spied an empty seat
between two men at the counter. Both wore black T-shirts with a
monochrome American flag on the sleeve. Maybe they were together.
It's the practice of such men to leave space between them. I sat in it.
Neither nodded. I tried the man on my right. His shirt advertised
Shooters, his red hat MAGA, the gun on his hip a certain sense of the
American threat level. He looked like he'd been left a long time in the
deep fryer. He had a notebook; he seemed to be doing figures.

"Manager?" I asked. He agreed that he was. "I'm a reporter." I
tapped my own blank page. He allowed that I might be. "Could I
talk with you about Shooters?" That he could not permit. The boss
lady wouldn't like that. He gave me a manager smile. It didn't feel
friendly. I studied the menu.

"I recommend the Guac Nine," said the man to my left. He *did* look
friendly, or maybe lonely, which sometimes amounts to the same. His
name, he said, was David, initial "G," and he was just shy of thirty,
unarmed. His gun, he explained, was "outside." I pictured a bike rack

of assault rifles, but I realized he meant something smaller, tucked into a glove compartment, one of the 393 million firearms privately held in America. David G didn't need his at Shooters. He nodded at a pistol passing by, holstered to a young woman balancing two platters. "Bacon and cheese," said David G of the burger he thought I should order. Or there was what the menu called "Glock-a-Mole."

I explained my notebook. David G glanced past me at the manager, as if to make sure he wasn't listening. He didn't look like a nervous man. Thick, square shoulders packed into his black Shooters tee, big neck, square jaw scrimmed by an earth-red beard. Square glasses, tinted red. This, combined with arched eyebrows and an underbite that set his thin lips in a permanent half-smile, gave him the appearance of a boy in band class who has come to accept that not many care about all he knows of twenty-sided dice.

"Things," said David G, "are going down the hole. *Fast.*"

The things that hold us together.

"Civil war?" I'd learned that with patriots the question needed no framing.

"That's right. We're going down fast." *We* were the *things* that were going down. I told him about Sacramento, and Antifa versus the Saviors. He nodded, chewing. He wasn't surprised. I told him about Ashli, how I thought some people had made her a martyr—

He interrupted. "Yeah, I know her." Present tense? He didn't explain. He just folded her into the things that were going down. The shit that was coming. That's why, he said, he was in Rifle. Refugee, from Denver. Just like Lauren. Boebert, he meant, who'd moved inward, up from the city.

"What happened in Denver?"

"I got into trouble." He did not care to say what kind. He stared at the television over the counter. Fox News. "MURDERS," it read in big white letters. "VS 2020: +17%." In a deepening red square of alarm: "VS 2019: +133%." "The guns," he said, still staring, "are the most important thing."

The manager, I noticed, wasn't happy about our conversation. Maybe because the boss lady wouldn't be. But I was. I'd made a friend. David G and I were the lonely men, the ones who want to talk, the ones who don't have anyone else to talk to. He seemed the least threatening presence in the room, including the children. He told me he kept his serious firepower ready—at his grandma's. Hidden. Where he lived, he had only BB guns. "Decoys."

Who did he mean to fool?

"I have two green cards acting as roommates."

I pictured two bureaucratic rectangles, printed on green card stock, with arms and legs, doing a little roommate dance.

"They barely speak a lick of English. And you can't trust someone you don't understand."

True enough. But wasn't it him who was trying to deceive, with his decoys?

"We are in a tinderbox situation." I thought of the smoke in the air. Something I'd heard on the radio. A fire warning, issued for the first time in ten years. "Critical extreme."

"What is it that will put us over the brink?" I asked.

Had he not told me about the guns at his grandma's? He thought that the fact that he had to hide his guns meant it might well soon be time to use them. "Veterans, myself included, will rise up when the moment comes." He'd had six months in the Army. What had he learned? "I was almost blown up." I didn't follow the lesson. It happened twice, in training. Mortars landed next to him. His mistake or the artillerist's? Not the point. Here he perched, polishing off another fat plate from Shooters. The point was that he'd been in the shit, even if the shit was self-inflicted. The point was, he was prepared. "I'm indestructible," he said. What ended his Army career? "Something like asthma." Now he was a UPS driver. "Not a single army in the world can stop us." The UPS drivers? The veterans. The men with hidden guns. The world pushes them, he said. It does. It pushes, this world. It takes. "Little bits at a time, taking little bits from us." Like erosion, like the wind. You don't notice. You think you're standing your ground, but the ground crumbles. You step back. You eyeball the green cards. Possibly, you tweet. Maybe you march. Up Constitution Avenue. January 6. Now the course of things is reversing: *You* take. You take ground. Press forward—

"Ashli Babbitt?" I said.

David G nodded slowly, looking at me through his red-tinted glasses. "I met her. I met Ashli Babbitt. It was a truck stop. Ashli Babbitt." This was before Ashli Babbitt became "Ashli Babbitt." How had he wound up talking to her? "Just like you and me, talking now." Nothing flirty. Just two people at a counter. Only later would he know her, would he himself understand his close contact with the spirit of history. "I never forget a face," he explained. He hadn't watched the video. He'd never seen her die. "It popped up on the Facebook." Her face. Such was his "feed," filled with the face of a woman he believed he had met, to whom he had been nice, who in return had been nice to him, as not many were, and now she was gone and everywhere at the same time. He dreamed he saw her. He wondered if it could have been him, in the broken window, leading the charge. He thought of the mortars. Maybe it almost had. "The way they killed her," he said, "made me feel like I don't like people anymore." Correction: He'd never really liked them. Individuals, yes, but not "people." "People" bullied him as a child. People do that sort of thing. He'd learned to fight. That's why he didn't carry. "I start with my fists." Where does it end?

I noticed on his shirtsleeve a Scripture citation running down the side of a monochrome American flag, Joshua 1:9. Same as on the patriot pastor's shirt at the Ashli rally, same as on Pastor Dave's AR-15 at Glad Tidings. The battle verse, *rak chazak amats*. It was on a lot of Shooters merch. The front of the shirt featured the fragmented snake of the Revolutionary-era "Join, or Die" flag, only, it read "Liberty or Death."

"Are you a man of faith?"

"Absolutely." He felt guided by Joshua 1:9. He wanted to say it from memory. " 'Have I not' "—his voice deepened and stumbled as if entering a dark cave. He closed his eyes. "Have I not commanded you? Be strong and—Be strong and—" He couldn't remember. It's all right, he said. Joshua 1:9 was the weapon he always carried. He pulled out his phone. Tapped and it was there.

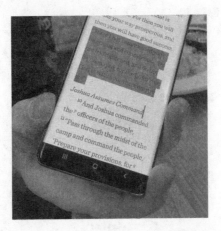

"How will I know when things are going down the hole?" I asked.

"You get into the city areas, you will see the people." Which people? The "instigators." I'd see them fighting in the streets. "When I say it's going down the hole fast, I'm talking about that. I'm talking about those of us who have less tolerance for the instigators." *The instigators.* "So some will resort to, let's just say, other methods." Militia? He smiled. "I'm not saying I'm *not* militia." He would say he was a man of peace. The militia movement, he said, stands for "any reasonable method to promote peace." Like guns. He offered his favorite quotation: "'People who know violence and are capable of violence are always the persons to pick peace.'" He didn't know who said this.

David G finished his meal, and I moved on to a table of five men. One grumbled for all: "You don't want to hear my point of view." The manager approached. I was small, he was smaller, but his chest appeared to have inflated. Did his hand hover near his sidearm? Impossible. It wasn't that kind of situation. Was it? He stood there. I stood there, too, eyeing my uneaten Guac Nine. It was time to leave. Not that I thought he was going to draw his gun. It wasn't like that. That would defeat the point of the gun. He didn't need to. The point of the gun was the promotion of peace.

7. Golden

Tséstho'e (Cheyenne) and Núu-agha-tʉvʉ-pʉ (Ute) land

In Golden, Colorado, where the mountains begin to ease into the plains, a friend took me to visit a garden shaped like a shield. It was at the heart of an intentional community—something like a commune with boundaries—presided over by a magnificent cotton-wood tree. One entered the garden by crossing a little wooden span over a stream. Within, a gardener guided us from herb to herb, this one to make you sleepy, this one to make you alert. The gardener told us about a novel he had written. It was called *Tickling the Bear*, and it was about a recurring nightmare he had endured for many years, of a bear breaking into his home. He hadn't known what to do. Then, in his dream, he tried tickling the bear. It worked—the bear laughed, and apologized, and moved on. The gardener said this might be a metaphor.

We'd been joined by a very old woman. She stayed standing on the bridge. The day was dry and hot. She wore a black winter coat. She looked ashen, her skin like parchment and her hair like a thin gray cap. She seemed not ancient but *after*. She was very beautiful. Her name, she said, was Lorraine. Her voice was like old silver. She had lived there a long time. I told her how much I admired the great cottonwood. "The mother tree," she said. She enjoyed think-ing about what to call things. About the names we lay upon things, and the bridges of perception between these names and the things themselves. She liked to think about the smaller parts of words. Lately she'd been thinking about a suffix, "-ness," and what hap-pens when you add "-ness" to a word. *Likeness. Hopefulness.* "How it brings you inside," said Lorraine. She was intrigued by what hap-pened when you add "-ness" to words with which it does not normally belong. "*Andness*," she said. "What does *andness* mean?" The conjunction, the joining of things.

"Treeness," I said, looking at the mother tree. A quality of being.

This delighted Lorraine. She was an artist, she worked on paper. She had been studying traditional Chinese and Japanese poetry, because she was interested in the way different paper takes water and ink. Silk paper, she had learned, had influenced the shape of certain letters. She thought about that. The flow of ink on silk, in contrast to the chiseling of stone. The difficulty of drawing a curve in rock. She wondered if the shape of letters formed the shape of words. "Do the words shape the ideas?" she asked. A concern for linguists, but we had come by it in the wild, or in the garden, on the bridge, over the stream. She was very old, she said. The world would carry on without her. But she worried about the letters with which we'll do so. Sharp edges; hard corners. Abstraction. The way we don't pay much attention to—"the *wordness* of things."

We talked about my travels. Some of the people I'd met.

"American personalities," she said. She didn't mean it cruelly. "They seem so . . . disoriented. They're not—*rooted* anymore."

Maybe they had unrooted themselves. I thought of that phrase, "rootless cosmopolitan," the slur by which the ancestors of today's conspiracy theorists spoke of Jews. "Cosmopolitan," a term by which the conspiracy theorists meant flowing, mixing, changing. Threatening. What is the opposite of cosmopolitan? The people I'd been meeting were the rootless *that*—rootless anticosmopolitans—and yet also threatening. They still believed they *were* rooted, in land that'd always been theirs, even if like Golden—Cheyenne and Núu-agha-t̶u̶v̶u̶-p̶u̶ land—it had once been someone else's. Even if they'd come there from elsewhere. David G in the mountains, up from the plains, Brian at the gun store, up from the bayou.

"Their talking points," said Lorraine. "The things they repeat from Fox News, have nothing to do with where they are. They draw them from air." The "talking points," like toxic balloons, lifted them off the land. Away from words that might come to be shaped like the things around them.

We considered the smallness of some words, through which so much meaning passes and is transformed. I told her I love prepositions.

"Yes!" she said. The sun, dappling through cottonwood trees, played over her skin. We considered where we stood. Were we on the bridge, or in the garden? "*On* or *in*," she mused, repeating the words as if they were the names of flowers.

8. In Omaha

On Očhéthi Šakówiŋ and Omaha land

Sunday morning, present tense now, on the brink of a plain of cracked and broken blacktop, parched almost to whiteness. The husks of a former strip mall. Pizza Machine, offering bumper cars and "thrill rides"; in what was once perhaps a JCPenney, a church, West Omaha Baptist; in what was once perhaps a Sears, another church, Heartland Hope; and in between, in what was once perhaps a Best Buy, or, at least, has since been reconstructed to look like a brand-new Best Buy, LORD OF HOSTS, the church I'm attending. Pastor Hank Kunneman, presiding, maybe the most militant of self-declared prophets on the national scene, who does not deny Covid-19 but celebrates it, who declares "this virus is the spirit of God," who channels messages from Christ that Trump will return. When? Soon. He's coming, sayeth the Lord. It might be Trump the man or Trump the idea, in another man's skin, because prophecy never errs but its truth takes many forms.

The sanctuary is full for the day's second service, believers standing or shaking or dancing, a crowd of singers and players onstage and a double bubble of glass for two drummers. There's a good ol' boy on bass, a Black man with a mohawk singing, a cast of White witches à la Stevie Nicks as backup singers. At Glad Tidings, the congregation only listened; here they sing. The worship band strips it down to a slow, thick beat. A Black man behind a bright-red keyboard takes over vocals: "Ain't no *rock*, gonna cry in my place..." This song is standard megachurch fare, but LORD OF HOSTS is doing what they will with it, and it is good. And frightening. Chills, the witchy women coming in like a chain gang. Nothing cute. Like they're breaking stone. A young Black woman across from me, tight jeans, tight tee, throws her head back, eyes closed; an old White man in front of me, work boots and buzz cut and skin like the cracked parking lot, bows his head, one fist up, stomping with the drum; the

Latinx dude next to me, long-haired and green-eyed and beautiful, moans. Just another Sunday. [17]

A big White woman grabs hold of the lead vocal. I hear a classic rock echo—"Total Eclipse of the Heart," by Bonnie Tyler, *"Turn around, bright eyes. . ."*—and then the drums, *boom! Ba-da-doom!* But this one goes out to the Lord. "Every man"—deep breath—"will booow down . . . " It's another "Contemporary Christian" standard, but LORD OF HOSTS has jam-band plans, segueing into a drum-driven, dirge-like chant. "All glory—all power—belong—to—*You*." Taking the congregation into trance time, the chorus no longer singing but testifying, the lead vocalist's comprehensible words falling away as the gift of tongues descends upon her.

And here's Pastor Hank. Crouch-walking onto the stage, like a tiger, an older White man well tanned beneath dark chestnut hair so perfect it looks snap-on. He's wailing on air guitar. "C'mon!" he shouts. "C'mon!" Eyes closed, doubled over. Thin belt, dark shirt, pocket square, cufflinks shining. The screen behind him a cosmic swirl. This is the part of the service when he prophesies, a *verb*, rocking back and forth, holding the mike like a joint. *Inhale.* A woman near me screams: "Papa! I love you, Papa! Paaapaaa!" She means God. Or Hank. She collapses into the arms of the ponytailed man

---

17 Right—but what's the point? Why go on about the barely sublimated eroticism and ecstasy of a congregation I've already let you know is in denial of death, embracing the virus, stoking the return of a fascism not really gone? Is it that they, too, have "feelings"? Like, "we're really all the same underneath"? No—we really are not. We've made different choices. We're on different timelines. The current year or 1776, the forever election of 2020 or 1619, backwards or beyond, past 2030—last chance, say some scientists, to keep the temperature down—into an age of elegy, in which this congregation's tears, or yours or mine, will all be equal: liquid milliliters added to the deepening ocean. I register the emotional temperature as well as the facts of the congregation, not because we are "all the same" but because the congregation's grief, like mine, like maybe yours, transubstantiates into the rising tide.

beside her, her body convulsing. "A release in the spirit realm," Pastor Hank murmurs over a simmer of synth and drum. His voice deep and comic, earnest because you hear that he doesn't need to be, that mockery is within his range. So, too, evidently, is the voice of God Himself, speaking now in the first person through His vessel, Hank, suddenly booming: "Therefore, pay attention, as they fill your sky." Pause, eyes closed, fingers up like antennae. Receiving. "Great warfare!"

In other prophecies Pastor Hank has said that sometimes Jesus reveals himself to Hank in combat fatigues and a trim white T-shirt. Once, he says, the roof of the sanctuary lifted clear off, and a warrior in "Indian headdress, the tallest feathers that I ever saw," hurled a flaming spear at Hank's feet, and told him, "Now, take this nation!" The warrior Christ, an old tradition surging again now in America. A Native Christ, in Hank's vision, passing his torch to a White man.

"Drought, great heat, will be upon the land!" Pastor Hank cries. *Yes, Lord,* says the man beside me, as if grateful for this renaming of the sizzle outside as not "climate crisis" but confirmation of the divine. That's how prophecy works. More diagnosis than prognosis. More description than soothsaying. It can be a means of deception or perception, or both at the same time.

"I am the God that separates light from darkness!" cries Hank-as-God, speaking the language of QAnon divorced from its source. Or returned to it, since Q, and the crisis dream of the Right in America, is trickle-down Book of Revelation. "You cannot run! You cannot resist!" God-Hank hollers. He vaults into the mysterious syllables of tongues. The instruments throb. He returns to English. "C'mon, keep screaming at me!" he calls to the church, and it does. Hank air-drums, the double-bubble drummers hit a military beat, and the chorus cries, "Let the army of the Lord arise!"

224 › The Undertow

Then we all sit down.

To say such frenzy is stage-managed does not mean that it is false. The frenzy is real, and the faith itself is fact, even as it displaces both reality and the subtler possibilities of belief. The body of the sermon is a montage of the same anxieties and furies that animated David Straight. But Pastor Hank can almost make it sound sane, which is why he's a regular on a Christian news show called *Flashpoint*, along with a rotating cast of the prophetic Far Right and their semi-secular counterparts, such as General Flynn and Congresswoman Boebert. Hank, though, is a book lover. Mixed in with calls for holy rage—"I *know* I'm making you mad!" he boasts—directed at the usual suspects—mask-mandators and vaccine genociders and all the many pedophiles—is a special venom for those who would read Scripture on Kindle, or some other wicked app, subject to Big Tech revision. "'Well, I got my phone,'" Pastor Hank says in a dummy voice—he is a great performer of voices. Then, in his angry own: "When's the last time you opened the book, cracked the book, read the book?" The Book. The Bible. He may love only one book, but he loves it a whole lot, paper, ink, and stitching. I look down at the phone in my hand.

And then, it seems, Pastor Hank is looking at *me*. I'd announced myself as a journalist on arrival, asked an usher before the service if I might meet Pastor Hank after the sermon. So maybe he's been warned. Or maybe he's receiving signals from God. A warning. About me. "I have a sense," he says, "there's a reporter in here!" Fee, fi, fo, fum. He chops his Bible through the air like an ax, like he's about to hurl it at—me? How could he see me beyond the lights? How could he know which one I am? Now the message is *for* me. "We *welcome* you! Report on! Write on! I hope you enjoy yourself!" The truth is, I have been. The music, the fantasia. Great material. "I hope," sneers Hank, "you enjoy working for people that pay you to *lie* and distort the truth." He fake-applauds. Here is his mockery. And now here is his earnest: "Your *sin* will find you out."[18]

But the real topic of today's sermon is the Pentecost, its "violent wind," as the Book of Acts describes the Holy Spirit coming upon the followers of Jesus, instilling in them "tongues of fire." The *fire* part is what Pastor Hank has come to tell us about, versus what he derides as the effete manners of so-called Christians afraid to take the Kingdom of Heaven by force. He mocks such manners by imitating the voice of a timid preacher, who apparently speaks with a Scottish brogue: " 'There came this gentle breeze . . .' " Then a piss joke: "Mary, Jesus's mother, felt the *trickle*"—a roll of the r—"of His presence." The flock is in full guffaw. Now he imitates an American dummkopf, a normie who thinks faith is a personal matter: " 'But Pastor, it's all about the heart!' " Gales of laughter. Here it's about power.

At nineteen, Hank says, God sent him to North Omaha—Black Omaha—to start a ministry. "I started knocking on doors, said, 'I'm gonna hold Bible studies.' They said, 'You can't do that! You're a White guy!' I said, 'I didn't know that!' " And he means it—he *was* a White guy. Past tense. "I grew up a little perpendicular"—he squares his shoulders, uptight. "Everything was rigid, reserved, quiet."

---

18 It's usually considered bad form to include moments such as these—when a subject of your story challenges the very terms on which the story is made. We tell ourselves—the journalists, that is—that we exclude such reversals because they make too much of ourselves, even in a first-person narrative. It might seem like we're highlighting our risk. Like we're trying to make ourselves seem brave. So we gloss over this reflexive turn, for the sake of decency, of modesty, of not mentioning the coercive collaboration that occurs whenever you enter a private space into which you're uninvited with a notebook in hand. "They write about you and all their fake news things," Pastor Hank preaches. "And then they reach out. 'We reached out to the LORD OF HOSTS church for comment.' No, you didn't! You liar!" But I did. I did reach out, and I was rebuked, and I did almost write this without mentioning this portion of Pastor Hank's sermon.

Then he went to a Black church. "Nineteen years old!" Born again, again. "All the sudden, I get there, and the preacher comes up"—the keyboardist lets rip a little snort of organ, meant to be Black gospel—"and he says, 'Aahyeahoooh!'" Big organ blast and cheers front row to back. Hank has brought the congregation—which is, after all, still mostly White—over into the Promised Land. Authenticity. Blackness. By way of a minstrel act. The Black preacher called young Hank up to preach. Hank mimes his former stiff-hipped self. He opened to John 3:16. "For God so loved the world." He started to read it like—his voices goes nasal and flat, nerdy and sanctimonious. Then he drops it down to deep velvet: "But there was an organ behind me." The synth player riffs. "And something came on me! And all of a sudden, I said—" He delivers John 3:16, in his best impression of a Black gospel preacher, which devolves into meaningless but ecstatic syllables, and then a James Brown coda: "Yeah! I feel good!" That's how Black Hank Kunneman is in his telling. Blacker than Black. "*You* feel like Michael Jackson," he says, speaking to the White people who can't handle his gospel. He starts to moonwalk in mockery. His voice becomes a high-pitched mince: "Worship is not my thing, so just beat it!"

On it goes, bouncing between pews' worth of different ridiculous White-man voices as channeled through Hank, to which Black Hank responds each time with his gospel howl. When he started his church, he says, he asked the Lord to spare him "people like this"—he means the prim honkies—and says the Lord gave him a gift. "You know what it was?" They do—"Black people!" And the people, most of them White, exalt, over the Black people they believe God has given them.

"Officer," calls Pastor Hank—there are men who look like cops in tactical gear stationed at the back—"you're not gonna put cuffs on me are you?" It's a joke. "That's another thing. People say"—yet another White-man's voice, this one like a cranky old shopkeeper from Long Island—"'Why do you have officers in the church?'" Oh, the flock finds this funny. Pastor Hank, to the shopkeeper: "Why don't you shut up!" Even better. But here's the real answer: "Because they get mistreated and lied about, too, out in public. They need to be honored. And don't let the media convince you through race wars that they're all bad!" The true church, preaches Pastor Hank, is armed. God's angels are warriors, and yet, Hank concedes, you can't always see the angels. That's why we need cops. "You sure see a cop with a gun!"

It is, says Pastor Hank, like Psalm 23. The people around me nod. Maybe they've heard this before. Not me—I thought 23 was a gentle one. Pastor Hank recites the version I know, in the voice of a country vicar sipping tea: "The Lord is my shepherd," Hank lisps. "He makes me lie down in green pastures." Eye roll. "Now watch this." Hank shouts: "Thy *rod*"—he wants us to feel the firmness of the word—"and thy staff do comfort me." Thy rod; thy gun. Whoever these men in the back are, they're carrying.

❯❮

After the sermon I wait in the lobby, near the merch, hoping to meet Pastor Hank. I've read online that his passion is model railroading, and I have this idea that maybe I can persuade him to show me his set, his little miniature world. We'll talk about how things ought to be as we survey his tiny towns and trees, he'll tell me his right ratio of steeple to store to prison. I don't imagine we'll see eye to eye. We won't try to. We'll look down on a land where he is sovereign, where the truth is entirely in his hands. I've met men like Hank before. "It's no accident you came here," they say. Pastor Dave had said it. They always do. They view me as a vessel. Even if I am deaf to their meaning, they believe, I'll be a carrier for the contagion of their words. God, they think, is a virus.

But in response to my request, ushers in blue blazers multiply. A White man in body armor, with what Pastor Hank calls a rod, a big one, stands by. An usher named Lester tells me, You're waiting for nothing. He's tall, older, a veteran pin in his lapel. "But, but," I say. Lester doesn't give ground. He takes it. Leans in. Looking down. A journalist can't be redeemed. I'm beyond infection. This, in a church, has never happened to me before.

I leave the church's bone-chilling AC. Outside, it's near ninety, sun straight up and crashing down into the broken blacktop. Huddled as if indifferent to the sweat beading their fair skin are three women who're willing to talk about what we've just been through. One, with bright blond hair and a flowing tie-dyed dress, I recognize as a barefooted dancer from within. Standing next to her is a woman with rich brown cascading curly hair, and beside her, much smaller, grown but built like a child, a woman who grins unceasingly and blankly. They're visitors, the woman in the tie-dye dress says. They've driven hours to be here.

"Like me," I offer.

No—"*we* came on purpose," Tie-Dye says, as if I'd arrived as flotsam. "Because we're spirit-filled Christians." My notebook suggests I'm not. How had they known LORD OF HOSTS was here? The middle woman, with the curly hair, takes over. She's a former student of Pastor Hank's spiritual father, Pastor Rod Parsley. I know the name—a self-declared "Christocrat" who once distributed swords in exchange for donations to a campaign he said would help Christian rebels in Sudan, sort of a knives-for-guns program. Curly had attended Parsley's Valor College, where Pastor Hank was a frequent guest to discuss God and politics, which in his telling are one and the same: *Authority*, that of the man who speaks for, or as, God. We have a "biblical right," says Curly, to a government led by such men. The ones God chooses.

"Look at the Constitution," says Tie-Dye. "The Bill of Rights is the

Ten Commandments!" (It's not.) Her face flushes red. "You have to get mad for the truth," she says by way of explanation.

How mad?

"It could get there," says Curly. The big bang, she means, the nuclear option of American history. Civil war, if not in fact, then in our hearts. She says the other side—she means people like me—has already begun. Look at the lockdowns, look at the closed churches, the way they try to "turn Christians off"—like lights. A switch. Click. They're gone. She's afraid of disappearing. They might do it with a bullet, they might do it with a law, or they might sneak into your phone. Erase you by changing the words.

"Critical—" I begin.

"*Race theory*," Curly concludes. An edit—two words instead of three—that may come closer to the truth she is mad at and for.

"The Midwest," says Tie-Dye. "It's not as"—she scans the parking lot for the word—"*diverse*."

"Mmm-hmm," murmurs Curly.

"We're still the Bible belt," says Tie-Dye.

"Mmm-hmm."

"Our roots are deep."

We're getting into it now. And we're soaked, Tie-Dye and Curly and me, sweating like it's a sauna. The three of us are practically a stew. Double, double, toil and trouble. The quiet little smiling woman on the side doesn't seem to feel heat.

Deep roots. Not like those other people, the ones on "the coasts," Tie-Dye says, the ones in "the cities," the ones—she stops, she needs another polite word like *diverse*.

Their grinning friend has it: "the edges!" she cries, thrilled to be heard.

But diversity, I say. Pastor Hank's church. Must be at least one-third people of color. And yet—

"Hey." A church usher, Marquise, has joined us, a skinny young

Black man, blue blazer and cornrows. Positioned behind him, hands crossed, is one of the armored cops, a White man standing a pace back, blank-faced. "How's it going," says Marquise. Not a question. A tattoo of what I think is a little girl praying, steepled hands, rises up his neck from the collar of his white dress shirt. "Are you conducting interviews?" he says. Also not a question. I want to say no—they're testifying. I'm witnessing. Instead, I smile. Marquise spreads his long arms wide, like he's holding us together. Like we're all guilty. The church, he says, "didn't authorize any interviews today. So, unfortunately, we can't have any interviews."

The ladies sweat.

"I'm sorry," I say. Then, to the man with the gun: "You're an officer?"

"I'm a security guard." He stares. He's good at the deadeye. Black combat gear head to toe. He appears to be wearing a tactical vest over body armor with what to my ignorant eye are two extra magazines. Big gun on his hip; on his chest, dead center, an American flag in black and gray. Not for this warrior the deceptions of color.

We're not members of the church, I say. Just four people in a parking lot. Talking.

The women don't move.

Marquise nods. "Well. You can do that." Except, he means, we can't. "But you're conducting interviews on the church's ground." It's a parking lot. But I stay silent. "So that's different," concludes Marquise. He says if we were talking about "today's game," it would be one thing. But he senses we're talking about God. And on this land, that topic belongs to Pastor Hank and his shepherds, with their rods and their staffs. He smiles. "There's a proper way to do things."

A proper way? I did ask, I say. I told them I was here. That's why he knows I'm here. That's why he saw four people talking outside and decided we required the intervention of a man with a gun.

But I don't say all that. Because he did bring a man with a gun. Instead, I hold up my notebook. As if to show him, just words. I hold up my purple mechanical pencil. Click, click, until the slender lead disconnects and tumbles to the broken ground. But I talk; I keep talking. As if there are words. I tell Marquise, and the gunman, that yes, it's true, I don't believe as they believe. I know it. They know it. But I did come to listen. I'm not from here, I say, and they know that too. But I am headed home, I tell them, only I'm taking the long way, and that's how I came here. "I don't really do interviews," I say. I show them the first pages of my notebook, in which I had not written any questions.

Maybe that would have worked. But then I say, "I meant no offense." Which is a lie. I know even in this moment that what I will do with Pastor Hank's words—"twist them," he will charge; "print them," I will say—will offend them. Marquise knows too. His lips curl. It is not a smile.

"I don't think you mean harm," he says, meeting my lie with his. "There's just a lot of evil media out there. Portraying the wrong things. Taking the things the pastor says. Putting him out there. So we have to be that way now." He nods back at the gunman, who is saying something into his radio. "That's who we are today."

A senior churchwoman arrives. White woman with towering blond hair, draped in what looks like rivers of gold. "C'mon, ladies, come with me," she whispers. *Leave the men to their business.* We are left to our business. The gunman steps forward. I feel my heart in my neck, my ears. I have learned, over the years, to be aware of my blood pressure. I like to keep it that of a lizard. But I know mine now is very high.

Which is where, in this story, I should mention that several years ago, at a young age, I had two heart attacks, that I attribute them to an accumulation of moments such as this, that I vowed then, on the table, as fentanyl dripped into me, that if I lived, I would thereafter run from trouble.

I look at the little girl tattooed on Marquise's neck. Her praying hands. I can see his veins. His pressure is high too. I look at the gunman. Still dead-eyed. I've met enough like him to know how they see themselves being seen when the crisis they long for finally arrives.

Marquise steps off the curb. Closing space. It's time for me to leave. I'm sweating through my shirt. I'm sweating through my jacket.

Marquise drops his left shoulder.

I raise my notebook.

"I guess," I say, "I have a question." He cocks his head. "I certainly—I—" I'm stammering. "I'm asking questions, and you're bringing a man with a gun, to tell me to get out of church?"

"Well," says Marquise, eyes flicking back to the man with the gun. "He didn't say anything. Yet."

"You brought law enforcement."

"No," Marquise says.

"Right there."

Marquise smiles. "He works for *us*."

"A man with a gun?"

"How do we know you're not some crazy person trying to do us harm?"

"I have a notebook and a pencil."

"Reporters twist words."

It's time for me to leave. I'm dizzy. It's so hot out here. I feel it crackle in my sternum. I feel it tingle in my left arm. I keep saying these two useless words: *notebook, pencil.* Holding them up. *Notebook! Pencil!* And, "You brought a man with a gun!"

Marquise comes forward. All of him. Not puffing up his chest—that's a posture, that's a bluff. Curling his chest in, protecting his core. It's his jaw that worries me, his lower jaw, jutting. Pulling the incisors back. It forces the mouth open, the teeth slightly apart. It forces a smile. A rictus. I've seen it before. Not performance; instinct. Anger, and something terrible, like joy.

"I mean," I say—very dizzy now—"I mean"—as if we might yet agree on a mismatch of terms, "pencil! Gun."

Marquise breathes. "How do you know," he says, "*I* don't have a gun?"

9. Holiday City, Ohio

Bodéwadmiakiwen (Potawatomi), Kiikaapoi (Kickapoo), Meškwahki·aša·hina (Fox), Myaamia, and Peoria land

An American question: "How do you know I don't have a gun?" Open carry, concealed carry, a backpack, a trigger, made of metal or in the mind. How did Marquise know *I* didn't have one? How did the cop who killed Ashli know that the woman climbing through the window was unarmed? One man wears ammunition strapped to his chest, beneath an American flag; another keeps it in his pocket. Ashli had a knife in hers. What are you packing?

I backed away from Marquise and the gunman, hands out, half-up. Part of me thinking "stay," thinking, "what a story." Thinking they wouldn't draw. Thinking what a strange verb—*draw*. Like together we might make a picture. Thinking of Ashli on the marble floor, illuminated, her bright blood, her blue flag, the gold of her hair.

The worst Marquise and the gunman were really likely to do was a throw jab, a cross, a shove. How easily I'd fall! I could almost hear the crack of my skull against the blacktop. My heart, the heat, the pounding already present in my brain. I pivoted away from them, willing myself not to look back and failing. The gunman in his black armor, Marquise in his blue blazer, watching me leave.

When I got to my car, the first thing I did was turn on the AC; then I reached over to the glove and opened it, to make sure they were still there. Fiona's ashes. My stepmother. A little wooden box.

I'd left the car unlocked. A thief in the sun reaches past my computer on the front seat, opens the glove. This is what he steals? Of course not. The ashes were still there. A dead woman's remains.

What was it I was really doing here, in a parking lot in Omaha, measuring my pulse with two fingers? What was it that was so frightening? I went looking for trouble and I found it and now I realized what a fool I'd been. We're past the days of "looking for trouble" in America. They were always an illusion. Trouble has always already been present. That's the fear I felt racing too fast under the skin of my left wrist. I left LORD OF HOSTS, drove out of sight, pulled into another mostly dead strip mall, and noticed I'd parked in front of a gun store. I put my hand on the little wooden box of Fiona's ashes.

A Scotswoman born in Jamaica, raised in Trinidad and Canada and Edinburgh. Came to New York as a young woman, harbored always that British dream of the desert even as she was alert to the formation of that dream by the empire, the aftermath of which was her life's exploration; dreaming it anyway, longing to drive west, even though she knew the land had been taken. She was a gladly rootless woman, a brilliant cosmopolitan. I'd planned to join her for the drive when, eighty-seven-years-old, she moved to Golden, to be with her middle son, after my father died. He had been her love across forty-five years. But I didn't; something came up. I can't recall.

I was driving away from Omaha, trying to remember. Why didn't I drive west with her? I would visit, I promised. Then lockdown, virus, her age, my heart, kids in Zoom school. I stayed home. Then her cancer—abrupt, like a sudden gust, weeks from diagnosis to death. One day she was climbing a mesa, the next she was in bed, soon she was gone. So her three sons climbed the mesa and put her ashes into the wind. They saved some for me. In Golden, I, too, put a portion into the wind. And I kept a portion in this box, which I tucked into my glove compartment, to carry home to my children. We would sprinkle Fiona's ashes in the duck pond to which she had liked to bring the kids. One of the last times we talked she said to tell them that yes, she was dying but by her bed she had a window. "I can see the dawn," she said, winded, each sentence standing alone.

"I can see the doves.

"The doves fly by.

"A drove of doves.

"I have a tree, the doves land, and they fly. And I watch the geese—the geese flying south."

I told her it sounded like a poem, but she misheard me. "Yes," she said, "I'm home."

The truth is this entire journey, from a rally for Ashli back to home, was conceived slant rhyme to the story I'm telling. Searching not for Ashli's ghost but for my own grief, and through it maybe something of the grief that is in us all now, if not often spoken of. Or maybe it is *on* us, like the smoky sun. The fire's ashes sift down into our lungs. All the dead whom we have not mourned. The passing of certain possibilities—democratic, ecological—imagine the gunman, feel the heat rising—which we still speak of in the present tense, as if they're not already gone.

We say we are in crisis. The crisis of democracy—the gun—the crisis of climate—the fire, the water, the rain—the crises of our own little lives—debt and Twitter and rage, and most of all the ordinary losses of love and loved ones that feel too vast. But that word, *crisis*, supposes we can act. It supposes the outcome is yet to be determined. The binary yet to be toggled, a happy ending or a sad one, victory or defeat. As if we have not already entered the aftermath.

Will we save democracy, or lose it? Will the earth boil, or will we all drive electric cars? Are the dead gone, or do they live in our hearts forever?

Such imaginations we have.

Fiona's ashes, in the wind and destined for the duck pond; Ashli's, which her family sprinkled from a simple wooden box, into swirling waters off Dog Beach, which she loved more than anyplace in the world. While a bagpiper played "Amazing Grace." A woman sang it at my mother's funeral, and we played a version at Fiona's memorial over Zoom, and maybe you have played it, or will play it, for your dead too. It's a beautiful song.

I drove east, thinking of ashes, Fiona's and Ashli's. Merging, in my mind. As they were in the world, let loose into the water and the wind. Nothing deep there—I was leaving Nebraska but thinking like a Kansas song, "Dust in the Wind," which really is a pretty little tune. In Iowa I stopped to visit a friend, another journalist who like me wanders sometimes, who like me has noticed that where once we were taken in as strangers by those we hoped to know, now we are received too often as enemies. She spoke about that common problem of journalism, "parachuting in." A reporter from the big city drops into a small town to collect color at the local diner. Why, I'd done it in Rifle. The opposite of such a practice is immersion, rooting yourself in one place, one story, for a duration. Parachuting, immersion—these are metaphors of the vertical. I was on the horizontal, cutting a line. Not an immersion, a cross-section. An incision. Draw a scalpel across the country, see if it bleeds.

The body's inert. All this simmer and civil-war talk—merely sifting the ashes. Fighting over bits of bone. How does a body come apart? It already has. The country's already gone. My metaphors are mixing here, I know, "ashes," "the body," as if they are not just different ways to name the same wordless ground. We lack a language that could encompass what this place—this land of stories—was and what it is, what it may become. So my metaphors are mixing. Rootless. Cosmopolitan.

><

The motels were full. So many trucks. I needed to sleep but it seemed it wouldn't be an option, until I came to a room in Holiday City,

Ohio. Pop. 47. Not much but a truck stop, and that was just a gas station with a glowing chamber of knives that made me think of Ashli's.

That suggests I think Ashli's knife mattered, but I'm not sure I do. It was part of the investigation—

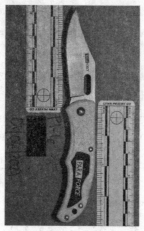

—but the investigation was closed. There were other investigations stemming from January 6, many hundreds, but I do not believe they will ever, in a true sense, be "resolved." This isn't that kind of story. The crisis kind. The kind in which the outcome is yet to be determined. It isn't a "crisis," January 6, any more than the fire and heat I'd been driving through all these miles. It's a condition. Our condition. The one we share.

10. The Book of Hot Dog

The Hub, Holiday City, Ohio

The tense is shifting again. The present tense.

In the morning I head out to my car, not really rested—there is no sleep on this drive—and across the road I see a black sign that reads in white letters:

Ohio Ablaze
REVIVAL IS NOW!

Behind it, three boys are stretching out the giant canvas of what will be their tent. "You're holding a tent revival?" I ask.

One of the boys shrugs. "I guess?" He doesn't plan to attend. It's just a job.

"Is there anybody from the church here?"

"I guess?" He nods at a metal door red with rust. "I saw some dude go in there."

It's locked. I walk round front and try another. Locked. But then, out comes the dude: big man, Brown skin, shaved head, thick goatee. He's wearing long black shorts and a giant black T-shirt featuring a screaming white skull breast to belly. "You looking for something?" he asks, neither friendly nor not, since I am, after all, rattling his locked door.

"Yeah," I say, "I am." I'm a writer, I tell him, working on something, but I'm not sure if I know what it is anymore.

"Huh," he says, which is exactly the right response.

I tell him I began in California, with a rally for a dead woman. "Ashli Babbitt?" I say. "The woman killed in Washington at the Capitol?"

"Uh-huh," he nods, like I'm saying nothing odd.

I'm driving cross-country, I say, following her ghost, as it were, trying to understand something about what's happening, or might be happening. Or maybe it already happened and now here we are.

"I feel you," says the dude, who I'm certain is the pastor. So I tell him also that Ashli is more like an echo now, one I keep hearing even when I know she's not there, and that my story is really about—and this is why I tried his locked door—how and why some of us believe some of what we're believing lately.

"Faith," he says, in that breathy pastor way.

"Yeah, I guess," I say. And how that "connects, maybe?" to the way things are coming apart—

"C'mon." He steps aside so I can enter. "Pete," he says. Pete Garza. Pastor Pete. A church called the Hub. Getting ready for revival. "Glad you saw our sign, man!"

›‹

Had I read the sign as a sign? I had. I set out on the road looking for evidence of Ashli's haunting, that which haunted her—the bastardized Holy Ghost she called "the spirit of 1776"—and the ways in which she now haunts us, whether we consider ourselves "us" or not. But simply *looking* is meaningless, a mechanical act. *Seeing* is interpretation. Or, *discernment*, as a preacher might say. I've tried to listen so that I could see it for a moment "their way," even as I kept seeing it mine. But somewhere in the miles past, the "frame" with which I—reason-bound, a sensible man, a citizen—filtered my discernment has lifted away. Caught in the wind, maybe. Gone up into the smoke.

I read Pastor Pete's sign as a sign because I've been awake a long time, because at 3:20 this morning I stared again at this snapshot from far back on the road—

—and because the night before that I had similar motel trouble, "no vacancy" mile after lightless Nebraska night mile, until somewhere shy of Omaha I found a room and parked my little rental between trucks and dragged myself in, trailing a sex worker. Not in my employ. Her client leaned bare-chested over the second-floor railing, watching without excitement as she teetered across broken blacktop on shiny black needle heels, heaving the giant shoulder bag in which she likely carried the sneakers into which she'd change after the fantasy had been fulfilled or at least adequately embodied. After the work was done. To save them both the trouble I let her in the door. She said "thanks," I said, "good night," and I hoped that the work would not be too loud, or, if it had to be, not take long. Pretty lonely.

Then, in my room, a surprise. Or a sign. Coincidence. מקרה. If looked at by anyone else, what I found would be meaningless. Seen by me, it was a wonder: a little stack of books. Amazing books. Maybe someone had left them. Maybe an ambitious manager, thinking to spruce the place up. Among them were four that startled me.

On top, a novel I loved as a child, about signs and wonders, aliens and strange messages transmitted through TVs.

Below it, a novel for adults about children who follow such signs into peril; at home it sits on my shelf of sacred books because in ways I can't name it makes me imagine my stepmother's life as a child.

Below that, a copy of the very book I'd planned to read that night, a Kindle copy on my phone. Also about a child, and an old woman, on an island, each learning to read the signs of their age, the child's ascendence and the old woman's decline.

Last, a novel I didn't know existed, the source material for an old movie which was the last good movie I watched with my father—a moviegoer—before he died.

The names of the books wouldn't mean much or anything to

you. None of this should—except, maybe, for the possibility that we do, after all, have some say over the patterns we choose to perceive. That we needn't simply receive signs and wonders, or "Q drops" and Trump tweets, that we needn't only acquiesce to verdicts as truth or to reports of carbon dioxide parts per million as foreshadowing. That we might instead collaborate with the data; that is, interpret. This what I want to believe that the preachers, even addled by their own filtered revelation, mean when they say to us, *discern.*[19]

19 The books were: *Lizard Music*, by Daniel Manus Pinkwater (1976); *A High Wind in Jamaica*, by Richard Hughes (1929); *The Summer Book*, by Tove Jansson (1972); and *In a Lonely Place*, by Dorothy B. Hughes (1947), the basis of a 1950 movie starring Humphrey Bogart and Gloria Grahame. I stole the copy of *The Summer Book*. It's on my desk as I write. Here—I'll open it at random (I swear): Page 139. Oh, this is—discern this: " 'Put anything you want,' said Sophia impatiently." The little girl, dictating a story to her grandmother. "Just so they'll understand. Now don't interrupt. It goes on like this: The worm probably knows that if it comes apart, both halves will start growing separately. Space. But we don't know how much of it hurts. And we don't know, either, if the worm is afraid it's going to hurt. But anyway, it does have a feeling that something sharp is getting closer and closer all the time. . . ." Too on the nose, I know, like the way in between Omaha and Holiday City a bird flew into my windshield at high speed—or, rather, don't blame the bird, *I* hit a bird, an explosion of feathers, and then the next morning, right before I look up and see that revival sign, I notice another dead bird, this one still perfectly formed, blocking my car's exit. "Lose the bird," a friend tells me when I relay this remarkable serendipity. "But the bird is a fact!" I say. My friend rightly points out that facts are things we choose. So, no bird in the body above. Just down here in the notes, where even more mysterious true-life coincidences may be revealed.

›‹

Pastor Pete and I sit at a high café table in a mostly empty hall. Before the Hub was the Hub it was another church—that sign, too, is out front, though it's been turned inward—and before that maybe a Howard Johnson's or some other roadside dining.

The first thing Pete says is "Plandemic," the term used by those who believe the pandemic has been as plotted as a pulp novel. But he must see my eyes, because big man that he is, he's light with his words and he pivots away. Toward the tent outside. He's raising it, he says, because he knows what it means to look at a church and see lies. "I have a crazy testimony, man," he says. Then he delivers it, as he has surely delivered it before, which makes it neither more nor less true, only more shaped and interpreted and reshaped until it has become a thing of vernacular beauty.

"And part of my testimony is because I grew up in the church and I saw everything." Everything awful, he means. "Some of my worst encounters was on my way to church. My mom and I would have these horrible fights. We'd go into the service, and it was like 'Hallelujah! Praise the lord.'" He twinkles his fingers in the air. "I'm like, 'You just got done slapping me around!'" His flat hand swings like his mother's. He discerned then that such must be the shape of God: the flat hand that slaps you. "So I turned, man." The usual story, sin and crime, but at high volume. "High trafficking," he says, "kilos." He stretches his hand wide as if measuring a whale. "I was full of rage, full of anger, full of hate. I didn't have a problem hurting people. This tattoo"—he holds out his arm—"it's the literal testimony of my entire life. This is the Angel of the Lord. He's got a sword."

"Do you mind if I take a picture?"

"Go ahead, man," Pastor Pete says.

"His arm is being stretched out," Pete continues. "This is the Angel of the Lord. You see how it's bright and blue up here?" Turquoise, to my eye. But I know what he means. Like the sky this morning. "But it gets really dark down here." He slides his finger to his wrist. The distance between, he says, represents not one but two heavens. "Heavenlies," a plural of heavens. Which is why, he tells me, the Bible says, "there was war in the heavenlies."

I think of something I heard two thousand miles back, in the parking lot of Glad Tidings. After Pastor Dave was done with me, I'd walked through the dark to my car. Just as I was about to pull away, there was a rap on my window: Thomas, the gentle curly-haired street pastor from the Ashli rally. He wanted to keep talking, even though it was after midnight and everybody else was gone. I wanted to go, too, but I got out of the car, shivering a little because a chill had settled on the fields. He needed me to know he'd heard the violence of the evening. He knew it was scary, and truth be told, it'd troubled him too. "The execution stuff," the trials and hangings the church hoped would come soon. But he was there because God had given him a dream in which it was revealed that Thomas was to go to Texas. Why Texas? What would he do there? This had confused him until that very evening in that very church—Glad Tidings, he'd realized, was the "Texas" of his dream. Consider, he said, what we'd heard "about execution and Old West law." The hangings. He did not love them, but there was war in the heavenlies, so now, "Texas—'Texas'—is what matters."

But it wasn't all that mattered. That's why he'd knocked on my window. He'd seen that I was shaken, and he wanted to tell me that there was more, a heaven of Texas and another one of "people who are what I call 'miracle chasers.'" Two heavenlies, or maybe just two Americas, one of those for whom justice is social, "Lefties," he said, and another of "people that are like prayer warriors," Texans, in spirit if not geographical fact, for whom justice is the sword. Thomas loved them both, the Texans and the miracle chasers. I think he knew I was not a Texan. He wanted me to know that God loves them both. Said they will meet soon, that we have come to "the season of preparation," a fact he'd learned from the pastor under whom he studied, Dutch Sheets, whom I'd later see on television trading prophecies with Pastor Hank. Preparation for what, I wanted to know. So did Thomas. He didn't have the answer. He wished me luck in my search for one. Then he let me get back in my car, and I drove two thousand miles, and now I'm looking at the Angel of the Lord on pastor Pete's arm.

"If you look closely," says Pete, "you could see the bullet holes where the angel took the shot." He lets go of his sleeve and reaches behind him. "I was shot here"—he points to the jaw of the skull on the belly of his T-shirt—"by an AK-47. It came in my stomach, from around my back." Pete follows my eyes. "I know you're looking at my shirt. You see the skull, right? So let me tell you about the skull. Ezekiel 37 talks about how he went to the valley of—"

"Dry bones," I say. I know it too. *Can these bones live?* A metaphor for faith where there is none.

"C'mon!" says Pete, grinning. We're in it now. He returns the story to the hospital, where as far as he knows he's dying. "I said what everybody says right when they're about to die. 'God, if you save me, I promise I'll change my life.' Right? Everybody does that."

Heart attack at forty-four, I tell him. I've said it too. Pete nods. We're definitely in it.

"You're like, 'Please, God!'" He stops. "There's fear-based evangelism"—the war angel on his arm—"but I believe there's another side." Miracle chasers. He asks my permission to offer a for-instance. It's three weeks ago, he says, he's holding a cookout in the parking lot. "A man drives up in his car and he parks right there across the street." Where my car's parked now. "He never gets out of the car." He doesn't, like me, try the door. "So I walk up to him. I said, 'Hey, buddy, how are you, man?'

"He says, 'I'm good.'

"I said, 'You look like you could really use a hot dog.'

"He said, 'Oh, no, no, I'm good, man.'

"I said, 'Are you sure, man?'"

Then Pete really looks at him. His whole face is covered in tattoos. "Under his right eye, it said 'Always Alone.' Right above his other eye, it said, 'Broken.'"

Maybe Pete was thinking about his own tattoos. Maybe he was just doing his job. He asked if he could pray for the man, and the man said yes, and Pete got in the car, and he prayed that God would take away his pain. Like an opiate. Opiates are powerful. Nobody's a tough guy—I'm thinking of my own heart and the fentanyl the doctors dripped into me—when they really need them.

"And he's weeping," says Pete.

"How did you know this guy"—*needed you*, is what I mean to say and don't.

Pete shrugs. "I didn't know."

"Was the car all beat up?" A guy down on his luck?

No. A sweet green Mustang with neon running along the bottom. The guy told Pete he'd been sitting in his car preparing himself. Preparing for what? This man had an answer: "I was going to run my car into a tree," he said.

Crush himself inside his beautiful Ford.

Green Mustang.

Suicide.

Pete stops. I remember the preacher on the radio, the undertow, the three sons lost at sea without an ending.

What happened?

"He's now a regular person!" He's coming to the revival. Always Alone, Broken, together with Pete, under the tent. And there'll be more hot dogs; there's going to be a whole lot of hot dogs at Pete's revival. "A simple hot dog," he says, "and loving people, is all it takes." He tells me to put that in my "theology." He means this book.

"The Book of Hot Dog," I say.

"The Book of Hot Dog!" He's delighted. "C'mon!"

><

He wants to know if I can stay in Holiday City so he can introduce me to the man with the tattooed eyes.

I wish, I say, but I've brought only so many heart pills with me on this trip. My supply is dwindling. "Gotta keep rolling."

So he keeps rolling too. Another story, a good one, he says. A miracle. It starts with a television ministry he once had. Five hundred people worshipping, "doing their thing, and this man, must have been late fifties, he was dancing, and then all of a sudden he grabs his chest, and he grabs my son by the arm and he says"—Pete pauses, shifts, body and voice. "Help! Heart!"

He says it in a White man's voice. It's my voice, I realize; he's lifted it right from me.

"He drops to the floor." They thought he was slain in the spirit, which is like speaking in tongues, only you "fall out," you fall down, like you've been killed. But this guy really is gone, Pete says. A regular dead person. For half an hour they don't notice. "His body had already turned cold. His face had already been blue. He's on the floor. He's like this." Stiff shoulders, zombie face, rigor mortis. "So check this out. Matthew 10:8 says this, it says"—with both hands he spreads out words like a marquee in lights, like one of those Jesus billboards that tick off the miles—"'Raise the dead, heal the sick, cast out the devil, and cleanse a leper, and freely give, and freely you can receive." Or, at least, that's what the Bible promises. And yet here is the dead man, and Pete a pastor, a real second-chancer, practically raised from the dead himself. "Lord, *you* said we would see the dead raised!" *You promised.* "But I haven't seen *nothing*!" His voice is angry, but his anger is grief, and over the dead man he began to cry. Because that is what we are called to do for the dead, to acknowledge loss. Loss is a fact. The miracle is mourning.

If only the story had stopped there, at solidarity with a stranger. But crouching over the dead man, Pete remembered: He, Pete, is a king. "It says that we have all the authority in heaven, right?"

Suddenly, we're not in it anymore, Pete and me. I can't follow him here. A king, he says, and I think of David Straight, the vanity of authority, at odds with the Book of Hot Dog. Raising the dead, Pete says, and I think of the ghost of Ashli, and those for whom the fact of her traitorous death is not enough to say that this dream of war is a sorrow, who insist that she was younger or smaller or braver or more generous than she was, who prop up her body for their own purposes, who put her likeness on flags and #sayhername like it's a spell to bring *them* power, like it's a curse with which to call for more corpses. Raise the dead? No; let them rest.

Pete did not. "I said, 'Everybody, go and grab a camera." The videographers, their bright light, assembled over Ashli's body bleeding out. "Follow me," Pete told the cameras. There was one sane woman among them. "What's the matter with you people?" she demanded. "Let this man rest in peace."

They did not. They prayed over the body, which was or was not dead, "and all of a sudden the breath of God is coming"—or the breath of a body, a regular person—"and he goes"—Pete sucks in a gallon of air—"and—"

You could tell the rest of this story as easily as me or Pete.

My turn to change the topic. "You're lying in the hospital," I say, picking up the story he'd dropped. Now I borrow *his* voice. "'God, if I survive, I'm going to change everything.'" Back to mine. An edge. "But a lot of people say that."

He hears it. "Right?" he says.

"Not a lot of people do it."

"Right." Pete didn't either. He's in the hospital, on the opiates, morphine or fentanyl, and he takes his vow and then he thinks of all the money he has on the street, his drugs out on the street, and he thinks about how he'll need it, the money, to change his life, how he'll need capital to follow Christ. So he says to God, "Hold on." As in, wait. And when he's up but only barely, "walking inch by inch, like a penguin, I literally had a grapefruit blown out of my back, a hole, a tunnel, where the AK-47 hit me," he goes to collect. His money, from the street. And right away, he says, he gets jumped.

By who?

That's not important.

"Stabbed!"

Why?

Leave that behind. No details. Just this thought: "Oh my God. I did it again."

And then?

"I think that's where I'll pause on that story."

We sit. We're in it again: the "it" that doesn't fit neatly. "I'll ask you this question," he says. "Who do you say God is?"

I'm about to say, "I don't." But I'm looking out the window. "I'm looking at the clouds," I tell him. "Not like 'up in heaven.' But— creation is beautiful. Even a parking lot—"

Across the parking lot, behind the gas station, there's a little yellow house. Really just a hut. Like lemon meringue pie, with a silver-gray roof. Nothing special, just a pretty little bit of color.

"That motel across the street," I tell Pete, "is not the loveliest place I've been in my life." A bleak place. The motel and me both. "And then, there's that revival sign." His sign, like a spark, even if I don't believe. Which I think means, I confess, "Keep your eyes open." I hesitate. Because his god isn't my god. *God* isn't even my word. And if it were, some of the other words he uses—*king* and *authority*—are the opposite of what it would mean to me. "God," I venture, trying to meet Pete on the ground he has invited me to share, "is someone who will show you things."

>‹

"Let me ask you a question," Pete says. Oh hell, here it comes. Just when we were in it together. He sees what I'm thinking. "Yeah," he nods. Smiling but determined. "What has stopped you from accepting Jesus? What is it?"

Christian mother, Jewish father, I say, trying to wriggle away.

"So, you have the Orthodox . . ."

No, I say. Not religious. "But I'm a Jew. I owe it to the dead."

"You owe it to the dead."

"You know what I mean?"

"Yeah." He does. Six million. OK, then. Maybe being a believer isn't what I'm meant for. In the Bible, he says, they talk about scribes.

In Ezekiel, I say. "A recording angel." My favorite angel, neither warrior nor cherub, doesn't even have wings. "The man clothed with linen, which had the writer's inkhorn by his side." Later I look up the whole verse, and it changes; the documentarian is tasked not just with making a record but inscription: "set a mark upon the foreheads of the men that sigh." I think of the cliffs of the Western Slope, streaked olive, rust, and purple. The way this reach of Ohio lies so flat you can see it bend at the horizon. The Earth curving. The geological record. Recording angels of the mineral kingdom. Indifferent to history, tender in the rain.

"Write it down and tell the story," says Pete.

I want to agree—"my faith is in stories" is my standard disavowal when pressed by believers for my religious convictions. But maybe it's the stories that're the problem. What if we *only* wrote it down? That is, we wrote it down but did not "tell the story." What if we wrote down—recorded—as much of the *it* of our lives, whether or not it fits in "the story," as we can? What if we didn't worry about endings, about crescendos? Maybe *it* stops with Pete crying over a dead man.

"Let me ask you," I say. My turn. "We've been through a bad time, in America." A lot of people sighing. "What just happened?" I tell him about Ashli's mother in Sacramento, how she cried. How she was angry. "You lose someone," I say, "you're angry." He knows it, anger and its costs. I tell him I've been listening to anger, writing it down, for two thousand miles. I haven't heard the costs. "Maybe you wouldn't be surprised," I say, "how many people think we're on the brink of civil war."

He nods. Slow. He wants to be careful. "I'll say this. I believe we're on the verge of seeing the greatest *will* of the goodness of God." What does that look like? "Churches, rising." I've already seen that, churches with guns. Is that what he means? Please no.

"There are tents going up," he says. Tents, literally. "You look in California." That's where I've been. "Mario Murillo just put up a ten-thousand-man tent." Oh no. Murillo. He shares a TV show with Pastor Hank. Another civil war man. "There's tents going up all over the nation," Pete continues. Tents, metaphorically. "There are pockets of fire," he says, "that God is birthing forth." A heavenly father birthing fire on the earth down below. "God is in control," he says. "Get ready." I'm trying. "And does it look like civil war?" he asks.

Say no.

"It might," he says. "It might."

It does.

"But I promise you this." He leans toward me. He wants me to write it down. "I promise you"—I am "the scribe," he says, it's "no coincidence" I've come to him—"God *will* have his glory."

11. Pockets of Fire

Civil War started.
—*Proud Boy leader Zach Rehl, 2:29 p.m., January 6, 2021*

Everything is different, but nothing has changed.
—*U.S. Capitol Police Officer Harry Dunn,*
testimony before the U.S. House Select Committee to
Investigate the January 6 Attacks on the U.S. Capitol

Near Niagara Falls, en route to Buffalo, I pulled over by a dump-truck depot.

Maybe Pastor Dave of Glad Tidings was right. No הרקמ. Only pattern and repetition. Who strung this prepositional phrase, "To God Be the Glory," across the blue in golden paint? What is the glory said to be meant for God? Glory, hallelujah—a pairing set by John Brown's body to the tune of civil war. Glory in battle. Glorious demise. I drove on, thinking of Ashli, "We the People" behind her, pressing her forward, "the politicians" before her, fleeing her fury. Her glory.

"It could have been me," a young man named Thomas Barayani boasted to an interviewer outside the Capitol, "but she went in first." He held up his hand, to show her blood. "It was one of us," he said. But this was not true. It was Ashli alone.

She was there to "#savethechildren." She'd gone to see her "#love." She was going to march, to storm, to push, to be "boots on the ground." To lay hands on the bodies in front of her and clear them from her path. To let them lay hands on her body to boost it into the window. Where she crouched. Seeing or not seeing the gun. Let's say, *not* seeing. Seeing or not seeing the barricade. Let's say, *seeing*. Calculating the leap. She believes in her body. She's already looking beyond.

What is she thinking? What has brought her here?

Guns. "Keep your hands off my guns!" she wrote on Twitter, but more often she just added "#2a" to other words about that which she called freedom. God. She declared herself faithful, to Trump and the Lord, her first tweet "#love" plus Trump plus a photo of a sign, CHRISTIAN DEPLORABLES LIVE HERE. Politics? She liked tax cuts. "My libertarian side is starting to peacock." She supported prison reform. She listed Great Lakes restoration, an Obama program, as a Trump achievement because her president had waxed poetic about the depths of Lakes Superior, Huron, Erie, and the rest. "They're big," he correctly observed. "Record deepness, right?" (Wrong.)

QAnon consumed her. She was a researcher, a rabbit-holer, a clicker of links, known in her circle for knowing things, facts and numbers beyond her friends' measure. She wanted to save the 800,000 children she incorrectly believed disappeared every year. She thought Disney was working with Jeffrey Epstein. Race haunted her so much she pretended it wasn't there. She scoffed at the notion that Trump's use of the word *lynching* evoked anything but a rope that knows no color. When pundits complained about the word, she vowed to say "lynching" herself every day. "FACTS!!!!!!!" she all-capped. "White liberals continue to support a party that tells them that they should regret being white." She would never regret her color. "I live 15 min from Tijuana," she tweeted often, furious with those who could not see what she believed she saw, the "atrocities" of the border, rape, murder, drugs, children drugged, raped and murdered. The wall was to her a romance. "FACTS FACTS FACTS," she thrummed, tweeting her president's 2019 State of the Union: "Why do wealthy politicians build walls, fences, gates around their homes? They don't build walls because they *hate* the people on the outside, but because they *love* the people on the inside." Love. He said love. He loved her.

Or maybe none of it meant anything at all. Consider the shaka. Her trademark gesture, the thumb and the pinky extended, the three fingers in between curled.

There was a photograph of her outside the Capitol that morning, flashing her "hang loose" sign. She had a motto, "Hydrate and Press On." She pressed on through a door kicked in moments before, after a Proud Boy used a stolen police shield to smash a window. Surging toward another set of doors that wouldn't open. Veering left, down a hall, the flow gathering force, until she crashed up against the doors through which she had to pass, if she were to save the children, or love her president, or defeat the mask, or get out of debt, or prove her mettle, her moxie, her all-American badassery. Hang loose. She wasn't charging, she was riding a wave. Surfing the current. Guns, God, what-have-you.

Her favorite movie was *The Big Lebowski*. It's laced through her Twitter: "The dude abides," she writes; "#Abide," she wrote. The movie's meaning, like that of any myth—like that of the Whiteness at the heart of Ashli's story, which has become fascism's story, which is becoming, whether we like it or not, our story—depends on its convergence of genres, on being many different kinds of story at once. Comedy and tragedy, bitter and absurd, spectacular and subtle.

The plot is not the point but I'll try: Jeff Bridges as Jeff Lebowski, aka, "the Dude," a stoned former college revolutionary who spends his days bowling, is drawn into an elaborate kidnapping plot by a rich old man also named Jeff Lebowski—the "Big" of the title—involving the rich man's wife, its twists and double crosses something like the 1944 film noir classic *Double Indemnity*. And yet, *The Big Lebowski* begins with tumbleweed and is occasionally narrated by a cowboy played by Sam Elliott, cast after the filmmakers, the Coen brothers, wrote the cowboy in the script as "looking not unlike Sam Elliott," because Sam Elliott looks not unlike John Wayne, had Wayne stayed lean as he grew old.

The film is anti- or maybe post-romance, but there is a sex scene, presented as an absurdist and surreal musical in which the Dude starts out a bowler and then becomes the ball, flying down the lane between the legs of countless lovers, an homage to Busby Berkeley's 1933 musical *Footlight Parade*, like the biggest, the grandest, the gaudiest—the Trumpiest—consummation of them all.

And yet, everything's filtered through the dark and druggy lens of a 1970s conspiracy thriller, something like *The Parallax View* (1974), in which Warren Beatty as a journalist investigating an assassination follows a trail of clues down a deep state rabbit hole, connecting dots as he goes. "I've got information, man," the Dude declares in *Lebowski*. "New shit has come to light." In *The Parallax View*—as with QAnon now—light is dark, down is up, like *Double Indemnity* but played out on a national stage. The arc of history may yet bend toward justice, but the American arc, as played out onscreen—in a movie theater or a viral video of Ashli Babbitt's killing on YouTube—took a sharp right turn from noir to paranoia to the hopeless absurd.

The Big Lebowski plays it all for laughs. Or maybe loss, because Walter, the Dude's best friend (played by John Goodman), is a Vietnam vet for whom every plot twist collapses back to the American dead of that war. "Has the whole world gone crazy?" he hollers, leveling a .45 at a fellow bowler he believes has crossed a line. "Am I the only one around here who gives a *shit* about the rules?" Ashli: "I will not be told by media personnel who work in New York thousands of miles away from my border that my reality is a lie #BUILDTHEWALL." Walter: "They're a bunch of fucking amateurs"; Ashli: "These ppl are clowns." Walter, who believes he can cut through all the conspiracies plaguing the Dude with firepower: "pacifism is not something to hide behind"; Ashli: "They can go gather their ppl and we can gather ppl—we will see who comes out on top. SAY WHEN!"

That was something she wrote often: "Say when." As in, "anytime, anywhere." As in, "try me." She was waiting for her war. "It is coming," she wrote. And she was tired of waiting. "Hard to be armed when you don't believe in guns," she taunted the libs. "Hard to mobilize when you live in safe spaces . . . you and your cronies will not overthrow we the ppl who are 2 war generations deep—say when." Two war generations deep.

Released in 1998, when she was twelve, *The Big Lebowski* is set in 1991, when she was five. It opens with President Bush, the first one: "This aggression will not stand!" he declares on a TV behind the Dude. What aggression? The details of the Gulf War don't really matter now, three decades on, just that "the aggression" marked the beginning: the long war in which as a young woman Ashli would serve in both Iraq and Afghanistan. Two "theaters" out of her eight deployments in the various fronts and rearguards of the forever war that will appear to end in 2021, nine months after she is gone. (And yet the drone strikes continue. The war abides.)

"New shit has come to light," declares the Dude, but it never does, because in this movie the plot is not the point. There is no point, just absurdity sprawling across the dead map of American myth. The exhaustion of genre. Noir, Western, musical, three great American story forms, and then their dissolution via paranoid thriller, itself reduced to less than a speck of meaning. The point at which details no longer matter. The point at which—for Ashli, and maybe America, "2 war generations" after *Lebowski*, on January 6, 2021—the why doesn't matter. Nor, really, the how: the rope, the gallows, the knife, or the mob. The body has come apart. No terms left to share. So, up into the broken window. Terrorism/patriotism. *A shot fired.* Cop/killer. Last words: "It's cool." It's not.

Ashli's favorite movie ends with Walter and the Dude, the old radical and the old reactionary, casting into the wind the ashes of their young and clueless bowling teammate Donny, dead of a premature heart attack brought on by a meaningless brawl. Only, the breeze blows the wrong way. Instead of into the ocean, Donny's ashes fly over Walter's shoulder and coat the Dude gray. Blowback, literally.

I can't tell if this is tragedy or farce.

Our condition, I mean.

1776 returns. 2020 never ends. Blowback carries not ashes but the

dream of those who make Ashli a martyr, which is the last story left
that might bring us together in the telling: civil war.

Say when.

><

Ho-de-no-sau-nee-ga (Haudenosaunee) and Onöndowa'ga:' (Sen-
eca) land. The Burned-Over District, so-called for the fire of its
nineteenth-century religious revival, the Second Great Awakening,
prelude to the present moment's Q Awakening, no qualifiers, aka
the Storm. Ashli, January 5: "Nothing will stop us. They can try
and try but the storm is here and it is descending upon DC in less
than 24 hours. Dark to light!" Palmyra, New York, now. Where the
Angel Moroni chose Joseph Smith to find divine tablets, which, when
peered at through seer stones, revealed a new myth of America as the
true and blooded Promised Land. At the western edge of town, at
an intersection of churches, kitty-corner from Zion Episcopal and
next to United Methodist, lurched a large yellow box of a house, the
color of goldenrod just before it goes to seed. Over its driveway a flag,
American, but stars and stripes all black. No blue line, no shades
of gray, stars and stripes visible only when the eye is turned just-so.
And strung like a banner over the side porch another flag, declaring
in bright-red letters FREEDOM. An abundance of text beneath: a com-
memoration of Robert the Bruce's determination to free the Scots
from England in the year 1320. The story, roughly speaking, of *Braveheart*. Mel Gibson, again.

When I knocked, a big White man in shorts and black braces
stretched over a green T-shirt featuring a wolf filled the door. Head
shaved, beard unkempt but squared, eyes blue like the cold east at
sunset. I explained my mission. A face loomed from the shadows.
Leslie, wife of Jason. No last names. "People aren't coming door to
door shooting," said Leslie. "But I see it set in motion." They were

prepared. Thus the black flag. It meant "no mercy." A Jericho flag, a total-war flag. "Either you have freedom or what's the use?" Her hair was dark red, her face sun-browned. She wore an undyed linen tunic she said was in the style of her ancestors, the "Border Reivers" who fought in Braveheart times. Skittish eyes, not because she was afraid of contact but because she was a scanner. She lived, she said, by discernment and intuition. There was a Buddha sticker on her door. She was Hindu, she said, but she'd say no more about how or why. They were moving soon, she said, after two decades in this house, "to the center of the country," but she wouldn't say where. She would talk about her flag, which, she said, I couldn't photograph. "Take no prisoners," she said it meant.

"Civil war?"

"Yes, definitely."

"Some way, shape, or form," mused Jason. Not like the last one, no North versus South. The map had been gerrymandered. "We've got all these pockets of witnesses." His voice was a gentle surprise. "No quarter," he said softly.

She said the war had begun. "The psychological operation." She tapped her temple. "You're fighting for your mind." It was, she said, "the feminine side of warfare." Emotional. "Consciousness."

I told her about my journey, Ashli—"Oh, yes," she said—and about Mikki's tears and fury. Leslie nodded in recognition. She was a mother, too, daughters, homeschooled and grown. One watched us now from a window, head pressed against the screen. Grinning.

What did Ashli mean to her? Leslie couldn't really answer. "I've seen so many people killed." For freedom, she said, "people who don't even get recognized." She wouldn't say much about them. She knew who I said I was, but did she really? "It's hard to trust." It is. Consider Ashli, whose death she attributed to "infiltration." Not Ashli's, of the Capitol, but the enemy's, which swept Ashli along. "How do you get rid of the infiltrators?" she wondered. "You have to have people with a lot of information. People that can see through facades." It's urgent. "We're losing," she said, sweeping me into her cause.

"All is lost?" I tried not to sound hopeful.

"No, no."

Jason stepped in. "No," he said in his gentle voice, "I don't think all is lost."

"There is hope, still!" said Leslie.

The daughter had left the window. Now she was in the driveway. I asked if I could make a family portrait. The daughter shook her head. "No," said Leslie. I asked again if I could make a picture of the flag. "No," said Leslie. The reason, she said, was that she had been "targeted." The daughter nodded. By whom? Leslie couldn't say. She was careful, she explained, not to claim to know more than she did.

That is the great truth of our paranoia now: Not knowing. Not needing to. Not knowing as its own dim, dreaming certainty.

><

I thought the last stop of my journey would be my father's grave, near Albany. He died nearly two years to the day before Fiona. She and I used to speak of our relief that he did not live to see January 6. He was a shared-terms man, a rule-of-law man—"ruleoflaw," I discovered after he was gone, was the password to all his accounts. A believer in the strength of institutions, even if flawed, since the flawed institution, he thought, requires our collaboration in its ongoing creation. He was a political scientist, a "Sovietologist," he knew great powers collapse. He'd watched the red flag come down over the Kremlin. But he could not dream of that happening to the flag that would drape his coffin, folded now into a red-white-and-blue triangle on a shelf in my closet. The insurrection, the gallows outside the Capitol—"it would have broken his heart," said Fiona, an immigrant who spoke also for her own.

But I'd taken longer than I planned, crossing the country, and stayed too long beneath Leslie's black flag, and that morning I'd taken my last heart pills. I needed to get home. I'd drive straight through. Pass him by, the flat headstone on which is carved as epitaph, "It's been wonderful." Last words. Only, he didn't say it like that. He died as so many of us will, short of breath. Three words, three sentences: "It's. Been. Wonderful." His eighty-three years. He felt privileged to be able to say goodbye. Not everybody gets to.

12. It's Been Wonderful

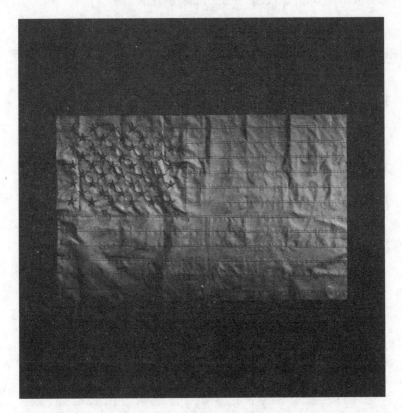

Ashli died at age thirty-five on a Wednesday afternoon, somewhere between the Capitol and the hospital. There's video of her being carried, outside, to an ambulance, but that may be just her body.

Ashli married Aaron Babbitt when she was thirty-three, on a Tuesday, less than a week before a court issued a judgment of $71,000 for an unpaid loan against the pool-cleaning business they ran together, and sometime after that they met a woman named Kayla at a bar and Kayla became their girlfriend. Ashli's debts did not concern her. "Nothing lasts forever," her brother Roger, who worked with her, would say she declared.

Once, she chased down a man who robbed a store.

Several times a week she took her aged German shepherd to the beach so it could soak its creaky bones in saltwater.

The dog died not long after Ashli.

Ashli separated from the Air Force when she was thirty, a senior airman. That's the word, *airman*, into which women such as Ashli are poured by a military that still does not fully recognize them. She'd been active duty four years and she wore a uniform across ten more and if her modest rank at the end may not seem to reflect the length of her service—it typically takes three years to achieve—perhaps it speaks well of her in other ways. She cared more for the well-being of her fellow airmen than for orders. She was demoted at least once. She tried, she said, to offer "comfort and knowledge." She was known for bucking authority. "She was," said an admiring airman who watched her rip into an inept commander, "like a dog with a bone." She was, the airman told a reporter after Ashli died, "like a chinchilla that had just done a line of cocaine." She served in Alaska, Abilene, and the United Arab Emirates. She served as a "Capital Guardian," tasked with learning the arts of riot control should trouble ever come to the building in which she would later roam the halls with a mob calling for the vice president to be hanged.

Her last active-duty post, when she was twenty-two, was as a "security forces controller," at Dyess Air Force Base in Texas, home to the 7th Bomb Wing. The motto of which is *"mors ab alto!"* Death from above. In 2006 she deployed to Iraq. July of that year was the war's deadliest month that far. The Baghdad Morgue alone received 1,855 corpses. Ashli's commanding officers, reported *The New York Times*, still believed that Iraqis could be "tamed."

That year, five U.S. soldiers raped an Iraqi girl named Abeer Qassim Hamza al-Janabi. Then they killed her and set fire to her body, and killed her mother, her father, and her little sister. At the end of the year, Saddam Hussein was hanged.

Ashli had already been to Afghanistan. In 2005. There she earned distinction by holding a "Merry Christmas" sign for taxiing pilots. That year, as in every year, the Americans killed more Afghans than Afghans killed Americans, but also that year Afghans killed all but one man out of two units of Navy SEALs. The lone survivor, Marcus Luttrell, wrote a disputed bestselling account—*Lone Survivor*—which became a hit movie—*Lone Survivor*—which in turn might be said to be the basis for Luttrell's opening-night speech at Trump's 2016 nominating convention. "Who among you," he demanded, "is going to step up and take the fight to the enemy? Because it's here." What fight? Which enemy?

Ashli first married when she was nineteen, to a staff sergeant named Timothy McEntee, and together they adopted a military dog, a German shepherd named Sorbon A333. There's a picture of Ashli and Timothy, Sorbon A333 draped across both their laps like a second sofa, Ashli's arm wrapped around the dog's shoulder, its head bigger than her own. Her face is open, her gold hair brushed out of her eyes, her smile shy.

Ashli joined the Air Force when she was seventeen. She had to persuade her parents to accompany her to the recruiting station. She was good at persuading. It was, she told them, what she'd always wanted, or maybe what she'd wanted since the attacks of September 11, 2001, when she was fifteen. "She came out that way," Mikki would say after she died. Mikki worked in a school. Ashli's father worked in flooring. They'd come to California from the Midwest. They didn't need or want politics. They had Ashli and four boys. Ashli was the "invincible" one. She liked contact sports. Water polo let her fight in the water. She was the smallest girl.

She liked being strong. She grew up in a "cowboy town." A "rodeo town," tucked into the foothills of the Cuyamaca Mountains. A White town. A myth town. She had a horse she rode to the store. She kept her horse in the front yard. I try to remember that when I read of how, close to her end, she'd rant, "I'm not going to have any homeless people crapping in my front yard." She remembered her first front yard. She remembered the horses, who surely shit in the front yard, too, but that was different to her, because they were horses, and she was a child.

I'm doing the same thing here as the martyr-makers when they age her backward, make her an innocent. But I know she's not. I know how old Ashli was when she died, and I've tasted the bile for which she died, the Whiteness of her crime and the Whiteness of her youth. And yet—her father would lift her high onto a horse's back, she'd kiss the horse's great neck. "She had a pony," said Mikki, "and my husband had a horse, and they used to ride all over the place." Picture the child, picture the pony. The father, a quiet man. The father, the daughter, they ride to the store, and there he buys his daughter a Baby Ruth bar, or maybe a Milky Way. "Yeah," Mikki remembered, "it was a lovely time." Or so the story goes.

><

My favorite book to read to my kids when they were younger was *We're Going on a Bear Hunt*, by Michael Rosen and Helen Roxenbury. A father and four children set out for an adventure: "We're going on a bear hunt. / We're going to catch a big one. / What a beautiful day! / We're not scared." The refrain repeats before each obstacle: tall grass, deep water, dark woods, a storm. Each time, the children reason, "We can't go over it. / We can't go under it. / Oh no! We've got to go through it!"

It's after midnight. I'm up in Vermont's Green Mountains, a narrow, steep road. I have gone neither over nor under America. I've gone through it.

The bear hunters find a cave, "a narrow, gloomy cave." What does one meet in a bear cave? A bear. The bear chases them back through the grass and the water and the dark forest, all the way home. Not a

Teddy or a Berenstain, a mad-eyed ursus horribilis. Its claws against the door's windowpane. "Into the bed," cry the kids. "Under the covers." That's my plan too. I'm almost home.

Then I see the bear, only it's a moose, too tall for me to comprehend, veering out of the darkness to clatter over blacktop beside me. I haven't been driving fast—I'm exhausted, bleary-eyed—but I slow down, watching the moose gallop in the high beams. I imagine I could drive under it, like the Arc de Triomphe. And yet it looks lean. Skeletal. Its skin ragged, splotchy. Ticks. They're eating the moose alive, I've read. The nights are warmer, there are fewer deep freezes, the ticks don't die. "Tick." It sounds so inconsequential, far removed from the concerns of a moose. But there are so many more ticks now than there ever were. They are part of our climate now. Our shared condition. They surge up the moose's long legs and drop onto its broad shoulders. They coat the moose, thousands upon thousands, as many as ninety thousand, and they drain the beast, drop by drop. The moose stagger. They will soon be gone. The ticks will consume them, slowly but as surely as fire.

This moose turns into the cool ink-dark night. Maybe this one will survive, live out its natural span. They're lonesome creatures, moose, so maybe this one will never notice how alone it is becoming, never know that its world is coming apart. Such is the hope— not for an end to this story but for the unknowing and maybe the unknown, the embrace of the undone and the undoing. It's too late to turn back, to wind time in reverse, to climb down out of the window, to retreat back through the Capitol halls, and the tall grass, and the Trump years, back to the pony at the 7-Eleven and the Milky Way bar. Too late because it was already too late then. It always has been. We've got to go through it. The Whiteness, this stolen land. Into the smoky, copper-bright uncertain, reckoning with the haunted past, which is hard, learning to love the smoldering days ahead, which is harder.

9

The Great Acceleration

> The thing to worry about is meanings, not appearances.
> —Michael Lesy, *Wisconsin Death Trip*, 1973

Cecil, Wisconsin

I went back twice to find out what the coffin meant, but though cars came and went in the driveway, nobody ever answered the door. Halloween in June, or a sign? Kitsch, or a warning? Both: a symbol, a symptom. I'd been driving for a week, since the first night of the January 6 congressional hearings, listening to them on the radio as I counted the flags. Not the American ones but the Trump ones.

Trump 2024, two years ahead of time; and the red, white, and blue of the Confederacy, the yellow Don't-Tread-on-Me Gadsden. There are so many now. And there's a new folk art in the land: hand-painted "Fuck Biden" placards, homemade "Let's Go Brandon" billboards and homespun "Never Forget Benghazi" banners. The cities and towns still ripple with rainbow pride, and their numbers are greater, but on many country roads the ugly emblems tick by like the miles.

What was the coffin, though? I saw it the night of what had been intended as the last hearing, before yet more evidence emerged. The one at which a handsome Republican congressman with no future left in Trump's party led the questioning. He'd shared a letter received by his wife, threatening to kill him, her, and their five-month-old baby. "You are one stupid cunt," it began. The witnesses he questioned were three Trump administration lawyers who had resisted the president's would-be coup. I listened to their testimony, their graying voices, their account of the pressure building, thinking, *This is the stress test of fascism.* Trump, probing prodding, feeling for weak links. *Will this bend? Will this one break?*

I was visiting friends in Wisconsin when we drove past the coffin. They let me out to make a picture. "Careful," they said, and, "We'll come back for you," because they didn't want to linger. Nobody home. I made my picture. I waited. I read on my phone that Kyle Rittenhouse, the dough-faced seventeen-year-old acquitted for shooting to death two men at a Black Lives Matter demonstration, was launching a video game in which players shoot at turkeys labeled "fake news." I read on Twitter that Wisconsin Republicans had refused an effort by the governor to convene a special legislative session to repeal a dormant 1849 law making any abortion—including for rape or incest—a felony. My friends returned, we fled. The next morning, the ruling came down: *Dobbs v. Jackson,* which overturned *Roe v. Wade,* and Wisconsin became the only "blue" state in which abortion was now effectively illegal.

><

The news spoke of the fifty years since *Roe* made abortion a constitutional right, but really the ruling only made it to forty-nine. I'm a year older, but like most men of my generation (whether they know it or not), I'm one of *Roe*'s children. I wouldn't have the life I do were it not for the 1973 Supreme Court decision. Now we're returned to a moment before, only this time we know better what we're losing.

Also in 1973, a book appeared called *Wisconsin Death Trip*, to which I'm looking now for guidance. *Wisconsin Death Trip* began as a staple-bound pamphlet and as a book became an unlikely mirror of its moment, even as it depicted the 1890s. History's like that sometimes, our faith in the forward motion of chronology suddenly evaporating, leaving us standing, disoriented, in a dry, still riverbed. *Death Trip* was, on the surface, a benign album of seemingly ordinary photographs—portraits, patriotic displays, happy youth—from one small town in Wisconsin, Black River Falls, during the last decade of the nineteenth century. Interspersed are excerpts from the town newspaper, the Black River Falls *Badger State Banner,* and whispers from a "town gossip." In 1973, a year of crises as varied and vast as those of this year, most White Americans still imagined the previous century as an idyll, apart from a brief interruption for civil war, fought for reasons they thought "romantic." Virtuous country life, bustling urban industry. American greatness. The *Banner* spoke other truths. Epidemic disease, whole families consumed; diphtheria, the formation in the throat of a "false membrane"; "astonishing bank failure"; "incendiaries," arsonists who loved to watch things burn; "vigilance committees"; "the private made public"; a woman, once a "model wife and mother," who traveled the state smashing windows; soul after soul remanded to the asylum; so many suicides; a woman who died "from a criminal operation performed upon herself" after she failed to find a doctor with the courage to help her.

There was beauty in the book, too, even in its carefully arranged photographs of dead infants. That's what you did then, when your baby died. If you had the money, you hired the town photographer to make the infant's picture, tucked into a little coffin with flowers, eyes tenderly brushed closed.

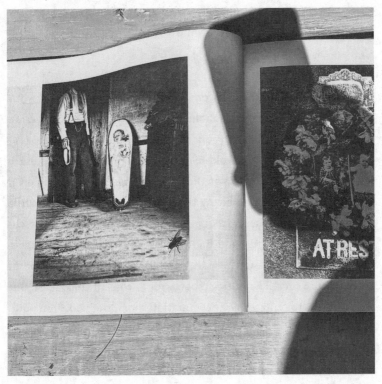

Thirty years ago, *Death Trip*'s author, Michael Lesy, was my teacher. The book, his first, has followed me ever since. "You can get as philosophical as you want," Michael said when I told him I was headed to Black River Falls. He mimicked cheap gravitas. "'From the deep ground grows the tree of life . . .'" Then comes the end, yours or worse, that of those you love—"and nobody likes it when it happens to them." A death trip is a memento mori, is a reminder that everybody dies.

If that seems obvious, consider the light-eating vanity of Trumpism, the delusion of a golden brand that will shine eternally. Consider this immediate post-*Roe* meme: "a thousand-year White Boy Summer starts today." But nothing lasts forever, not even White boys. A death trip, meanwhile, summons us to the precarious real. Not the myth of greatness. The pulse—the life—of uncertainty. The living, such as we are.

><

I got the news through a Wisconsin man I'd stopped to speak with that morning, who got it by phone from his wife, who heard it from her doctor, to whom she had gone not to end a pregnancy but to prepare for one. "Mary," who told me this story on the newly necessary condition of anonymity, was on the table when the ruling came down. Feet up in the stirrups, receiving a vaginal ultrasound. She wanted a baby, and this was the next step in the assisted reproductive technology she and her husband had chosen—until suddenly it wasn't. Following a course of fertility drugs, Mary was in the possession of three mature eggs. The nurse stepped out to consult the doctor. But when the doctor entered the examination room, she said, "I'm holding back tears."

"Then I started crying," Mary told me later that day, remembering the moment she learned *Roe* had fallen.

"I can't recommend you continue," the doctor said. Three eggs meant a risk of "multiples." Twins Mary could handle. Triplets she could not. Neither her finances nor her body. If she went forward, there was a minuscule chance all three eggs would be fertilized. One embryo might have to be removed. And that, as of 9:11 a.m., local time, on June 24, 2022, in Wisconsin, where Mary lived and into which she hoped to bring a new life, could be—according to the resurrected 1849 law—a felony.

›‹

I was driving north from Mary when I stopped to take a picture and found myself invited into the home of a militiaman. At first, I just wanted to photograph a "Fuck Trudeau" flag—an eccentricity in America, in Marinette, Wisconsin—serving as a curtain in a house. Quick work; I left the car running. But I tripped a motion sensor. A woman with cascading honey curls, broad-armed in a tank top, appeared on the back porch. "Whatcha doing?" she asked. I didn't know then that Megan Brumm had clocked me as soon as I'd pulled up to the curb, that by the time I squeaked "Hi!" I'd already breached two of what the family Brumm calls its "frontiers." I was a stranger on their lawn, which is to say I was one of three things: (1) a Fed (don't shoot, yet); (2) an intruder (be prepared to shoot); or (3) a fool (until proven otherwise).

I aced the third option without even trying. I said I was a writer wandering Wisconsin, making pictures of flags, asking questions about the division of America. Megan brightened. Her husband was a photojournalist! (Also a wedding photographer.) She was joined by a lean, sharp-shouldered young woman wearing an oversized pink tank top that read PINK. Her eldest stepdaughter, Athena. Baroque ink spiraled round Athena's thin bones. Megan went to fetch her husband, Rob. Athena gazed down on me, dead-eyed. Her aim, I'd learn, was the best in the family's. Rob emerged: big, buzzcut and camouflaged, a .45 holstered on his hip. I explained again about the flag. "Want one?" Rob asked. It felt unwise to say no, so I stood dumbly while Rob fetched me my very own "Fuck Trudeau" banner, still wrapped in plastic. He'd bought them two-fers in solidarity with his Canadian friends. He had a lot of friends, he said, and he had nothing to hide, even if some things would remain "classified," so he invited me in. Inside, on a pool table, there was—well, I asked if I

could take a picture of their cat. "Twitch," said Rob, smiling at the
kitty. He clicked on the overhead for better lighting—

The Brumms had four cats, and in addition to Athena there was a
three-year-old with streaming blond locks zipping around the table.
Everybody shoots, even the little one. How many guns between
them? Classified. But those that I could see, said Rob, were as legal
as his combat-grade body armor. He hoisted it to demonstrate its
weight, far greater than that used by the police, which he deemed
unfit for real battle. "You can shoot me with a nine-millimeter in the
chest all day long, and I will laugh at you." He shouldered the armor
sometimes eight hours a day. Training, he said; "I am the head of a
local militia." Rob slapped a red patch onto the pool table's felt. 4TH
WISCONSIN INF-RED ARROW MILITIA, it read. LEGIO IV FELIX FORTUNATA—
Fortunate Bearer of Thunderbolts. (I find no record of it online.
"That's the idea," said Rob.) The gear was for an upcoming training
operation. "Last Friday," he said, "we did night ops." He showed me,
finger on the trigger, and Megan laughed at my wide eyes.

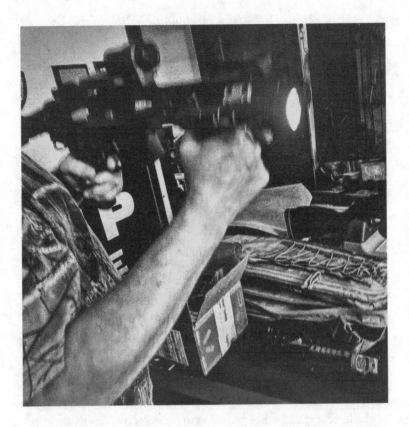

When Rob thought about abortion, he started with guns. The question for him was not whether abortion is right or wrong. The question was: When will China invade? The question was: Can we *afford* to spare potential infantry? "If you make the top ten of things that keep your country running, abortion is not in the top five hundred. But ten years down the road, if I have a war and I'm a leader, and you and the Black population have aborted forty percent of their babies for the past thirty years, I'm running out of foot soldiers. Abortions are bodies that never make it to my front line."

(It's true that a higher percentage of Black pregnancies end in abortion than White ones. Rob's even right about the number 40.

But not the percent: It's 40 out of 1,000, according to the *American Journal of Public Health*. That is, 4 percent.)

Rob called himself "pro-choice," but that term, too, meant something different in his vernacular. He meant that the choice of whether or not to murder a baby is up to you. "If you choose to do something that's medically possible, I'm going to leave it between you and God, until it affects me in the state of readiness of my defense." *Readiness*. It required panopticon paranoia, looking for threats down every sightline. Rob looked at falling birth rates. He looked at what he considered Mexico's invasion. He looked at what he suspected will be civil war according to a rural/urban divide—in which, even though he lived in town, he would side with the land he held outside of it. He looked at China, he noted they ended their population-control program in 2021, he contemplated 1.4 billion Red Chinese divided by half and then by some factor again to account for age and thought of hundreds of millions of Chinese wombs churning out multiple Chinese babies— in fact, the Chinese birthrate is dropping—and he thought, "they're getting ready." For the future war. "You start prepping several generations ahead to have bodies when you lose so many bodies that you need a level of fresh bodies you never dreamed you'd have to dig into."

This way of thinking was, he acknowledged, "macabre." But the macabre has flowed into the mainstream, and Rob's convictions are more moderate, in fact, than much of Fox News. Rob did not recall having heard of "Great Replacement Theory," the idea that the Left seeks to make conservatism—read, Whiteness—demographically dwindle even as it opens U.S. borders to non-White "invaders." Rob just thought it up all on his own. His ideas are no longer marginal. He knew this, felt it—the gravity drawing men with guns to the center—on January 6, his photographs of which played in a loop on a screen mounted in the corner of the living room, over his youngest's toys, next to a *Call of Duty: Black Ops* poster. Did he carry at the Capitol? "I would not answer that question." What he would say is: "I did not get robbed by 'joggers' coming out of D.C."

He claimed his militia numbered 6,700. Later, on the phone, he made it 7,500. Were the numbers real? Inflated, perhaps, but maybe also real enough. As I'd been driving, I'd been listening to a book called *How Civil Wars Start,* by a political scientist named Barbara F. Walter, who, in a final chapter, projects a hypothetical commencement in Wisconsin. Like Rob, I wanted to be prepared. I'd learned that we're in a golden age of militias—if you like militias—and that there are more citizens armed and organized now in varying postures of incipient insurgency than at any time since the last civil war. "Right-wing terrorism used to rise and fall depending on who was president," writes Walter, surging in response to Democrats and subsiding with Republicans. "President Trump," writes Walter, "broke the pattern." Trump said *more,* and the militias heard, all the new little armies formed in panicked response to Obama metastasizing. Trump said, "stand by," and they gathered.

Rob called January 6 a false flag—a hoax, staged—even though he was there. I'd been listening to the January 6 hearings, but who else had? Nobody I'd met on the road. Everybody seemed to know someone who'd participated (or, like Rob, had participated), and yet nobody believed it'd really happened. If, as F. Scott Fitzgerald suggested, "the test of a first-rate intelligence is the ability to hold two opposing ideas in mind at the same time and still retain the ability to function," such cognitive dissonance is the awful genius of our ecstatically disinformed age. "Pro-life." "Free speech." Athena, for instance, embraced fascism and yet bridled at the name. "They call me a Nazi," she muttered, sitting stooped on a tall chair beside the pool table. "Just because of my German-flag tattoo." Sometimes, she said, they told her to kill herself. She didn't say who "they" were. She bent her shoulder to show proof of "their" idiocy: "They" couldn't even tell the difference between a swastika and the Iron Cross. Yes, it's true that the Iron Cross in conjunction with a German flag was last used by the Third Reich; but before that it was a symbol of Imperial Germany, and it was to that long-gone nation, she said, that she had dedicated a swath of her left shoulder. "Honor and Glory for Germany," she said, her voice a low drone. Which was complicated, because Rob considered himself Jewish. "I'm *not*," Athena said. "You're Jewish by blood," Rob said. Athena ignored him.

Raised Lutheran, Rob said he discovered that his immigrant forebears had converted upon arrival in the late nineteenth century, fleeing pogroms. Pogroms he could understand; he feared they'll be directed against gun owners. He decided to reclaim his heritage. Details of how and when were classified, but he was, he said, a man of God. He said he was not a Rothschild, which is true, and that Hitler was Jewish, which is not. He said four cats purred through the armory because four is one of the numbers of God, and when I said I'm a Jew, too, but I'd never heard that, he laughed and told me, "You're a *baaad* Hasid," which, fair enough. (He was right, though, sort of, about four, especially if you're into gematria, the Jewish code of numbers and words and hidden meanings popular now with anti-Semitic conspiracy theorists.) He said his anti-Semitic comrades in the militia respected him despite his Jewish blood because they're like a wolf pack. He was the alpha. He ruled by strength. "They will depose me, if I deserve it." A radio on a shelf behind him crackled. "And I don't deserve to be deposed." Such was democracy in the Wisconsin Fourth Inf. Red Arrow Militia.

"Are you in the militia too?" I asked Athena.

"I guess," she said. She wasn't the eye-contact type.

"She's one of the people who can actually shoot," Rob said proudly. He'd already explained his belief that of every 100 soldiers (he'd said he'd been 82nd Airborne) only twelve are capable of killing another human being, and only two are good at it. "She would be one of the two out of a hundred that I'm absolutely certain of." When, advising me on home defense—the broad pattern of a shotgun wouldn't work, he said, if the bad guy was holding your daughter hostage— he demonstrated by sighting an inch from Athena's face. She didn't flinch. She agreed that were she being held as a shield she'd want her father to use an AR. That's what she'd use if the tables were turned. She had ideas of her own about firepower, seemed to be murmuring calibers to herself as Rob spoke, too low for me to comprehend. He pointed to the ARs on the table. He said the three-year-old had

282 › The Undertow

already trained on them. "Shooting prone," the little guy lying on his belly, blasting away. "It's really kind of cute."

"How old were you, Athena, when you started?" I asked.

Rob answered for her. He picked up a very large handgun, a Taurus Raging Bull, .480 Ruger, which, he thought, looked like the mile-long barrel seen in *Dirty Harry*. "She was holding this revolver when she was two and a half."

"Two," Athena corrected.

"How?" I asked, incredulous.

"Two hands," said Rob, a proud papa.

"Favorite thing to hold," Athena said.

Rob cocked it. "God, I love this."

Athena too—I caught just two words of her undercurrent commentary: "An elephant gun," she said, smiling, nodding, thinking of its uses.

><

The Family Brumm is, admittedly, a special one. Jewish and "German," given to guns and powwows. Looping with Rob's January 6 footage was his video of the Standing Rock pipeline protest. Rob said he's sometimes mistaken for Indian online, but the truth was that the only indigenous ancestry in the family belonged to his daughter-in-law, who he said was a Lakota woman. Still, Rob loved powwows; and he lined up with the water defenders at Standing Rock. Yes, the Brumms are unusual. Their flags are not. Their "Fuck Biden" and their "Don't-Tread-on-Me" and their blacked-out American flag, meant to signal the deepest distress, the fullest "readiness"—like those window decals I'd been seeing on trucks that said TRY ME with a gun or a skull—was the visual drumbeat the whole of my long drive, the lawn décor cosplay of a populace preparing itself for an imaginary war that threatens to will itself real.

Gadsden flags—

—and God flags—

—and guns.

The old—

—and the new—

—and the what-might-come-next:

><

I kept driving. Near Mountain, Wisconsin, a local took me to meet his "favorite billionaire." A rich man who had made a fortune, my friend said, by inventing the jalapeño popper. He had plowed it into a small empire of good barbecue and guided hunts and, illuminated at night, a curiosity cabinet of magnificently antlered bucks, dozens of heads expertly stuffed. The rich man said it was all for God. He was also interested in artificial intelligence. His brother was invest-

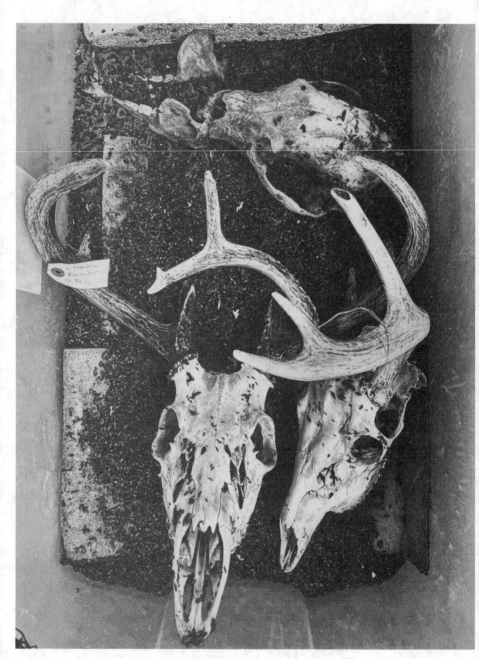

Mountain, Wisconsin

ing heavily in Tesla, he said, to get closer to Elon Musk, so he could bring him to Christ. "Imagine," said the Popper King, "what Elon Musk will be able to do when he knows Jesus!" The Popper King wondered if we might yet discover the ghost in the works, whether a God-fearing Elon might build for us robots with souls. I thought of a recurring theme in *Wisconsin Death Trip*'s local news clippings of the 1890s: men driven mad—taken off to the asylum—by their attempts to invent a perpetual-motion machine.

"I did programs for computers," a retired steelworker named James Schmidt told me when I dipped across the border to Michigan. "Robots and machines and shit." I'd pulled over to snap a picture of his black Second Amendment flag, flying in front of the yellow school bus his wife drove. He thought of himself as a big-picture type. The picture, as he saw it, was about technology. Its decline. He thought the nation's dying for want of invention. He was dying, too, faster than most of us. "Stage four terminal lung cancer." The black flag was likely his last. He was fifty-nine, two years into a prognosis with an outside chance of five. He measured his life by technological collapse. "They"—the elites, the communists, the city-dwellers—try to tell us we live in an age of innovation. This, he said is a ruse. "What has been invented in the last fuckin' hundred and some years?" I suggested a few notable items. James dismissed each as derivative, wan commentary on an age of American genius a hundred years gone.

Except, he said, for Elon Musk. I didn't argue. I never do, with the well-armed. "He wants to colonize Mars," said James, pulling from within himself a skein of hope for his nine children's seven children. A mission to colonize Mars, James let himself hope, would make us great again. It'd be like the Old West, like our forefathers. A chance to be men with guns again—as, despite the fact that he and most he knew were armed, he thought "we" no longer are.

"What has destroyed every great civilization?" James demanded. "The most powerful force in the universe?"

I shrugged. James smiled, because such a cluelessly tepid response from another man was to him just more evidence of the answer. He pressed his thumbs and fingers together, the way teens do to suggest a heart, and lowered the construction over his crotch. He pulsed it open and closed.

"*This*," he said, "and greed."

"What's 'this'?" I asked, even though I didn't want to.

"Pussy."

"And greed?"

"Women in power," clarified James. "Making *allll* these decisions." For which he had a solution.

In Ashippun, Wisconsin, I pulled over for a display of American flags and a yard sign, REBECCA FOR GOVERNOR. That meant Rebecca Kleefisch, a GOP candidate, the "moderate" who merely agreed with another politician's declaration that pregnant rape victims should "turn lemons into lemonade" by bearing a rapist's child. In the minds of the abortion abolitionists—those who would outlaw it in every instance—it's a matter of finding beauty even within suffering. To Peggy Morrisey, who'd put up the sign, it was the liberals she said drove by and yelled foul things at her flags who brought ugliness into this world. There is so much ugliness, said Peggy. They shouted even when her daughter was in the yard. As a mother, Peggy feared that the ugliness was growing. Getting closer. Milwaukee, Madison, cities threatening her immaculate lawn. Ugliness, everywhere. "Education," she said, by which she meant indoctrination. "The border," she said, by which she meant—we were close to Canada—the other one, 1,500 miles south, across which, she said, "they waltz." I didn't ask who "they" were.

In How, Wisconsin, I broke my rule of never approaching a house hidden from the road if it advertises itself with Trump flags, which is why I found myself backing up, very slowly, before two barrel-chested barking black Labs. Their owner was Jerry Pinchart, a fit former contractor with white hair and skin almost exactly the same color as his salmon T-shirt. It was the afternoon of *Dobbs*, which Jerry told me was good news but also bad. Good for God, bad for the nation, which now faces "chaos." He was a proud no-exceptions man. Rape, incest—God let it happen for reason. Life of the mother? No, sir. That's up to God. Prayer was all the medicine a mother needs.

Jerry didn't consider himself a zealot. Almost nobody I met was particularly pious. Jerry liked wearing his Trump shirt, he said, because the ladies gave him hugs. James, concerned about the exile of God from the schools, growled many times that he didn't give a fuck what anybody else thought. Christian nationalism reaches far beyond the pews.

Jerry said he'd heard "they" were calling for riots. Part of the Democrat plan for "total control" that began with killing babies and would end with war in Wisconsin. "It's bled through here too."

Not a word Jerry said was fully his own. I'd been listening to Fox, to right-wing radio, as I drove, and I'd already heard variations of every syllable he uttered. Jerry followed the news. That was the word for it: he followed. He was a follower. He had not been a good student as a boy, he said. But now he had learned his lesson. The lesson was fear, the lesson was bitter, the lesson was that other people were getting more than their fair share. That grievance flowed naturally for him from his feelings about baby killers—as if women, by getting to choose, were getting more than their fair share too. He fretted about the Menominee Reservation, two miles away from the country home to which he'd retreated from Green Bay, because, he said, the city had grown "too risky." Not just due to crime but to those he claimed would barely allow a White man to speak anymore. The Menominee, though, were worse in his view. "A lot of them I believe are the type of people who want what you and I have. And they're willing to take it."

What you and I have. He didn't ask whether my politics were like his. The latter to him was implied by what he observed, correctly, as the Whiteness we had in common.

"It's coming," he said, of war. With the Menominee? The Democrats? The aborters? The name of the enemy didn't matter, just that it existed. Jerry was prepared. "We are"—he paused—"*well-supplied*. We can defend ourselves."

The anger kept twisting. Rob and Peggy and Jerry and James. Abortion and guns and God and Whiteness and women and cities and borders and then guns again. The intersectionality of fascism: all perceived threats, across all time—"Indian wars" and new Cold War and critical race theory—brutally interconnected.

><

Rosholt, Wisconsin

"Wisconsin Needs Farmers." Brian Bushman was a farmer, a potato culturist, owner of much land and many trucks that supplied taters to Walmarts far from his little town. A prosperous man. On his porch I spoke first to an old woman who said Trisha raised the Trump flag, and then to Trisha, a handsome if tentative woman in perhaps her late thirties. Trisha had not yet heard the news. *Dobbs.* But she was glad when I told her. She thought she'd better fetch Brian, her boyfriend, gray-haired and square-jawed and smiling. He wore crisp blue-and-white striped bib overalls—he always wore bib overalls, had worn them to weddings, had named one of his businesses Bibs Transport—and his voice was like honeyed tea. He carried a beverage. Yes, he had heard the news. How could he not? "You'd have to be a deaf and blind man!" He'd been celebrating.

"Deaf and blind man!" Trisha repeated. She laughed after her man.

"It's been a Christian thing forever," said Brian, marveling over the inevitability of God's time. "A gentleman was just telling me a story today about what he told a young woman who said"—Brian pressed his knees together as if to curtsy and raised his hands with fluttering fingers, mincing: "'My body, my choice!'" The gentleman in question was inside. Brian summoned him. "Wayne!"

Wayne was younger, bigger, and bushier, one of Brian's employees. He settled down in one chair while Brian took the other, vacated for him by the old woman. She stood. The story was secondhand to Wayne, too, but he thought it such a good one he told it as if it was his: "You know how it is—twenty-four-, twenty-five-year-old little smartass girl." He did his own imitation, same fluttering fingers. "'Y'all keep your hands of my body, my body, my body!'" Wayne's clever friend had said, "'It's just you're out runnin' around and you spread your legs for every gentleman round, and chance of you getting pregnant is very high whether or not you use protection.'"

Brian laughed hard—a forced laugh. I'd heard it from other men when they spoke of sex and women's bodies. It wasn't that they found it all funny, it was that they wanted to. They willed themselves into becoming men for whom women are a joke, not a threat. They couldn't imagine other possibilities.

Wayne's friend was, in Wayne's view, relatively liberal: Wayne said he told the woman that sure, he'd keep his hands off her body, but she'd better get herself an IUD or pills or a condom, because there'd be no excuse now for an unwanted pregnancy, nor any way out for smartass little girls knocked up through their own careless ways.

The moral, to me, was unclear, the point irrelevant—the majority of people seeking abortions are already mothers—but the Bushman porch laughed uproariously. These, they believed, were days of victory. I ask if they'd been listening to the January 6 hearings. They laughed harder. "There might be a civil war!" said Brian.

"That's true!" agreed Trisha, giggling.

"What would you do to keep yourself safe?" I asked.

I'd lobbed a slow easy one right over the plate, and Brian swung with perfect timing: "We got all the guns in the world!"

><

At a gas station in Tomah I got to talking with a young family from Eau Claire about the "Let's Go Brandon" decal on their truck, the Trump-world euphemism for "Fuck Joe Biden," which they said they'd chosen because as parents they didn't think it appropriate to use the *f*-word. Mom said yes to a family portrait—

—but Dad said no to names. He worried about what's going to happen when the Second Amendment falls, which he viewed as likely, perhaps soon, and the government comes for their arms. "We have a gun in the truck and guns in the house and the kids know how to use them," he explained. Mom and Dad owned roughly thirty-five between them. Dad was thirty-six years old. The older he got, he said, the angrier he became about abortion. He said it's the second most important issue—after guns. He spoke of a singular picture he couldn't get out of his mind, although there seemed to be many. Government knocking on his door, demanding his weapons, and the question that haunted him of what he'll do then ("I won't be handing them in, that's for sure"); and boys dressed as girls and girls dressed as boys and furries—"kids who identify as animals"—and litter boxes for such creatures in schools, which don't exist but had become a piece of permanent fascist folklore since a clip of a Nebraska state lawmaker lamenting the practice went viral. ("How is this sanitary?" the legislator demanded.) But the worst picture—the killing picture—was of an abortion. An imaginary one. "When I picture these doctors, sticking wires in their—crap—and—literally cutting their arms off, so they bleed to death?" He spoke with White-man vocal fry: "Killing the chunks? Throwing them in a garbage can?" And White-man fury: "I tell you what. Put that doctor in front of me—I'll do the same to him."

This was also his answer to the question of exceptions for rape: men killing men. He had an idea of good men gathering to kill bad ones, God-fearers executing rapers. To spare the mother the pain, so she might raise the rapist's child, because every child is of God.

I thought of the man's brightly smiling son. A father's protective euphemism, "Let's Go Brandon" for "Fuck Joe Biden." His anger growing with age. What he described as the quiet pro-life views of his childhood. The murderous fantasy of now. I thought of the brightly smiling son and my own children, who must now forge their future selves at the precipice of rage to which we've brought them.

><

I had, in fact, brought my eldest child to Wisconsin. I'll call them Y. They are thirteen, nonbinary, bright and funny and kind, and furious at the world into which they're coming of age. What should they do with that anger? They were in Wisconsin for a residential program they hoped would help them find some equilibrium. They like to follow the news. They read our local paper. First the horoscopes, then *Dear Abby*, then local reports. Schools, arson, selectboards, murder, zoning, fentanyl. Covid-19. Then the wire, the national: "Don't Say Gay" in Florida, the January 6 investigation in Washington, the heat, everywhere. The fires, the floods, the extinctions, the collective inaction of Y's elders—me, writing this, you, reading it—to save this withering world.

After *Dobbs*, Y showed me a drawing they'd made: a woman jumping to her death from a hot-air balloon. Because, Y explained, the woman in their drawing was pregnant and did not want to be. I was alarmed. "*Look*," said Y, pointing down the page. They'd drawn a story in pictures, a vertical comic strip. The would-be suicide lands, alive, in an inland ocean, where a wave carries her from Wisconsin to Vermont, our home state, where abortion remains legal. Where she would not have to live a life others decided for her. "It took me a while to get her there," Y told me. In their imagination, Y meant. It's getting harder, they said, to think up happy endings.

><

In Wisconsin, a woman bled for more than 10 days from an incomplete miscarriage after emergency room staff would not remove the fetal tissue . . .

—*Washington Post*, July 16, 2022

The accounts you're about to read were considered neither sensational, nor exceptional, when they were printed.

—*Wisconsin Death Trip*, as originally published as a staple-bound booklet, 1972

I came across a copy of the original *Death Trip*, published before the book, the movie, the operas (there are two), the many shadows it has since cast across music and literature and film. "Look what I found," I wrote Michael.

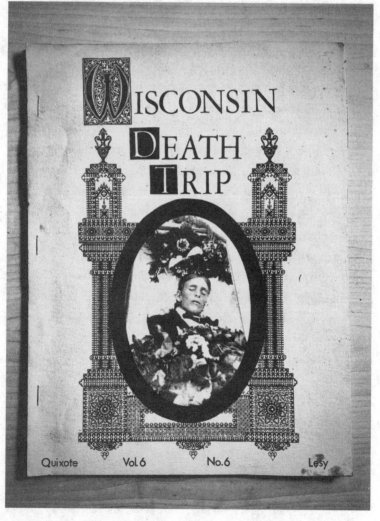

He called a few hours later.

"The issue is," he said, "why is this book still fucking breathing?"

He'd made the book as a young man, fifty years ago, and now he was old. His "hinges," he said, were breaking. He'd had a shoulder replacement and he needed new knees. His doctor had prescribed him a small daily dose of morphine. He'd made many books since *Death Trip*, but it was the one that followed him, the book that wouldn't leave him alone. To wit, my email with the picture. He said he genuinely didn't know why this book endures. He'd been training as a historian when he'd made it, but instead of writing what he'd studied how to write, he'd stumbled into something else. "The arcane and actual history behind and within conventional 'history,'" he said. Behind and within. The "Trip" in the book's title, he said, had been a youthful journey. "If you drop acid, every once in a while—God forbid it should be often—something happens to you. You think that you've been obliterated, and then you realize that you're still alive, and not only still alive, but you look around and it's like a Hollywood movie. You thought you were dead. Now you're not, and you can hear the birds sing. That's exactly what a death trip is like. Where you touch bottom."

Michael, a very Jewish man, liked rabbinical tales. "There's a lot of stuff about touching bottom among some of the Hasidic masters. There was this one great man who used to convene his classes in a cemetery. One of his followers asked the master, 'Why are we meeting here of all places?' And the Hasid, the tzaddik, said, 'You have to go down to the bottom. In order to realize what the light is. And that's why we're here.'" In the cemetery, the living among the dead. The book wasn't all so deep. Very little of it was, in fact. Instead, "all sorts of chatter, absurdity, and dark humor, and all that shit," he said. But the light, behind and within, could be beautiful.

While he was making the book, he told me, he'd get in his car and slide into traffic. "The guy in front of me, I just followed him. I didn't turn away. I didn't turn right, I didn't turn left, unless he did. I just gave myself over to the current. It was like giving yourself up to a stream. Once he got to where he was going, I did it again. And again, and again. As a kind of surrender. It was amazing." He stopped, mocked

himself for saying "amazing," a term he deemed sentimental. He settled instead on *primal* for the current that carried him to the "news"
of another century. Or maybe for the news itself, as recorded in the
Black River Falls *Banner* and the archive of the town photographer:
suicides and incendiaries and "religious derangement," con artists
and would-be inventors and star-crossed lovers. A woman was pho-
tographed draped in snakes like feather boas, her face illuminated by
a grin that crossed decades; a strongman stood buck naked for the
camera and flexed. A Mrs. Friedel commissioned a photograph of her
baby "in its coffin"; then, an enlargement of the baby's face alone, on
which she further commissioned an artist to paint the infant's eyes,
open and alive. "Frederick Schultz," reported the November 15, 1900,
edition of the *Banner*, "cheated his undertaker by suddenly jumping
out of the coffin in which, supposed to be dead, he had been placed."

Such things happened then; adjusted for period detail, they happen now. Michael thought they'd always been happening. Persephone,
Mrs. Freidel's wide-eyed dead baby. Looked at one way, such an image
is a nightmare; turned another way, it's a consolation. "And if you read
more, or talk to learned people, you realize this primal shit is archetypal
shit." That is, you never need to make anything up. "It's just right there."
He meant the patterns. "It isn't like you dress up like a shaman, or light
some sage, or bow to the four compass points. But you do have to give
yourself over." To the current, into the river. "That's the deal. It isn't like
the world is divided between stuff that is kosher and stuff that is treyf"—
the Yiddish word for that which isn't kosher. A death trip doesn't honor
such distinctions, no simple good and bad and that's the answer.

Remember *Alice in Wonderland*? Michael asked. "She's chasing a
white rabbit, if memory serves." He didn't need to spell out the rest:
down a rabbit hole, the mind-ruining metaphor of our times, in
search of certainty. No such luck. Instead, "Tweedle Dee and Tweedle
Dum, pointing in opposite directions." This is the death trip: "possibilities of almost unremitting suffering, and also of clear-minded

understanding, even in the presence of this kind of craziness and very bad odds." Our odds, he meant. Our very bad American odds. This was what he had called to tell me.

>‹

Wisconsin Dells, Wisconsin

The shirt, the back of which featured a black-haired skull and the legend LIVE FOR NOTHING OR DIE FOR SOMETHING, represented Rambo, with whom the young man—maybe eighteen, nineteen, mullet and black bandanna and the whisper of a mustache—identified. The cross? God and guns, his passions. He belonged to a trap-shooting team. In a contest the day before he'd shot 90 out of a 100, bested by only one man who'd scored 92. He was happy to talk about God and babies—maybe someday he'd be a father—and he began to pose for a portrait. But his girlfriend intervened with a hand in front of the camera. "Protect your face!" she snapped and turned to glare at me. *Go away, Fake News.*

She was right—Wisconsin Dells, where I met them, isn't a town for hard questions. It's a tourist trap, titillating attractions, a lot of water slides—Noah's Ark Water Park—and escape rooms and a shooting range where you can rent a fully automatic AR-15. A friend's son tried to convince his mother to retain a magician advertising his "CLOSE-UP magic in your hotel room" with a mysterious blurb from Ray Lewis, the Baltimore Ravens Hall of Fame linebacker indicted for (and acquitted of) an unsolved double murder: "Holy shit! Here's my card, call me." What did that mean? I fed a dollar into the Trump fortune-telling machine, one of those racist "Zoltar" attractions refurbished with a talking Trump mannequin—"Every man has a right to decide his own destiny" it declared, a pointed message post-*Roe*—and got out of town.

In Springville, Wisconsin, I pulled over for what I thought was going to be a waterskiing show—I desperately wanted the loveliness of which kitsch is capable—but it wasn't happening, then or maybe ever. So I wandered into an adjacent trailer park, counting Trump flags. I got lost and cut through a field looking for a way out. Instead—

Glock under the left arm. Two flags and on the porch inside, a Confederate windsock. What was I doing on his lawn? I explained my mission. I asked for his name. "Just a guy," he said. An Average Guy. One with another gun in his right pocket, a tiny .380 that almost fit in his palm. One you could see, one you couldn't. He was a city man, Milwaukeean, native-born. Nothing to do with Confederate anything, he said of the red flag, which belonged to his stepson. HERITAGE NOT HATE, it read, though in the dank heat only the latter word could be seen. He recited the right-wing rosary—borders, crime, stolen elections, stealing our guns, *"our" guns*—and added his own variation to my growing toxic bouquet of reproductive disinformation: *man trap*s. The dark marriage plot. Abortion as "birth control," he thought, allowed women too much leverage. He pitched his voice high: "'I got pregnant because I wanted this guy to marry me'"—so many men I met discussed abortion by imitating voices they considered feminine—"'and now he's found out I'm pregnant and he doesn't want to marry me. So I'm going to have an abortion done. Until the next guy comes along that I can maybe chicken into marrying me because I'll get pregnant with his baby.'"

"Have you ever seen a woman pull something like that?"

He stammered that he hadn't—but he did know a lot of single mothers, an outcome he deemed somehow made less likely by outlawing abortion.

It was an ethos if not a logic, a fundamental belief in the deceitfulness of women and the necessity of their control. (Other people with wombs were beyond his imagination.) How did it work? He couldn't say, exactly, but he knew that it did. He was right. It does. It "works." Control. A man, a gun, a flag, a law: add it up, he thought, and we could return to order without any shooting.

Some friends, rural Wisconsinites, queer, left, and armed, wanted me to stop talking to angry people. "Why talk to Nazis?" asked one of their children, a six-year-old of strong common sense. "Well, they're not exactly *Nazis*," I said, but I knew that wasn't a real response.

In Quincy, Wisconsin, as the evening sun turned the fields gold, I saw a long-haired man who seemed to be making a fishing rod. He was happy for my company, so we stood together until the sun was gone. We spoke of the tornado that had sliced around his house and the fire that had eaten the surrounding fields and how fortunate he felt that the house still stood. How he loved fishing so much he'd made a little business for himself fixing other people's old rods and reels. He didn't charge much. He nodded at a rack of dozens, more than he'd ever get to, an abundance that brought him as much joy as a trout on the line. He never ate them. Always threw them back. Fish love life, too, he observed. He was very gentle, until he spoke of the deep state, and then something foul ate at his mind. He had a theory about abor-

tion: it is not just murder but worse, a plot to replace American new-borns with adopted foreign ones. Soon, he predicted, they will try to make us all speak one language, a one-world government tongue, an evil Esperanto that will rob us of that which is particular to our lives, our places, our pasts. It's coming, he said. No, he said, it's here. There will be no civil war, he said; he will never bring out his guns, though he, too, was armed, well-armed, he too had prepared his children—because we have already lost. All that remains is our accommodation.

><

To Waukesha, then, dense White-flight suburb of Milwaukee, where in 2021 a man who called himself Mathboi Fly plowed through a Christmas parade, killing six. Where, in 2014, two twelve-year-old girls took a third to the woods and stabbed her nineteen times. They wanted to ingratiate themselves with Slender Man, an Internet meme made real, or real enough, through the knives of children who believed what they read online.

Off the highway, where one might typically find a welcome sign boasting of past championships, there's a hillside on which stand dozens of hand-painted billboards. They rant against Joe Biden (MR. BEIJING BITE ME) and before him Obama, against local and state politicians, against tyranny and taxes and education (creeping critical race theory, warns the newest member of the Waukesha school board, "is intertwined, and it is soft, and it is subtle.") A fresher sign declares COVIK in bright red, bracketed by the jagged lightning bolts of the Nazi SS. It is all the work of one man, a Waukeshan told me. His discontent is said to have begun some two decades ago when a road project threatened his property—or failed to cross his property and raise its value. Which was it? Nobody I spoke to was certain. It didn't matter. Memes and grievances rise and fall according to the currents of sublimated mourning, eddying around this talking point or that. Sometimes without sense—like a man up the hill who, when I asked about his Trump '24 flag, cursed the Democrats for outlawing abortion [*sic*]—and sometimes in open defiance of reason. Slender Man; Let's Go Brandon; the Christmas Parade. And the Highland Park Fourth of July mass murderer, Bobby Crimo III—seven killed just days past—who once attended a Trump rally dressed as Waldo of "Where's Waldo?" fame, and who may or may not have been truly aware of "politics" as such at all. His online life rippled with right-wing hatreds, but he dedicated the panicked days before his crime to a sped-up aesthetic of images and ideologies crashing into one another, sometimes called "schizowave." It is a vile term, a grotesque romanticization of mental illness; an awful metaphor for the quickening of our fragmentation: the great acceleration, a simultaneous explosion and collapse of meaning.

Up the hill from the signs, in the vast empty parking lot of Elmbrook, which is said to be the biggest church in Wisconsin, I spoke to an old man named Terry. He said he remembered his sorrow the day *Roe* became law. "Life begins at conception," he declared. "When the sperm meets the egg, there's an explosion!" He raised his hands from his walker, threw them in the air. "It's not the baby's fault," he said. He kept saying this, over and over. He believed in "life," because it is never our fault that we're alive.

Like "schizowave" and its verb form, "schizoposting," "accelerationism" is a relatively recent term, allegedly coined or at least brought into contemporary use in 2013 by two Marxist political scientists via the influence of a two-volume work of 1970s French theory called *Capitalism and Schizophrenia*. "While crisis gathers force and speed, politics withers and retreats," the political scientists' *#ACCELERATE MANIFESTO for an Accelerationist Politics* announced. And: "The overwhelming privileging of democracy-as-process needs to be left behind." It was a rejection of the slow, small work of solidarity in favor of a "future more modern."

Yes, said fascist "intellectuals," adapting the concept to their own ends. *Yes, let's leave democracy behind.* The new fascists liked the idea of hastening the end of a liberal order. They repurposed the term for the speeding up of decay—deconstruction or destruction of the old to make way for the new, an idea that in turn bounced left again and found supporters amongst the anarchist ranks, schizowaving around a dizzying ideological loop. The instinct to burn it all down is understandable. But here's what fascism does with those matches: January 6; *Dobbs v. Jackson*, a decision seemingly tailored to provoke conflict; a long line of mass shooters. Christchurch, El Paso, Buffalo, and Bobby Crimo, of the Fourth of July, whom Marjorie Taylor Greene—accelerationist congresswoman of Georgia—suggested may have acted in a "false flag" capacity, perpetrating a hoax "designed" to promote gun control. "That would sound like a conspiracy theory, right?" she asked. Chuckling, she answered herself: "of course." Meaning, exploding and collapsing.

I drove to the woods in which Slender Man received his sacrifice (the girl lived), but the trees had been replaced by playing fields, which were filled with children, so I moved along, ashamed for looking. But shame didn't stop me from walking the Christmas Parade route. It was similarly devoid of any sign of the nightmare just recently past. I stopped for a drink, and the bartender told me that four of the victims, the "Dancing Grannies"—a delightful group that was just as it sounds—had been killed out front. "But you'd never know it now."

Predicting violence the night *Dobbs* came down, Fox News pundit Monica Crowley described pro-choice America as a "death cult." The Left calls the Right a death cult too. But for all its guns and Punisher skulls and actual killers, fascism is actually worse than a death cult: It's an innocence cult, the belief that one might be as innocent of history—read, race—as a fetus is of the world. Perfect and pink (White); unbloody in the Dobbsian imagination of the womb. The gun, too, is made clean by the cult of innocence, born again not as tool of aggression but of defense, as the protection of purity, inscribed by a growing number of manufacturers with Stars and Stripes and biblical verses; advertised as a form of evangelism, a means of spreading God's goodness in the world. Like a baby. The fetus and the gun. Small marvel nobody's yet put them together on a flag.

›‹

More poetry is said to come from Wisconsin than from any other state in the Union.
—Black River Falls *Badger State Banner*, April 10, 1885

So what do you think? Do you think maybe Jesus teachings [*sic*] is coming true right before our eyes?
—Black River Falls *Banner Journal*, June 22, 2022

Black River Falls, Wisconsin

I'd met a woman trying to conceive, and I'd met a soldier, and the soldier's daughter, who, he'd boasted, was a killer. I'd met a dying man, a mother and a father, a farmer. I'd met a boy and an angry man, and a brokenhearted man. I'd brought to Wisconsin with me my own hurting child. Then, when I felt like I most needed to, maybe because I felt like I needed to, I met some heroes. That word—*heroes*—makes me uneasy. The way it has come to require unalloyed virtue. That I did not find. Instead, the older sense of the term, having to do with courage, which is never simple.

The protest began with one woman, standing alone on the Main Street Bridge over the Black River, down a gentle slope from the Catholic church, holding a sign. Some cars honked, others revved; Black River Falls is a small town, 3,500, and Maddie Diehn, whose father was a county judge, recognized many of the drivers. She knew who honked because they believed like her that her body was her own, and who revved because they saw her there on the bridge, right out in the open with a sign that declared, YOUR MISOGYNY IS SHOWING, and thought her profane. She watched a man she knew—"the town extremist," with whose eldest daughter she'd been figure-skating friends since first grade—drive back and forth in his truck, filming her with his phone over the steering wheel. Then he got out, big-bellied and bearded, looming over Maddie, who at eighteen stands 4'11". He told her she was going to hell. "See you there," she replied. He insulted her mother. "Get the fuck out of here," she said. "I'm done with your ugly ass."

Her friend Paige joined her, and then Theta and Lilli drove by and stopped and made signs, and Paige went to gather others. A cheerleader for the Black River Falls Tigers named Peyton arrived with her FUCK OFF sign. "It means if you don't believe in women's rights, you can just literally go fuck off—you ain't getting no pussy, you ain't getting nothing!" It meant, she said, "rage." The town extremist returned with his wife and two of his younger children.

They also took up positions on the bridge, waving giant placards of aborted fetuses. That's what some people do now. Their dead-baby pictures.

Wisconsin Death Trip is about Black River Falls. Everybody I met there knew about it, but only one man cared to speak of it—

For twenty years Don had been walking the main street of Black River Falls, between the church on the hill and the bridge over the river, which is where he joined his fellow townspeople. He drifted between the teenagers with their clever signs and the extremist's family with their bloody ones. And me. He wanted to discuss *Wisconsin Death Trip*. He had not read the book, but he had seen the movie, made by the Academy Award–winning director James Marsh in 1999. He'd watched it over and over, studied it, after a fashion. "Beautiful, beautiful," he said. He told me to watch it on VHS if I wanted to see its true essence; he was certain secret truths came through only on tape. I told him I had, that the author, Michael Lesy, was a friend and that he'd shown me the film when I'd gone to his house to offer condolences the day of his wife's funeral. Michael had wheeled a television out of the room in which his wife, Liz, had lain dying, into the center of his living room, in front of a picture window. He'd placed a chair before the television and pushed in the advance VHS tape the director had given him. "Look," he'd said. He hoped I would see. I watched, the movie and the picture window. Delivery men coming and going with flowers. I thought I knew what Michael wanted: a witness, to life within death. "It is intertwined," as the Waukesha school board member had said—she hadn't yet realized the kinder possibilities of her words—"and it is soft, and it is subtle."

It can be—

Black River Falls, Wisconsin, circa 1900

"I remember," said Don, rolling the VHS in his mind and rolling out words, as he always did, very fast, "a lady that was having problems, she was walking around breaking windows." Mary Sweeney, described by the Black River Falls *Banner* in 1892 as a "model wife" and window smasher, walking and riding trains since she "ran away from home 2 years ago," jailed 100 times, "serving short sentences for indulging in her wild sport." She would claim to have smashed $50,000 worth of glass around Wisconsin, and she never did say why. Rage? "Every time she would get out of jail," theorized Don, "she'd break the window and they realized there was nothing they could do about it. And what did they do? They gave her a bus ticket somewhere." They did not; there were no buses in 1892, but there are buses now, and sometimes cities and towns dispatch those whom they have no call to imprison and yet wish gone with free tickets. I've seen it happen. I wanted to ask Don if he'd seen it, too, but his river of speech kept rolling: "And they had no choice but to be kind to her." *No choice but to be kind.* "They realized she had a condition." Our condition. "They had to accept it and move on and do something about it and figure it out. And they gave her a bus ticket somewhere and hugged her and made friends with her and I think they gave her a meal. This is a beautiful story."

Don had a word for beautiful stories: *math.* I thought of Mathboi Fly in Waukesha. Don's math was on a different plane. To a mother who had come out to protest with her daughter, he praised the teenagers for doing good math. He so mildly tangled with the extremist—whose name was Brian Aish—that Aish nodded meekly when Don told him that Aish needed to work on his math, "do your math and eat your breakfast"—*breakfast* being in Don's deep code another term for the things we do to hold on when the world is accelerating too fast. Eat your breakfast. Slow down. Consider, carefully, what lies ahead. Try to choose your path instead of being led down it. "We don't know how to act, as Americans," said Don.

Aish did not. It was a balmy summer night in Black River Falls and the thin arms of his children, dutifully holding up placards for a long time, were wilting. They had been promised soft-serve and could they please be done with dead-baby pictures now? Their mother took them. Aish remained, glaring at the teenagers and preaching at me. You could fill most of it in—stolen elections and furries and what he saw as widespread masturbation in schools (why was he imagining masturbation in schools?). On and on about rape's innocent children.

We'd drifted over to the parking lot and he was saying something about Trump when a big, apple-cheeked boy with jolly eyes and a thatch of blond hair swooped over on a tiny scooter and asked in the sweet voice of a choir soprano, "Do you guys know what this is?" He pointed at the teens.

"They're pro-choicers trying to advocate for murdering babies," snapped Aish.

The boy grinned; nothing wicked, pure delight. "Aw, hell, yeah!" he cried, and scooted a loop-de-loop around the preacher, cheering the pro-choicers.

"How'd you like to be his parents?" Aish snarled, and then to the boy: "You can't be a Christian and be pro-choice!"

"Good thing I'm an atheist," squeaked the boy, not missing a beat.

Aish sputtered something about Jesus judging him.

"Going to hell anyway!" the boy said brightly.

Aish harrumphed, double-defeated by the town meshuga and a laughing boy on a scooter.

>‹

Faster now.

The golden sky turned violet then blue, so the teens declared victory—with plans to return to the bridge the next day—and decided to retire to Perkins. One of their mothers, Catie Delcerro, invited me to join them for late-night waffles. The conversation was talk one might hear at such a table in any American town—college plans, summer jobs, social drama, crushes. There were multiple past and present student-government officers at the table. It would look like to anyone passing by to be a group that might have convened with only minor fashion adjustments in 2012, the Obama years, or, for that matter in 1982, the age of Reagan. But it was 2022, and these kids had lived through pandemic and insurrection and the slow boil of climate disaster. We remained mired in the Trumpocene, arguably

314 > The Undertow

deeper post-*Roe* than at any time in these young people's lives. So, after an enthusiastic exchange about possums—Catie, the mom, had rescued a wounded one and shared pictures of the creature cuddling with a pet skunk—and local elk—there was a herd I could witness, they promised, if I drove slow in the night on the dark roads past the casino—the conversation turned to civil war. Or, as Theta, the eldest, put it, "revolution."

Theta had a year of college behind her. She was tall and sure, honey-skinned and gorgeous, because they were all gorgeous, there is innate loveliness in young people celebrating the fight for their rights over late-night diner plates heaped high with calories for the struggle. There was also Karsen, deep-voiced and funny, a mixed martial arts fighter, a woman who took no shit; and Paige, who is Ho-Chunk and whose father moved the family there from Arizona to take a job for the Ho-Chunk Nation; and skinny, blond Reese, the youngest, who had just recently won a court case against another teen who'd assaulted him in a homophobic hate crime; and Lilli, second youngest, a keen student of political currents; and Peyton, the cheerleader with the FUCK OFF sign. Sitting across from me was Theta's mother, Catie. "Community mom," she said, crackling with pride for all, her daughter and her daughter's brave friends.

"Personally," said Theta, "I am for some kind of revolution. I think people should be prepared to arm themselves, because it's been shown to women that we can't trust our government to protect us."

"Not at all," said Karsen.

"Sometimes I take a Malcolm X approach to it," said Theta.

"I heart Malcolm X," agreed Karsen.

"Like," said Theta, "if they're showing violence to us, or not caring about violence that's happening to us, why not reciprocate that?"

"My take," said Karsen, who was Navy-bound, "is I plan on using the government to my full advantage. If we do get into a civil war."

"It's something you worry about?" I asked. Civil war?

"I'm waiting for it!" said cheerleader Peyton, fiercest of all. "And then I'm gonna—"

I thought of *Death Trip*. Michael had been a graduate student at the University of Wisconsin when he made it, working on an underground paper. Cartooning, collaging. Revolutionary art. Some took it further. There was a group called the New Year's Gang. They stole a plane and dropped a bomb on an ammunition plant. They set fire to a ROTC center. On August 24, 1970, they drove a stolen van packed with two thousand pounds of explosives to the campus's Army Mathematics Center and detonated. It wasn't supposed to hurt anybody, but it did, killed a young physicist, father of three. Michael watched it all happen, and then he'd return to the paper's office—under federal investigation by then, because they'd published the killers' communiques—where he began making *Death Trip*, which "means whatever you want it to mean," he told me.

Catie, Theta's mother, clarified that, to her, "arming" meant knowledge. Peyton clarified that to her it meant guns. Her family had them and she'd known how to shoot since she was a girl.

"That's what I'm here for," said Karsen. "My dad is a Republican"—many of their parents were—"and we have a lot of guns. I'll defend everyone else."

"You know how to shoot?" I asked her, wincing at my sexism and the condescension of age even as I said it.

"I hunt," Karsen said. "I do a *lot* of hunting."

Theta mimed aiming a gun.

"I don't share that feeling," said her mother. But she knew her daughter was of age. She believed she must make her own choices about what's to come.

Perkins was closing, and Theta's mom had to get to Walmart to pick up a prescription for her own mother. The kids and I walked into the night, and as one does in such a town if you're a teenager,

316 > The Undertow

316 > The Undertow

we sat on the curb. I did the same when I was their age, only then we argued about war in Iraq, not Wisconsin.

"It's not that I'm like, 'Ooh, yeah, war,'" said Theta. "It's like, we *need* a different system. As soon as possible. Because the planet is literally dying. Honestly, it's like when I make my plans? I'm going to be in school for another eight to ten years"—she used to want to be a politician, now she wanted to be a scholar—"and do I have that long?"

I thought of others my age who'd roll their eyes at such a question. Nothing's happening that quickly.

Unless it does.

"I have a hot take on how it'll start," Paige said. She'd been sitting quietly, listening to her friends.

"Go, Paige," said Lilli.

"I've been thinking," she said. "It's unfortunate, but I feel the revolution won't start until something happens that affects White men. Like BLM, that came close"—it was, they all agree, the summer of 2020, the murder of George Floyd and the demonstrations, that opened their eyes to the state of things—"but it didn't take off because it's Black people. This"—the fall of *Roe*—"probably isn't going to take off, because it's women. But when something happens to a White man?"

"They ban golf," said Karsen. We all laughed.

"They ban golf," agreed Paige, "and that's when the revolution starts."

I told them about some of the other people with guns I'd been meeting, Rob Brumm and his militia, the man who wanted to personally execute doctors. The kids said they weren't scared of them. Climate? That's scary. Trump is scary. The Supreme Court, they agreed, is very scary. They were afraid they wouldn't be allowed to love who they wanted, that contraception was next, that the adult lives they'd barely or not yet begun were already being bound, taken, in ways neither they nor their parents had ever imagined. They were just kids. This was just talk on the curb outside a Perkins in Black River Falls. They were scared of so much, because they had to be, but they chose not to be frightened by all the little men with their big rifles.

"You know," said Theta, "it's either we fight against them, we possibly get killed in a civil war—or we suffer like this, our rights stripped away from us by the minute. And I don't know if that's a life worth living."

›‹

Mary and her husband are going ahead with trying to have a baby. Because if not now, when? Because they know it's no longer impossible to imagine IVF criminalized. Because they're used to the kind of men who tell them what they can't do and they're used to doing it anyway. Because they love each other and they want to love and raise a child together and they're willing to take a lot of chances to make that happen—more, now, medically, legally, knowing they won't have access to abortion should three eggs be fertilized, might not even if Mary's life is at risk. "I'm ready to be a mom," said Mary. "I'm making that choice." They're going forward—it's Wisconsin's slogan, *Forward*, coined for a state that was once the union's most progressive—because that's all there is.

10

The Good Fight
Is the One You Lose

In 1950, Lee Hays sent his family the first proof of his existence they'd had in longer than a decade. It was a record: little Lee—all three hundred pounds of him—harmonizing his deep, dark bass voice on "Goodnight, Irene," the number-one hit in the nation. Lee was thirty-six, but his voice sounded old and smooth, and also hard, exposed: an oak shivered open. "Stop rambling, stop your gambling," Lee sang, a verse ironic in more ways than one:

> Stop staying out late at night,
> Go home to your wife and family
> Stay there by your fireside bright.

The last any Hays had heard of Lee, he was on his way to getting lynched, a gentle fool of a giant running after lunatic dreams: lily-white Lee planning a Black Boy Scout troop in Mississippi, pinko Lee organizing a mixed-race union of sharecroppers in Arkansas, "Professor" Lee teaching Yankees how to put on communist plays in Southern churches. And then he'd gone missing. In a ditch? In a river? To Moscow? No; he resurfaced: on top of the charts, in *Time* magazine, singing on television. He was the foundation of a "folk sensation," a hillbilly quartet by way of Greenwich Village, the Weavers: Lee's bass, Freddy Hellerman's neat baritone, Ronnie Gilbert's fire-alarm alto, and the wry tenor of Lee's old friend Pete Seeger, all soaked in the syrup of an orchestra imposed by the record company and loved only by Lee. He appreciated a sound as big as his belly and as grand as his politics. He called himself a socialist, but he liked to say he didn't know what kind. That wasn't quite true; he was the singing kind. To him, collectivism meant four-part harmony. He hated to sing alone, took no solo bookings, insisted on sharing credit for his songs. "Sharing made him a little less vulnerable," remembered a guitarist who backed him. "Lee needed a group to be Lee Hays," says one of his protégés, the singer Don McLean. "That's why he invented the Weavers." They were all lefties, but it was Lee's longings—one part Red, one part religion, one part the angry empathy of a closeted man raised holy roller in rural Arkansas—that provided the tilt that made "Goodnight, Irene" lilt so lovely out of jukeboxes across the country.

Lee and Pete had borrowed the song from an idol of theirs called Leadbelly. A good many of the Weavers' songs were Leadbelly's. Lee and Pete likely first gleaned "Midnight Special," "Rock Island Line," "Stewball," "Goodnight, Irene," and the tune to which Lee wrote "Kisses Sweeter Than Wine," all huge Weavers hits, gathered round Leadbelly's twelve-string guitar and a bottle of bourbon in Leadbelly's Lower East Side apartment. Leadbelly was a font of American songs. Not just the blues but also ballads and folk and gospel and reels, country, jazz, and pop. "Art is a weapon," went a radical slogan of the day. Leadbelly was an armory. He remembered every-thing he ever heard and mixed it together as the spirit led, as the hour demanded. Leadbelly taught Pete what Lee already knew: "authenticity" was a trap, purity was a dead end, no song belonged wholly to anyone. Pass the song along, he told the White boys. Lee didn't appropriate Leadbelly's songs, he made "sub-versions," each variation both new and noisy with the ghosts of those who'd sung it before. Pete memorized the notes, Lee felt them. He was loose with language. Not careless; agile. Before he went north, he specialized in what he called "zipper songs." He'd make them out of Christian hymns and sing them at the secret meetings of the sharecroppers' union back home in Arkansas, "zipping" radical words into a song like "The Old Ship of Zion." "It's that union train a-coming-coming-coming," he'd sing—prepared, he explained, "to break into the old hymn words if gun thugs should appear."

That was back in the '30s, when Lee led with a movie-star chin and followed with bluebird eyes, when he was still filled with enough Holy Ghost—Lee always had the Ghost—to believe that racism would soon fail. "See the lynch-rope a-swinging," he'd write,

see the torches burn.
The people said, wake up, it's time to learn,
Time to get together, drive the evil men out
And make a new land in our own South.

But it was Lee, no fighter, who got driven out, running north by stages. To Cleveland, where he educated himself working in a library, reading all the books marked by a special black rubber stamp as unsuitable for respectable people—*Lady Chatterley's Lover*, by D. H. Lawrence; Upton Sinclair's *The Jungle*; Walt Whitman, sus-pected of desires similar to Lee's; tales from a renaissance said to be taking place in Harlem. From Cleveland to Philadelphia, where he became "Uncle Lee" to the household of the avant-garde poet Walter Lowenfels; and from there to New York City, where he shared a place on West Tenth Street with a gangly green banjo picker named Pete Seeger, cataloguer of five hundred songs, enthrallee of Lee's Southern storytelling bona fides.

Lee's signature song was "State of Arkansas," a mournful dirge about the miseries of his home state that shifted effortlessly to hillbilly humor. The song's narrator pays for a pint of whiskey with a mink skin and gets "three possum hides and fourteen rabbit skins for change." Then the song turns again, ending, like most of Lee's thoughts, somewhere between mournful and funny:

If you ever see me back again
I'll extend to you my paw
But it'll be through a telescope
From hell to Arkansas.

Pete, built like his long-necked banjo without the curves, emptypocketed scion of the New England Seegers, got up in sharecropper drag, became the straight man to Lee's shambling, smoky lush, bigeared and bag-eyed, with a black suit draped over his giant frame. "I was relatively shy and inexperienced in many, many ways," Pete recalled. "So we took bookings together." Joining them came along an Okie already of some renown, Woody Guthrie, with whom Lee liked to share a bottle nightly. Woody was not easy on Pete's workingclass affectations. He'd point his nose in the air in imitation and drip Harvard vowels. Pete—known as "The Saint"—couldn't or wouldn't come up with a response, so Lee would find himself defending the Yankee barely out of his teens. Together they called themselves the Almanac Singers. "If you want to know what's good for the itch, or unemployment, or Fascism, you have to look in your Almanac," Lee declared. "That's what Almanac stood for."

Soon there were more Almanacs than Lee could keep track of, singers and songwriters and guitar pickers and accordion squeezers crowding into unheated urban communes Lee called Almanac Houses. Pete would rise at dawn and sprout ten songs before Lee pried open his eyes. But when Lee finally woke he'd sift through the ten and pluck out the one worth singing. They sang "Which Side Are You On?" in churches, "Get Thee Behind Me, Satan" in union halls. "Songs about peace, white-collar workers, air raid wardens," catalogued Lee, "the sinking of a destroyer, love, unemployment, coal miners, songs about the Almanacs themselves." They sang the party line, although often as not they fell out of tune. As "orders-takers," Lee confessed, they were a failure. "If the Communists liked what we did," Lee summed up his orthodoxy, "that was their good luck."

><

But even up north, Lee couldn't escape "the torches burning." In 1949, after the Almanacs had dissolved because of the war and because Pete kicked Lee out (some would say it was politics; Lee would say it was because he'd been lazy), and after a union of radical folk singers they'd created called People's Songs folded (Pete kicked Lee out; Lee *was* lazy), a mob of lowercase people, actual workers and farmers and especially veterans, attacked an outdoor concert Lee and Pete had helped organize in the Hudson River town of Peekskill, just north of New York City.

The headliner was Paul Robeson, the stage and screen star of *Showboat, Othello, Emperor Jones*. The "Russia-loving Negro baritone," the local *Evening Star* called him. The paper considered him an advance man for Moscow and urged the citizenry to stop Robeson and his Red friends by any means necessary.

The scheduled date, August 27, was one of those Hudson River days when the sun seems too sleepy to set. The concert ground was a meadow at the end of a dirt road, its entrance a bottleneck; gathered round it like a noose was a crowd of boys, jeering each passerby. The radical novelist Howard Fast was early on the scene. He found a group of teenage ushers. "Just keep cool," he told them. He was sure there wouldn't be trouble; the weather was too sweet, a goldenrod evening, Robeson too big a star. "Nothing will happen," he told the ushers.

Then another usher came running around the bend. Trouble, he hollered, men gathering. Fast and a few dozen followed the boy back to the entrance. Up on the banks of the road had gathered a mob, more than Fast could count, hundreds, veterans in American Legion caps, businessmen in shirtsleeves, teenagers grinning.

Fast was a sophisticated man, an artist, but he'd grown up in street gangs. He knew as much as anyone there about fighting. He pulled his little group of men and boys into a line at the entrance to the concert grounds and surveyed his comrades. Soft material. Skinny boys from Harlem in church clothes, summer-camp counselors, bohemian hoboes whose fingers were more used to plucking six-strings than making fists. "We stood in a line in the gathering dark, arms locked, singing 'Freedom is our struggle, we shall not be moved'"—one of the songs Lee had helped popularize. "Every few seconds there was a sickening thud as a rock crashed against a skull of one of our boys," Fast later wrote. "Some held their places with blood pouring from their torn scalps; others went down."

Night fell. A lull followed. The policemen were no longer there. The mob shifted shape. Then it charged, through the dark in waves, men with billies and men with bottles, fools with posts ripped from white picket fences.

Lee and Pete later memorialized the fight in a song "Hold the Line," which would become an anthem of the civil rights movement:

Hold the line, hold the line,
As we held the line at Peekskill
We will hold it everywhere.

But the truth was that they held the line only by backing it up, foot by bloody foot, till they were pushed into a ring around the stage. Someone smashed the lights. Women led crying children in "The Star Spangled Banner." The mob chanted, *"Kill a commie for Christ!"* The night turned brilliant with a bonfire of two thousand folding chairs. A wooden cross flared into flames. Three government men in suits, who had likely come to observe Red Robeson—impartial, they later told the wounded concertgoers who begged for help—stood taking notes as the townsmen, now some seven hundred strong, gathered up songbooks and sing-along sheets and threw them into the fire.

The concert's organizers rescheduled for the following week. This time they knew it'd be a fight. So up from the city, from Brooklyn and the Bronx and the Lower East Side, they recruited an army of three thousand union men to form a perimeter. Instead of the originally planned audience of two thousand, twenty thousand showed, determined to show the fascists that they would not be beaten. Pete brought his banjo and belted out Lee's lyrics to their new "Hammer Song," later to be known as "If I Had a Hammer"—"I'm hammering out DANG-ER!" And Robeson took the stage guarded by a circle of Leftist veterans and sang his famously radicalized version of "Old Man River"—

I must keep fightin';
Until I'm dyin'
And Ol' Man River,
He just keeps rollin' along.

Then, after a few more numbers, point made, the crowd was ready to declare victory and get out of Peekskill.

But the townspeople had made plans. With the help of some nine hundred local and state police officers, another mob—a militia five thousand strong, pre-planned and organized into units—funneled the concertgoers onto Division Road, "a long gray tunnel" Lee would call it. Thousands of protesters waited, pre-stacked rock piles at the ready. State troopers looked the other way. A police helicopter thumped overhead. Local deputies cheered as each car had its windows smashed. A CBS radioman broadcast the scene. "The police—are beating up a Negro. They're clubbing him." The rioters screamed. "White n----s go back to Russia!" Or, reduced by rage to one word, "Jew! Jew! Jew!"

They began flipping vehicles. They dragged out first men and then women for beatings, with clubs and brass knuckles and most of all shoes, work boots and wingtips and women's pumps swinging into the bellies and teeth of schoolteachers and garment workers and railroad porters.

Lee made it out on a bus with Woody. Big Lee shaking and close to tears, little Woody cracking wise. "Anybody got a rock?" Woody called. "There's a window back here that needs to be opened." That made Lee laugh. Then Lee began to sing. The new song he and Pete had just written. He began in the middle of the lyric, his great barrel of a voice transcending his terror. *I'll sing out danger! I'll sing out a warning!* Woody joined in. *I'll sing out love between my brothers, all over this land....*

The next day started late in Peekskill. The sign at the outskirts that declared PEEKSKILL IS A FRIENDLY TOWN was joined by another, hastily printed, replicated in store windows up and down Main Street. WAKE UP AMERICA! PEEKSKILL DID.

If this is America, Lee thought, it's not mine.

"Sometimes I live in the country," went the number he sang after Peekskill, "Goodnight, Irene," a subtler, sadder song.

Sometimes I live in town,
Sometimes I take a great notion
To jump in the river and drown.

Pete's banjo plucks the rhythm, Ronnie Gilbert's alto slips into the water, Lee's big bass aches the lullaby. That's all it was to the hit parade, but to Lee, especially, "Goodnight, Irene" was a secret language, "a great notion" all that could be said of a nation that responded to folk songs with burning crosses, the drowning as much of an allusion to Leadbelly's darker words—an addict's lament, a love gone cold—as Decca Records would allow. For those who could hear, though, the simple song was thick with brokenhearted meanings, an elegy for wrong choices and defeats, a hope for the sweet revolutionary bye-and-bye.

Irene, goodnight. Irene, goodnight.
Goodnight, Irene, goodnight, Irene,
I'll see you in my dreams.

><

In 1950, when Lee sent out three records of "Goodnight, Irene," one to each of his siblings—brother Reuben, a banker; brother Bill, a salaryman; Minnie Frank, a newspaper poetess in a little North Carolina town—he attached a note relaying as much as he thought they'd be able to understand. Where he had been, what he had seen, the revolution that did not happen, the signals he still transmitted: radio free Lee for those with the ears to hear him. His letter was just six words long: "This is what I've been doing."

That was as true as the three minutes and twenty-two seconds of "Goodnight, Irene," from the first swell of the strings glued on by a hit-conscious record company to the fade of four voices.

After Lee had left home years before, after he'd given up on Reuben, Bill, and Minnie Frank as hopelessly bourgeois, he had found new brothers and sisters among the labor organizers who became his heroes. It was in their company, he would say, that he learned to hear himself sing: One night, late 1930s, riding with organizers through a cold Arkansas night, the sound of his voice mixing with others, those who sang along with him and those who had sung before him.

Lee was not a brave man. Despite his size, his mastiff shoulders and the head large and hard as a tree stump between them, he shrank from physical confrontation. From physical activity, in general. He was tubercular, though he did not know it then, and the diabetes that would piece by piece rob him of his legs in later years may have begun to set in. He had run away from home, but he believed his family had abandoned him. His father, an itinerant preacher, dead in a car crash when Lee was thirteen, his mother gone insane shortly thereafter. Bill, ten years his senior, was ill prepared to take in a younger brother. Hunger and loneliness aged Lee early. And fear, because beneath the big bass and behind his hillbilly routines, Lee was afraid, as permanent a condition of his constitution as the sexual desires he referred to in published writing only once, obliquely, in a pseudonymous review of now-forgotten novels by gay writers he deemed too "defensive" about their longings. "Have you ever been married?" friends who didn't know better would ask, and Lee would crack his broad thin lips in a grin, his little liquor-soaked teeth like a row of corn on the cob, and tell a tale about his first time, way back when, with a "golden- haired girl," in a Confederate cemetery; no more questions, please.

His old fears were strong that night in the rump-sprung car. It was marked for violence, and so was its owner, an organizer who had once been whipped by bosses with the belly band of a mule harness. "The organizer drove warily, hunched over the wheel," Lee wrote. "The young Negro boy beside him watched the road just as carefully, and his feet pressed the floorboards every time the organizer stepped on the brakes. The Negro man and the White woman who sat in the rear with me were tense, and I could feel their bodies tightening up every time we passed a car or went through a town.

"The organizer started singing."

Ordinarily, they would have sung union songs. "But in this cold night we sang hymns." They had all been raised in the Church and all had converted to unionism. They believed in deliverance, here and now, not salvation. But they remembered the old words, and they sang them, "harmonies swelling and breaking ('Floods of joy o'er my soul like the sea billows roll') bass voice giving way to sweet soprano, the organizer's raspy baritone coming in with a verse or a chorus, one hymn after another, and all the voices searching for harmonies unheard and unknown, perfect blends of tones and feelings and fears. I wondered about this, why we found such comfort in the old hymns, we whose eyes were fixed on a new day and a new way of life. For a while, it was possible not to be scared, even."

"But the answer was there, and it came to me that the words of the song didn't matter. They were there and we sang them, but what mattered was that we were singing."

><

Lee was a believer. Like his father who died pinned to the wheel of his overturned open-top Ford on a two-lane outside of Booneville, Arkansas, making his pastoral rounds; like his second father, Claude Williams, a radical minister known as the Red Preacher, a White Arkansan beaten and jailed for the same Christian hope that Martin Luther King Jr. would die for decades down the road.

But Lee's god wasn't God, it was "The People," that great abstract, many-faced mass, deified fetish of a faith since forgotten in America. You could call Lee's religion communism with a small *c*, and Lee sometimes did, but he'd just as soon call it a song. "One dreams of a great people's song," he wrote in 1948, as close as he ever came to declaring a creed, "of our marching song which will come again, but hasn't yet; of the great song which is still unsung."

"I never knew but one person in my life that didn't like singing or music in any form," went a story he liked to tell between songs. "He was a Southern preacher who belonged to a church that thought all music was sinful, etc., etc. I would argue with him about it by the hour and say, 'Preacher, I just can't understand your point of view. Music is divine, it's the language of the angels. It defines the indefinable, expresses the inexpressible.' But he would just say, 'I wouldn't care if it unscrewed the inscrutable, it's sinful and I don't like it.'"

Lee's gut was with the preacher—not on the matter of sinning, but in shared disregard for that which seemed exclusive—but he longed to sing like the angels. He believed that the unsung song of "The People" would be remembered for generations, a victory song, like John Brown's glory. He tried zipping labor and race into "We Shall Not Be Moved." He wrote the words to Pete's melody for "If I Had a Hammer." He wrote in a fury and rang his aching vocal cords like two-ton church bells on "Hold the Line."

But he didn't hold the line. He couldn't. In 1950, Lee alone among the Weavers realized that the battle was lost. The war was lost. Maybe someday they would fight another. When the Weavers hit the top of the charts and Pete seethed over being booked in swanky clubs in Hollywood and Vegas instead of union halls in Arkansas, Lee ordered room service and toasted every jukebox in America that made the Weavers' "So Long, It's Been Good to Know Ya" one of the most-played tunes of the summer of '51.

It wasn't that Lee had sold out. He just didn't think he'd be marching on Washington anytime soon, and he figured he could do more good at the head of the hit parade. He knew it wouldn't last. It was only a matter of time before some goon dug up their past and reported that the tuxedoed quartet was in truth a singing sleeper cell direct from Moscow. He was right. There was an actual Judas, an FBI informer named Harvey Matusow, aka "Harvey Matt," Lee's friend, the very head of the People's Songs Music Center.

Matusow would later describe his betrayal in a book called *False Witness*. He and the directors of a group called "Counterattack"—three former FBI agents who functioned as a faucet for J. Edgar's leaks—found themselves frustrated as they mulled over the success of the Weavers. They loathed Weaver hits such as "On Top of Old Smokey" and "Pay Me My Money Down" and "Midnight Special"—America-hating music, they believed, commie code. Seeger they had already tried to blacklist, unsuccessfully. And they had nothing new on the Weavers. That didn't matter. "Having known all four of them, not as Communists, but as friends, I triumphantly said, 'I know them, and they are Communists.'"

And that was it. Bookings disappeared. Records disappeared. Top of the charts in 1950, by the end of '52, the Weavers' names weren't safe to whisper. Before HUAC in 1955, Pete invoked freedom of speech, a move that earned him a prison sentence of a year. Lee wasn't so brave. The committee was especially interested in a song he'd written called "Wasn't That a Time," an earnest exercise in musical socialist realism that ran a red thread of Left patriotism from Valley Forge to People's Songs. "Our faith cries out," went the words. "We have no fear!" The biggest lie Lee ever told. After Pete's hearing, Pete sang Lee's song for the television cameras. Lee, lacking Pete's puritan pride, was too scared to admit he even knew his own words. "We have just heard one of your songs, entitled 'Wasn't That a Time,'" said the committee's counsel. "Are you the author of that song?"

"I decline to answer," Lee murmured, pleading the Fifth, which was precisely what HUAC wanted—the Fifth Amendment, as far as they were concerned, was a confession. "I don't think I have ever felt so damned alone as on that day," he'd remember in 1981, the year he died. He would sing again, but there was a sense in which the rest of his life was a long, slow exhalation. Don McLean, a folk singer of the next generation, recalls Lee circa 1968. Lee lived then on a half-acre up along the Hudson, on a hillside of Cold War casualties. His neighbors were fellow blacklist veterans. His visitors were young musicians who heard the love but not the danger in the song that paid for Lee's liquor, "If I Had a Hammer." Some days were very fine; he still had his legs then, and he loved to garden and tell stories about a South to which he could not return.

Some days he was afraid of what lay beyond, what he'd left behind. Some days he was just mean. He would disappear into his cottage, while away the day filling an ashtray as big as an urn. "He still had his voice," remembers McLean, "but he was shrinking. Like air was coming out of him." One day, McLean went to Lee for help with an album to be called *American Pie*, after the song that would become its great hit. But McLean needed a closer, a bookend to the good old boys drinking whiskey and rye. Lee said he knew just the song. He began to sing, his big voice filling his smoky living room. Nothing folksy; a psalm, number 137.

> B-y-y-y the waters, the wa-a-aters
> of Babylon. We lay down and wept and wept for thee, Zi-on.
> We remember thee We remember thee Zi-on.

><

At the end of 1955, the Weavers regrouped. Their manager beat the blacklist by renting Carnegie Hall for a nameless quartet and then selling it out before anyone could complain. Their opening number was "Darling Corey." If you have ever wondered what the Left once was in America—the Old Left that organized American labor and gave rise to the Black revolt that would grow into Black Power, and fought fascists in Spain in 1936 and in Peekskill in 1949, and was killed by committee just a few years later—listen to "Darling Corey," as the Weavers sang it in 1955. It's a ghost, a memory even then, but still it's more thrilling than anything that played on the radio that year—or last year, for that matter—a punk battle hymn for four voices.

Pete tears it open with a single note hit hard over and over, spitting bullets out of his long-necked banjo, usually the happiest-sounding set of strings in the world. But Pete was mad and proud and bitter, playing for the fallen and the falling, Leadbelly and Woody—two-thirds gone now, dying of Huntington's disease in Brooklyn—and the Weavers themselves. It was a new sound for Pete, Woody's sound—not the jokes, but the anger. The difference between Pete and Woody could be seen on their instruments. In a neat circle bordering his banjo, Pete wrote, THIS MACHINE SURROUNDS HATE AND FORCES IT TO SURRENDER. Across the hips of his guitar, Woody scrawled, THIS MACHINE KILLS FASCISTS. That night in 1955, Pete turned his banjo into Woody's old killing machine. The first spray of notes is followed by a plummeting spiral like a man falling—leaping—off a cliff. Then in come all four voices:

WAKE UP, WAKE UP,
DARLING COREY!

The song is about a free-loving, moonshining mountain woman, but as Lee would say of his favorite hymns, the words don't matter. The opening blast of harmony is Gabriel's horn, an air-raid siren, a mash-up of the Red Army Choir and the Mormon Tabernacle Choir and an Alabama chain gang, the First Amendment and the Fifth and all the others side by side singing out the most joyous fuck-you ever drawn up from the well, the deep, dark shaft of rage and terror and heart-hurting and love and defying.

The first booming verse, of course, belongs to mighty Lee Hays:

Well first time I seeeeeeen Darlin' Corey,
She was standing by the sea,
Had a .45 strapped 'round her bosoooom,
She had a banjo on her knee!

Maybe the words do matter.

Like these, the beginning of the third verse, Ronnie Gilbert's alto whooshing in like cannonballs:

OH YES OH YES, MY DARLING!

Lee was the reader of the group, a student of banned books and a secret writer of pornographic tales, so maybe he heard the Irish echo of James Joyce's Molly Bloom. "Yes I said yes I will Yes," the last words of *Ulysses*. Joyce thought Molly Bloom's *Yes* signaled the end of resistance; acquiescence. Lee heard the *Yes* of "Darling Corey" differently, louder, even, than Molly Bloom's transcendent submission, heard it to the end of his days, when he was legless in a little cottage up along the Hudson, not far from Peekskill, where he came to know and even befriend some of the men and women who'd had blood in their throats and rocks in their fists back in 1949. He heard that opening number in Carnegie Hall in the winter of 1955—sang it—like a hymn on a cold night in Arkansas. For a while, it was possible not to be scared, even.

Acknowledgments

Thanks to the illuminati—that is, those whose brilliance and generosity as readers, interlocutors, or hosts lit up the neural pathways of this book's composition. Some of the many have been Gretchen Aguiar, Michelle Aldredge, Jeff Allred, Aimee Bahng, Karen Beard, Bill Boyer-Bahng, Bill Boling, Blair Braverman, Matt and Yoko Burde, Anthea Butler, Bill Craig, Tracy Pizzo Frey, Rebecca Holcombe, Cynthia Huntington, Kathryn Joyce, Sarah Khatry, Andrew Kulmatiski, Michael Lesy, Lucas Mann, Peter Manseau, Quince Mountain, Ann Neumann, Tommy O'Malley, Sarah Posner, Randy Potts, Steve Prothero, David Rabig, Don & Jude Rabig, my wife and favorite historian, Julia Rabig, Jeff Ruoff, Joe Saginor, Seth Sanders, Nathan Schneider, Rianna Starheim, Meera Subramanian, Inara Verzemnieks, Stewart Wallace, Elizabeth Wildman, Diane Winston, Pete White, and JoAnn Wypijewski. Melanie Shornick shared the photograph of her dog, Louie, that appears on page 184; Matt Virden, even knowing that we did not see the events of January 6 in the same light, gave me permission to include the post-surgery photograph that appears on page 194. Thanks also to the activists and subtle scholars who, deep in the struggle, ask to remain unnamed; my colleagues at Dartmouth College, too many to name; and all the splendid artists and staff with whom I shared dinner, talk, and work across the several MacDowell residencies that made *The Undertow* possible. My children, X the Fantastic and M the Magnificent, made it worth writing, for the sake of its last words.

There are no honest books without great editors. Mine have been Alane Salierno Mason at W. W. Norton; Claire Howorth, Claire Landsbaum, and Eric Bates at *Vanity Fair*; Eric Sullivan, first at *GQ* and then *Esquire*; Paul Reyes, first at *Oxford American* and then *VQR*; Bill Wasik at *The New York Times Magazine*; and Chris Lehmann at *Bookforum*. I am indebted also to Mo Crist, Susan Sanfrey, Will Scarlett, and many more at Norton, and to Allison Wright, Sean Woods, and so many others at each of these publications. Will Gerrish and Kira Parrish-Penny provided research essential to the title essay. Thanks to Dartmouth College for research funding, particularly Elizabeth Smith and Barbara Will, and the Society of Fellows. And then there's Kathy Anderson, agent, friend, and comrade.

My most reliable and insightful reader was my father, Robert Sharlet, who died in 2019. I still hear his voice when I revisit the early essays in this book. His life partner, Fiona Burde, who died in 2021, was the inspiration for the best and brightest moments contained herein.

The title essay, "The Undertow," in which I embraced land acknowledgments, was one of the last I wrote. But as I look back across the map of this book, I know now there are other names for the places in which these events occurred: Manhattan, where the book begins, and Peekskill, New York, where it ends just up the Hudson River, which the Lenape called the Mahicantuck, are on Wappinger, Munsee Lenape, and Schaghticoke land. Camp Robert Smalls, where Harry Belafonte began his radical education with the help of older Black seamen and a local library, is on Peoria, Bodwéwadmi (Potawatomi), Myaamia, Očhéthi Šakówiŋ, Hoocąk (Ho-Chunk), and Kiikaapoi (Kickapoo) land. Greenwood, Mississippi, where he outran the Klan, is on Chahta Yakni (Choctaw) and Chakchiuma land. Montgomery, Alabama, is on Mvskoke (Muscogee), Koasati (Coushatta), and Alabama land.

Youngstown, Ohio, is on Osage, Erie, and Kaskaskia land. Fountain Hills, Arizona, where a White Trump supporter ominously whispered "Indians" to speak of the adjacent reservation, is on Akimel O'odham (Upper Pima), Hohokam, and Yavapai Apache land. Miami and nearby Sunrise are on Seminole, Taíno, Tequesta, Miccosukee, and Mascogo land. Detroit is on Peoria, Anishinabewaki, Bodwéwadmi (Potawatomi), Myaamia, Meškwahki·aša·hina (Fox), and Mississauga land. Bossier City, Louisiana, is on Osage), O-ga-xpa Ma-zhoⁿ (O-ga-xpa) (Quapaw), Caddo, and Yatasi land. Hershey, Pennsylvania, self-declared "sweetest place on earth," is on Susquehannock land. Austin, Texas, is on Jumanos, Coahuiltecan, Comanche, Ndé Kónitsąąíí Gokíyaa (Lipan Apache), and Tonkawa land.

In Wisconsin, I crossed Očhéthi Šakówiŋ, Omāēqnomenewahkew (Menominee), Anishinabewaki, Peoria, oθaakiiwaki·hina·ki (Sauk) & Meškwahki·aša·hina (Fox), Bodwéwadmi (Potawatomi), Myaamia, Hoocąk (Ho-Chunk), and Kiikaapoi (Kickapoo) land.

I must acknowledge my source for these acknowledgments, native-land.ca, a project of an Indigenous-led nonprofit organization called Native Land Digital, which emphasizes that its map is very much a work-in-progress, subject to change as new information and understanding develops. The past, like the future, remains unfixed, unsettled.

THE UNDERTOW

Jeff Sharlet

THE UNDERTOW

Jeff Sharlet

DISCUSSION QUESTIONS

1. Jeff Sharlet bookends *The Undertow* with pieces devoted to musicians—Harry Belafonte and Lee Hays and the Weavers. What roles do you think art and music play in times of cultural discord and dissolution? Which artists or performers today will be looked back on as revolutionaries or truth speakers?

2. Did these essays confirm or challenge your understanding of what is happening in America at this moment? Did any essays surprise you?

3. "Movements are born from the problems of everyday lives, but they're not limited by them" (p. 37). What do you think this line means? Do you agree? Which movements feel relevant to your own life—what problems have they tried to address?

4. How did these immersive essays make you *feel*? What did this intimate perspective provide that a more removed, traditional political essay could not?

5. "Democracy is a practice. It may not be real yet, but it is not a dream. It's something you do, something we could make, in this life" (p. 144). Do you agree with this statement? How do you engage with the practice of democracy?

6. "I wondered if I should press him. That's what journalists do. We're worse than the media haters can imagine. We leave a message and when we don't get an answer, we leave another and sometimes we just knock on a door on the other side of which, we know, is fear, or grief, or anger that does not want our ques-

tions. Our measuring gaze. But we want it. Their fear, their grief, their anger. Our measuring gaze. So we soothe, we cajole. We seek 'access'" (p. 199). Do you agree with Sharlet's assessment of journalists here? How does it influence your reading of these essays?

7. Do you think Sharlet has done a good job capturing this moment in time? Are there any other spaces or times you wish you had similar insight into?

8. What did you think about Sharlet's capitalization of "Whiteness"? Did this small shift feel impactful?

9. "'Let me ask you,' I say. My turn. 'We've been through a bad time, in America.' A lot of people sighing. 'What just happened?' I tell him about Ashli's mother in Sacramento, how she cried. How she was angry. 'You lose someone,' I say, 'you're angry.' He knows it, anger and its costs. I tell him I've been listening to anger, writing it down, for two thousand miles" (p. 254). How would you answer the question "What just happened?" Do you feel angry? Do you think that the people around you feel angry? Do you know why?

10. "'What I did,' Belafonte says, 'what made conscious political sense was to say, "Let me have you love me because I will show you my deeper humanity."' . . . 'If you like this song so much that I can engage you into singing it, delighting in it, I've sold you a people, a region, a culture'" (p. 20). Do you agree with Harry Belafonte that art is a conduit to empathy and greater humanity? Whose work has expanded your worldview?

11. "History's like that sometimes, our faith in the forward motion of chronology suddenly evaporating, leaving us standing, disoriented, in a dry, still riverbed" (p. 272). Which movements or moments from the past do you feel reverberating now? What lessons or guidance do they offer you?

12. Sharlet writes that "There is a difference, though, between delusion and imagination—that's the hope of this book. I've tried to pull a thread of imagination through these pages, to notice moments of

generosity, small solidarities, genuine wit, actual funny, real sorrow and love" (p. xi). Do you think Sharlet is successful? Where do you feel generosity and "small solidarities" in your own life?

13. "'Write it down and tell the story,' says Pete. I want to agree—'my faith is in stories' is my standard disavowal when pressed by believers for my religious convictions. But maybe it's the stories that're the problem. What if we *only* wrote it down? That is, we wrote it down but did not 'tell the story.' What if we wrote down—recorded—as much of the *it* of our lives, whether or not it fits in 'the story,' as we can? What if we didn't worry about endings, about crescendos?" (pp. 253–54) What connection do you see between storytelling and leading a meaningful life? Which stories guide you?

14. What is your greatest takeaway from *The Undertow*?

Diana Abu-Jaber	*Life Without a Recipe*
Diane Ackerman	*The Zookeeper's Wife*
Michelle Adelman	*Piece of Mind*
Molly Antopol	*The UnAmericans*
Andrea Barrett	*Archangel*
Rowan Hisayo Buchanan	*Harmless Like You*
Ada Calhoun	*Wedding Toasts I'll Never Give*
Bonnie Jo Campbell	*Mothers, Tell Your Daughters*
	Once Upon a River
Lan Samantha Chang	*Inheritance*
Ann Cherian	*A Good Indian Wife*
Evgenia Citkowitz	*The Shades*
Amanda Coe	*The Love She Left Behind*
Michael Cox	*The Meaning of Night*
Jeremy Dauber	*Jewish Comedy*
Jared Diamond	*Guns, Germs, and Steel*
Caitlin Doughty	*From Here to Eternity*
Andre Dubus III	*House of Sand and Fog*
	Townie: A Memoir
Anne Enright	*The Forgotten Waltz*
	The Green Road
Amanda Filipacchi	*The Unfortunate Importance of Beauty*
Beth Ann Fennelly	*Heating & Cooling*
Betty Friedan	*The Feminine Mystique*
Maureen Gibbon	*Paris Red*
Stephen Greenblatt	*The Swerve*
Lawrence Hill	*The Illegal*
	Someone Knows My Name
Ann Hood	*The Book That Matters Most*
	The Obituary Writer
Dara Horn	*A Guide for the Perplexed*
Blair Hurley	*The Devoted*

Meghan Kenny	*The Driest Season*
Nicole Krauss	*The History of Love*
Don Lee	*The Collective*
Amy Liptrot	*The Outrun: A Memoir*
Donna M. Lucey	*Sargent's Women*
Bernard MacLaverty	*Midwinter Break*
Maaza Mengiste	*Beneath the Lion's Gaze*
Claire Messud	*The Burning Girl*
	When the World Was Steady
Liz Moore	*Heft*
	The Unseen World
Neel Mukherjee	*The Lives of Others*
	A State of Freedom
Janice P. Nimura	*Daughters of the Samurai*
Rachel Pearson	*No Apparent Distress*
Richard Powers	*Orfeo*
Kirstin Valdez Quade	*Night at the Fiestas*
Jean Rhys	*Wide Sargasso Sea*
Mary Roach	*Packing for Mars*
Somini Sengupta	*The End of Karma*
Akhil Sharma	*Family Life*
	A Life of Adventure and Delight
Joan Silber	*Fools*
Johanna Skibsrud	*Quartet for the End of Time*
Mark Slouka	*Brewster*
Kate Southwood	*Evensong*
Manil Suri	*The City of Devi*
	The Age of Shiva
Madeleine Thien	*Do Not Say We Have Nothing*
	Dogs at the Perimeter
Vu Tran	*Dragonfish*
Rose Tremain	*The American Lover*
	The Gustav Sonata
Brady Udall	*The Lonely Polygamist*
Brad Watson	*Miss Jane*
Constance Fenimore Woolson	*Miss Grief and Other Stories*

Available only on the Norton website